AVID

READER

PRESS

HUNT, GATHER,
PARENT

What Ancient Cultures Can Teach Us
About the Lost Art of Raising
Happy, Helpful Little Humans

Michaeleen Doucleff, PhD

Illustrations by Ella Trujillo

AVID READER PRESS

New York London Toronto Sydney New Delhi

Avid Reader Press
An Imprint of Simon & Schuster, Inc.
1230 Avenue of the Americas
New York, NY 10020

First Avid Reader Press hardcover edition March 2021

Avid Reader Press and colophon are trademarks
of Simon & Schuster, Inc.

This publication contains the opinions and ideas of its author. It is intended to
provide general guidance and information about parenting, including parenting philosophies, advice, and techniques. It is sold with the understanding
that the author and publisher are not engaged in rendering medical, health,
or any other kind of personal professional services in the book. The author
and publisher specifically disclaim all responsibility for any liability, loss, or
risk, personal or otherwise, which is incurred as a consequence, directly or
indirectly, of the use and application of any of the contents of this book.

For information about special discounts for bulk purchases,
please contact Simon & Schuster Special Sales at 1-866-506-1949
or business@simonandschuster.com.

The Simon & Schuster Speakers Bureau can bring authors to your
live event. For more information or to book an event, contact
the Simon & Schuster Speakers Bureau at 1-866-248-3049
or visit our website at www.simonspeakers.com.

Interior design by Joy O'Meara

Manufactured in the United States of America

10 9 8 7 6 5 4 3 2

Library of Congress Cataloging-in-Publication Data has been applied for.

ISBN 978-1-9821-4967-3
ISBN 978-1-9821-4969-7 (ebook)

In memory of Mango,
the best book shepherd a writer could have

To Rosy

CONTENTS

PROLOGUE

I remember the moment I hit rock bottom as a mom.

It was five o'clock on a chilly December morning. I lay in bed, wearing the same sweater I had worn the previous day. My hair hadn't been washed in days.

Outside, the sky was still dark blue; streetlights still glowed yellow. Inside, our house was eerily quiet. All I could hear was our German shepherd, Mango, breathing on the floor below our bed. Everyone was asleep, except me. I was wide awake.

I was preparing for battle. I was going over in my head how to handle my next encounter with the enemy. What will I do when she strikes me again? When she hits? Kicks? Or bites?

It sounds horrible to call my daughter "the enemy." Goodness knows, I love her to death. And in many ways, she's a wonderful little person. She's whip smart, wildly courageous, and has the strength of an ox, both physically and mentally. When Rosy falls down at the playground, she gets right back up. No fuss, no muss.

And did I mention her smell? Oh, I love the way she smells, especially right on the top of her head. When I'm on a reporting trip for NPR, that's what I miss the most: her smell, like a mixture of honey, lilies, and wet soil.

That sweet fragrance is beguiling. It's misleading, too. There's a fire in Rosy's belly. A red-hot fire. The fire drives her, makes her march through the world with ferocious purpose. As one friend put it: she's a destroyer of worlds.

When Rosy was an infant, she cried a lot. Hours and hours each evening. "If she isn't eating or sleeping, she's crying," my husband told the pediatrician, in a panic. The doctor shrugged. She had clearly heard this all before. "Well, she is a baby," the doctor replied.

Now Rosy was three years old, and all the crying had morphed into tantrums and a torrent of parental abuse. When she had a meltdown and I picked her up, she had the habit of slapping me across the face. Some mornings, I left the house with a red handprint across my cheek. Man, it hurt.

That quiet December morning, as I lay in bed, I allowed myself to acknowledge a painful truth. A wall was rising between Rosy and me. I had started dreading our time together because I was afraid of what would happen— afraid I would lose my temper (again); that I would make Rosy cry (again); that I would only make her behavior worse (again). And as a result, I feared that Rosy and I were becoming enemies.

I grew up in an angry home. Screaming, slamming doors—even throwing shoes—were all basic means of communication for my parents, my three siblings, and me. And so with Rosy's tantrums, at first, I reacted as my parents had treated me, with a mixture of anger, sternness, and sometimes loud, scary words. This response only backfired: Rosy would arch her back, screech like a hawk, and fall onto the ground. Besides, I wanted to do better than my parents. I wanted Rosy to grow up in a peaceful environment, and to teach her more productive ways of communicating than throwing a Doc Marten at someone's head.

So I consulted Dr. Google and decided that "authoritative" was the "optimal parenting approach" that would help curb Rosy's tantrums. From what I could tell, authoritative meant being both "firm and kind." And so I tried my best at doing just that. But I never got it right because, time and time again, the authoritative approach failed me. Rosy could tell I was still angry, and so we'd get trapped in the same cycle. My anger would make her behavior worse. I would become angrier. And eventually, her tantrums turned nuclear. She'd bite, flail her arms, and start running around the house upturning furniture.

Even the simplest of tasks—such as getting ready for preschool in the mornings—had turned into battles royale. "Can you please just put your shoes on?" I would beg for the fifth time. "No!" she would scream, and then proceed to take off her dress *and her underwear*.

One morning I had felt so bad, I knelt down below the kitchen sink and screamed silently into the cabinets. *Why is it all such a struggle? Why won't she listen? What am I doing wrong?*

If I were honest, I had no clue how to handle Rosy. I didn't know how to stop her tantrums, let alone begin the process of teaching her how to be a good person—a person who is kind, helpful, and concerned about other people.

Truth is, I didn't know how to be a good mother. Never before had I been so bad at something that I wanted to be good at. Never before had the gap between my actual skill and the skill level I desired been so crushingly wide.

And so there I was lying in bed, in the wee hours of the morning, dreading the moment when my daughter—the beloved child I had spent many years longing to have—woke up. Searching in my mind for a way to connect with a small person who seemed, many days, like a raging maniac. Searching for a way out of this mess I'd made.

I felt lost. I felt tired. And I felt hopeless. When I looked ahead, all I could see was more of the same: Rosy and I would remain locked in constant battle, with her growing only taller and stronger as time went on.

But that wasn't what happened, and this book is about how that unexpected and transformative shift in our lives happened. It began with a trip to Mexico, where an eye-opening experience led to other trips, in different corners of the world—each time with Rosy as my travel companion. Along the way, I met a handful of extraordinary moms and dads who generously taught me an unbelievable amount about parenting. These women and men showed me not only how to tame Rosy's tantrums, but also a way to communicate with her that doesn't involve yelling, nagging, or punishing—a way that builds up a child's confidence instead of building tension and conflict with a parent. And perhaps, most important, I learned how to teach Rosy to be kind and generous to me, her family, and her friends. And a part of why this was all possible is because these moms and dads showed *me* how to be kind and loving to my child in a whole new way.

As Inuit mother Elizabeth Tegumiar told me, on our last day in the Arctic, "I think you know better how to handle her now." Indeed, I do.

———————

Parenting is exquisitely personal. The details vary not only from culture to culture, but also from community to community, even from family to family. And yet, if you travel around the world today, you can see a common thread that weaves across the vast majority of cultures. From the Arctic tundra and the Yucatán rainforest to the Tanzanian savanna and the Filipino mountainside, you see a common way of relating to children. This is especially true among cultures that raise remarkably kind and helpful children—children who wake up in the morning and immediately start doing the dishes. Children who *want* to share candy with their siblings.

This universal approach to parenting has four core elements. You can spot these elements in pockets of Europe today, and not that long ago, they were widespread across the U.S. The first goal of this book is to understand the ins and outs of these elements and learn how to bring them into your home, to make your life easier.

Given its pervasiveness around the globe and among hunter-gatherer communities, this universal style of parenting is likely tens of thousands, even a hundred thousand, years old. Biologists can make a convincing argument that the parent-child relationship evolved to work this way. And when you see this parenting style in action—whether you're making tortillas in a Maya village or fishing for char in the Arctic Ocean—you experience this overwhelming sense of "Oh, so *that's* how this parenting thing is supposed to go." Child and parent fit together like a tongue-in-groove joint—or even better, like a Nejire kumi tsugi Japanese wood joint. It's beautiful.

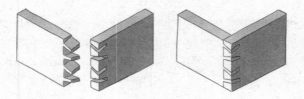

I'll never forget the first time I witnessed this parenting style. I felt my whole sense of gravity shift.

At the time, I'd been a reporter at NPR for six years. Before that, I had spent seven years as a Berkeley-trained chemist. So as a reporter, I focused on stories about medical sciences—infectious diseases, vaccines, and children's health. Most of the time, I wrote stories from my desk in San Francisco. But every now and then, NPR would send me to a distant corner of the world to report on an exotic disease. I went to Liberia during the peak of the Ebola outbreak, dug through Arctic permafrost in search of thawing flu viruses, and stood in a bat cave in Borneo while a virus hunter warned me about a future pandemic of coronavirus (that was in the fall of 2017).

After Rosy came into our lives, these trips took on a new meaning. I began to watch the moms and dads around the world, neither as a reporter nor a scientist, but rather as an exhausted parent, desperately searching for a tiny morsel of parenting wisdom. *There just has to be a better way than what I'm doing*, I thought. *There just has to be.*

*There just has to be a better
way than what I'm doing.
There just has to be.*

Then, during a trip to the Yucatán, I saw it: the universal way of parenting, up close and personal. The experience rocked me to my core. I returned home from the trip and began to shift the entire focus of my career.

Instead of studying viruses and biochemistry, I wanted to learn as much as possible about this way of relating to little humans—this tantalizingly gentle and kindhearted way to raise helpful and self-sufficient children.

———————

If you are holding this book, first of all, thank you. Thank you for your attention and time. I know how precious those are for parents. With the support of a fantastic team, I have worked hard to make this book worth it for you and your family.

Second, chances are you've felt a bit like me and my husband—desperate for better advice and tools. Maybe you've read several books already and, like a scientist, experimented with several methods on your kids. Maybe you got excited at first because the experiment looked promising, only to feel even more wrung out after a few days when, alas, the experiment failed. I lived through that frustrating cycling for the first 2.5 years of Rosy's life. Experiments failed, again and again.

One big goal of this book is to help you stop this frustrating cycle. By learning the universal parenting approach, you'll get a view into how children have been raised for tens of thousands of years, how they are hardwired to be raised. You'll start to understand why misbehavior occurs, and you'll become empowered to stop it at its root cause. You'll learn a way to relate to children that has been tested for millennia by moms and dads across six continents—a way that is currently missing from other parenting books.

———————

Parenting advice today has one major problem. The vast majority of it comes solely from the Euro-American perspective. Sure, Amy Chua's *Battle Hymn of the Tiger Mother* gave us a riveting look at a Chinese approach to raising successful children, but by and large, contemporary ideas about parenting are based almost exclusively on the Western paradigm. So American moms and dads are stuck looking at the parenting landscape through a tiny keyhole. This narrow view not only blocks much of the most captivating (and useful) landscape, it also has had far-reaching implications: it's one of the reasons why raising kids is so stressful today—and why children and teens in the U.S. have grown lonelier, more anxious, and more depressed in the past few decades.

Today about a third of all teenagers have had symptoms that meet the criteria for an anxiety disorder, Harvard researchers report. More than 60 percent of college undergraduates report feeling "overwhelming" anxiety, and Generation Z, which includes adults born between the mid-1990s and the early 2000s, is the loneliest generation in decades. And yet, the predominant parenting style in the U.S. is moving in a direction that exacerbates these problems instead of curbing them. "Parents have gone into a control mode," psychotherapist B. Janet Hibbs said in 2019. "They used to promote autonomy. . . . But now they're exerting more and more control, which makes their kids more anxious and also less prepared for the unpredictable."

If the "normal" state of teenagers in our culture is anxious and lonely, perhaps it's time for parents to reexamine what "normal" parenting is. If we really want to understand our precious bundles of joy—to really connect with our children—maybe we need to jump out of our cultural comfort zone and talk to parents we rarely hear from.

Maybe it's time to open up our narrow viewpoint and see just how beautiful—and powerful—parenting can be.

That's another goal of this book—to start to fill in the gap of our parenting knowledge. And to do that, we're going to focus on cultures that have an enormous amount of useful knowledge: hunter-gatherers and other indigenous cultures with similar values. These cultures have honed their parenting strategies for thousands of years. Grandmas and grandpas have passed down knowledge from one generation to the next, equipping new moms and dads with a huge chest of diverse and potent tools. So parents know how to get children to do chores without asking, how to get siblings to cooperate (and not fight), and how to discipline without yelling, scolding, or using time-outs. They are master motivators and experts at building children's executive functions, including skills such as resilience, patience, and anger control.

Most striking, in many hunter-gatherer cultures, parents build a relationship with young children that is markedly different than the one we foster here in the U.S.—it's one that's built on cooperation instead of conflict, trust instead of fear, and personalized needs instead of standardized development milestones.

So while I raise Rosy with essentially a single tool—a really loud hammer—many parents around the world wield a whole suite of precision instruments, such as screwdrivers, pulleys, and levels, that they can bring out as needed. In this book, we'll learn as much as possible about these super tools, including how to use them in your own home.

And to do that, I'm going to go straight to the source of the information—to the moms and dads themselves. We'll visit three cultures—Maya, Hadzabe, and Inuit—which excel in aspects of parenting with which Western culture struggles. Maya moms are masters at raising helpful children. They have developed a sophisticated form of collaboration that teaches siblings not only how to get along, but also how to work together. Hadzabe parents are world experts on raising confident, self-driven kids; the childhood anxiety and depression we see here in the U.S. is unheard of in Hadzabe communities. And Inuit have developed a remarkably effective approach for teaching children emotional intelligence, especially when it comes to anger control and respect for others.

The book devotes one section to each culture. In each section, we'll spend time meeting several families and getting to know a bit about their daily routines. We'll see how parents get kids ready for school in the morning, how they put them to bed at night, and how they motivate kids to share, treat their siblings with kindness, and take on new responsibilities at their own personalized pace.

On top of that, we're going to give these supermoms and superdads a challenge, a parenting puzzle they could solve right before my very eyes. We're going to give them Rosy.

Yes, you read that correctly. To write this book, I embarked on an epic—and, some may say, insane—journey. With my toddler in tow, I traveled to three revered communities around the world, lived with families there, and learned all I could about the nooks and

crannies of their parenting. Rosy and I slept in a hammock under a full Maya moon; helped an Inuit grandpa hunt narwhal in the Arctic Ocean; and learned how to dig for tubers with Hadzabe moms in Tanzania.

Along the way, I check in with anthropologists and evolutionary biologists to understand how the parenting strategies being shown aren't just specific to these families and these cultures, but are widespread across the world today—and throughout human history. I'll talk with psychologists and neuroscientists to learn how the tools and tips can impact children's mental health and development.

Throughout each section, you'll find practical guides for trying the advice with your own kids. We'll give you tips for "dipping your toes" into the approach to see if it resonates with your children, as well as a more expansive guide to begin integrating the strategies into your daily life. These practical sections delve into and are taken from my own personal experience, as well as my friends' experiences, raising young kids in San Francisco.

As we move outside the U.S., we'll start to see the Western approach to parenting with fresh eyes. We'll see how our culture often has things backward when it comes to kids: We interfere too much. We don't have enough confidence in our children. We don't trust their innate ability to know what they need to grow. And in many instances, we don't speak their language.

In particular, our culture focuses almost entirely on one aspect of the parent-child relationship. That's control—how much control the parent exerts over the child, and how much control the child tries to exert over the parent. The most common parenting "styles" all revolve around control. Helicopter parents exert maximal control. Free-range parents exert minimal. Our culture thinks either the adult is in control or the child is in control.

There's a major problem with this view of parenting: It sets us up for power struggles, with fights, screaming, and tears. Nobody likes to be controlled. Both children and parents rebel against it. So when we interact with our children in terms of control—whether it's a parent controlling the child or vice versa—we establish an adversarial relationship. Tensions

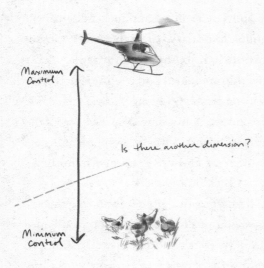

Maximum Control

Is there another dimension?

Minimum control

build. Arguments break out. Power struggles are inevitable. For a little two- or three-year-old, who can't handle emotions, these tensions burst out in a physical eruption.

This book will introduce you to another dimension of parenting that has largely fallen by the wayside in the U.S. over the past half century. It's a way to relate to children that has nothing to do with control, either in terms of seizing it or in surrendering it.

You may not have even realized how many of your parenting struggles were, at their base, about control. But when we remove control from the parenting equation (or at least curtail it), it's amazing how quickly the struggles and resistance melt away, like watching butter in a hot pan. Hang in there! Try what's here and you'll find that the incredibly frustrating moments of parenting—the hurled shoes, the grocery store tantrum, the fight at bedtime—happen a lot less often, and eventually disappear altogether.

———

Finally, a few words about my intentions with this book.

The last thing I want is for any part of this book to make you feel bad about the job you are doing as a parent. All of us parents already have so many doubts and insecurities—I don't want to add to yours. If that ever happens, please email me and let me know right away. My goal is the exact opposite—to empower and lift you as a parent, while also giving you a whole new set of tools and advice that is missing from parenting discussions today. I wrote this book to be the one I wish someone would have given me when I was lying in the dark that cold December morning, feeling like I'd hit rock bottom as a parent.

My other desire is to do right by the many parents introduced in this book, who opened up their homes and lives to Rosy and me. These families come from cultures different than my own—and likely different from yours, too. There are many ways to navigate those differences. In the U.S., we often focus on these cultures' struggles and problems. We even scold parents of different cultures when they don't follow our culture's rules. At other times, we swing too far in the opposite direction and romanticize other cultures, believing they contain some "ancient magic" or live in some "paradise lost." Both types of thinking are categorically wrong.

There is no question that life can be hard in these cultures—as it can be in every culture. Communities and families have suffered and do suffer through tragedies, illnesses, and hard times (sometimes at the hands of Western culture). Just like you and me, these parents work incredibly hard, often at multiple jobs. They make mistakes with their children and wind up regretting decisions. Just like you and me, they are not perfect.

At the same time, none of these cultures are ancient relics, frozen in time. Nothing could be further from the truth. Families in this book are as "contemporary" (for lack of a better word) as you and me. They have smartphones, check Facebook (often), watch *CSI*, and love *Frozen* and *Coco*. Kids eat Froot Loops for breakfast and watch movies after dinner. Adults rush in the mornings to get kids ready for school and share beer with friends on lazy Saturday evenings.

But these cultures do have something that Western culture is missing right now: deeply rooted parenting traditions and the wealth of knowledge that comes along with it. And there's no question that the parents in this book are incredibly skilled at communicating, motivating, and cooperating with children. Spend just an hour or two with these families and the evidence will be crystal clear.

And so, in this book, my explicit goal is to focus on these parents' excellent abilities. During my travels, I wanted to meet other humans, connect with them as genuinely as possible, and learn from their vast experiences (and then bring it to you, the reader). As I share these stories, I want to honor and respect the people in this book (and their communities) as best I can. And I want to give back to them. As such, 35 percent of my advance for this book will go to the families and communities you are about to meet.

To value everyone's opinions equally throughout the book, I will use first names on second reference for everyone.

———————

Okay. Before we hop on a plane and immerse ourselves in three of the world's most venerable cultures, we need to take care of one more item of business. We need to take a look at ourselves—and learn why we raise children the way we do. We'll see that many of the techniques and tools we take for granted—and take great pride in—have quite surprising and flimsy origins.

SECTION 1

Weird, Wild West

CHAPTER 1

The WEIRDest Parents in the World

Back in the spring of 2018, I sat at the Cancún airport, almost in a state of paralysis. I was staring at the planes as my thoughts raced back to what I had just witnessed. Could it possibly be true?

Could parenting really be that easy?

Just a few days earlier, I had traveled to a small Maya village in the middle of the Yucatán Peninsula. I went to report on a radio story about children's attention spans. I had read a study suggesting that Maya children are better at paying attention than American kids in particular situations, and I wanted to learn why.

But after spending a day in the village, I quickly spotted a bigger story underneath the thatched roofs. A much bigger story.

I spent hours upon hours interviewing moms and grandmas about how they raise children, and watching their skills in action—how they handle toddler tantrums, motivate kids to do homework, and coax kids to come inside for dinner. Basically, the families' version of the daily grind. I also asked them about the tough parts of parenting, such as how they make it out the door in the morning or get ready for bed.

What I witnessed blew my mind. Their parenting approach was totally different than anything I had ever seen. It was different from the methods used by the uber moms back in San Francisco, different from what I had experienced as a child, and it was 180 degrees away from the way I was raising Rosy.

My own parenting was like a white-knuckled ride on Class 5 rapids, with drama, screaming, and tears galore (not to mention the endless rounds of negotiating and bickering on both sides). With the Maya moms, on the other hand, I felt like I was on a wide, serene river, meandering through a mountain valley, smooth and steady in its flow. Gentle. Easy. And very little drama. I saw no screaming, no bossing around (in either direction), and little nagging. Yet their parenting was effective. Oh, so effective! The children were respectful, kind, and cooperative, not just with their mom and dad but also with their siblings. Heck, half the time the parents didn't even need to ask a child to share her bag of chips with a younger sibling. The child did so voluntarily.

But what *really* stood out was the children's helpfulness. Everywhere I went, I saw kids of all ages eagerly helping their parents. A nine-year-old girl hopped off her bike and ran over to turn on a watering hose for her mom. A four-year-old girl volunteered to run to the corner market to pick up some tomatoes (with the promise of a piece of candy, of course).

And then, on the final morning of my visit, I witnessed the ultimate act of helpfulness, and it came from an unlikely source—a preteen girl on spring break.

I was sitting in the family's kitchen, talking to the girl's mother, Maria de los Angeles Tun Burgos, as she cooked black beans over a coal fire. With her long black hair tied in a sleek ponytail, Maria had on a navy A-line dress, cinched at the waist.

"The two older girls are still sleeping," Maria said as she sat to rest on a hammock. The previous night the girls had stayed up late to watch a scary shark movie. "And I found them all in one hammock, at midnight, huddled up together," she said, laughing softly and smiling. "So I am permitting them to sleep more."

Maria works extremely hard. She handles all household chores, makes all the meals—we're talking fresh tortillas everyday made from stone-ground corn—and helps with the family's business. And no matter what chaos whirled around her during our visit, Maria was always cool as a cucumber. Even when she admonished her youngest daughter, Alexa, not to touch the charcoal fire, she spoke in a calm voice, and her face remained relaxed. There was no sense of urgency, anxiety, or stress. And in return, her children were awesome to her. They respected her requests (for the most part). They didn't argue or talk back.

We chatted for a few more minutes and then, as I stood up to leave, Maria's twelve-year-old daughter, Angela, emerged from her bedroom. Wearing black capris, a red T-shirt, and gold hoop earrings, she looked just like a preteen in California. But she did something that I've never seen in California. She walked right past me and her mom and, without saying a word, grabbed a tub of soapy water and started cleaning the dishes from breakfast. No one had to ask her to start washing. No chore chart hung on the wall. (In fact, as we'll learn, chore charts may actually inhibit such voluntary acts.) Instead, Angela simply noticed the dirty dishes sitting in the sink and got to work, even though she was on spring break from school.

"Oh, wow!" I exclaimed. "Does Angela volunteer help often?"

I was totally surprised, but Maria didn't seem to be at all. "She doesn't do it every day, but many days," she said. "If she sees there is something to be done, she doesn't wait. One time I took her younger sister to the clinic, and when I came back, Angela had cleaned the whole house."

I walked over to Angela and asked her directly why she started doing the dishes. Her answer melted my heart.

"I like to help my mother," she said in soft Spanish while scrubbing a yellow plate.

"And when you're not helping your mother, what do you like to do?" I asked.

"I like to help my younger sister," she said proudly.

I was standing there slack-jawed. *What twelve-year-old gets up in the morning and before doing anything else starts washing the dishes—on her spring break, nonetheless?* I thought. *Is she for real?*

And so several days later, while waiting at the busy Cancún airport, staring at the planes, I couldn't stop thinking about Angela—about her genuine desire to help and her gentle love for her family. How did Maria and the other Maya moms do it? How do they raise such cooperative, respectful children?

These women made parenting look—dare I say it—easy. And I wanted to learn their secrets. I wanted my relationship with Rosy to be that calm and relaxed. I wanted to get off the white-knuckle rapids and onto the wide, meandering river.

Then I turned away from the planes and looked at the American tourists sitting across from me, getting ready to board the plane back to San Francisco. And it struck me: Maybe I've had such trouble with Rosy, not because I'm a bad mom, but because I just haven't had someone to teach me how to be a good mom? Has my culture forgotten the best way to parent?

———————

Here's a quick experiment. Take a look at these two lines. Which one is shorter? Figure A or Figure B?

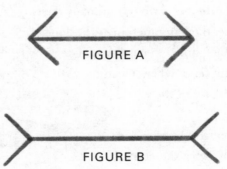

The answer is obvious, right? Or is it?

What if you were to give the test to a cattle herder in Kenya? Or a hunter-gatherer on a tiny Filipino island? Who would answer the question correctly? And who would be fooled by the illusion?

Back in the 1880s, a young German psychiatrist, Franz Carl Müller-Lyer, wanted to study how the human brain perceives the world. Only in his early thirties, he was already a rock star in his field. At the time, optical illusions were all the rage in psychology. And Franz thought he could leave his mark on the field. So he started doodling. He drew two lines of equal length—one line had regular arrowheads pointing out, such as A in the figure opposite, while the other line had the arrowheads pointing in, such as B. Franz soon realized that even though the lines were exactly the same length, they looked very different. The shape of the arrows tricks the brain into thinking B is longer than A.

With that doodle, he created what would become the most famous optical illusion in history.

Franz published his illusion in 1889, and immediately scientists began to try to figure out why our eyes—or our brains—fail us. Why can't we see the lines as they are, with equal length? The illusion seemed to reveal something universal about human perception.

Then, more than a century later, a team of researchers turned the field of psychology upside down and forever changed the way we see the Müller-Lyer illusion—and understand the human brain.

In 2006, Joe Henrich had just moved into his new office at the University of British Columbia, Vancouver, when he struck up a friendship with another psychologist down the hall. Little did he know that this friendship would eventually lead to a fundamental shift in the entire field of psychology—or as Joe puts it, "a real stab at the heart of psychology."

Joe is a big thinker. He studies what motivates people to cooperate with each other—or conversely, to start wars with one another—and how those decisions to work together have helped our species become the most dominant one on earth.

Joe is also a rare breed of psychologist, called "cross-cultural." He doesn't just run experiments on Americans or Europeans; he also travels to distant places, like Fiji or the Amazon, to see how people in other cultures perform in these same experiments.

Down the hall from Joe worked another cross-cultural psychologist named Steve Heine. He studies what gives people "meaning" in their lives and how that idea varies around the world. Like Joe, Steve wanted to figure out how the *human* brain works—not just how the *European American* brain works.

Given their common appreciation for other cultures, Joe and Steve began to meet for lunch each month. They'd head to the university's food court, grab Chinese takeout, and then discuss their current research. Again and again, Joe and Steve noticed a pattern: Europeans and Americans tended to behave differently than other cultures. "We were outliers in experiments," Joe said. "Steve and I were stunned. We started to wonder: 'Could North Americans be the weirdest people in the world?'"

At that point, the idea was just a hypothesis that popped up over lunch. But Joe and Steve were so intrigued that they decided to run a few tests. The pair roped in their colleague Ara Norenzayan, a psychologist who studies how religions spread and spur cooperation. Together, the trio began to methodically review dozens of studies in psychology, cognitive sciences, economics, and sociology.

Right off the bat, the team noticed a big problem. Psychology has a massive bias. The vast majority of studies—about 96 percent—examined only people from European backgrounds. And yet people of European descent make up only about 12 percent of the world's population. "So the whole field of psychology is studying only a thin slice of humanity," Joe said.

Such a Western bias isn't a problem if the goal of the research is to figure out how Western people think and behave. But the bias becomes a major issue if the goal is to figure out how *humans* think and behave, especially when the slice of humanity you're studying is really, really strange—as Westerners turn out to be. It's a bit like walking into a Baskin-Robbins ice cream store, trying only the Pink Bubblegum flavor, ignoring the other thirty flavors, and then publishing a paper that claims all ice cream includes chunks of chewing gum.

What happens when you sample the other thirty flavors?

To figure it out, Joe, Steve, and Ara analyzed the handful of experiments performed on people outside the U.S. and then compared them to the ones performed on Westerners. Oftentimes, the results didn't match up. Westerners stuck out at one end of the spectrum of behavior, while people from indigenous cultures tended to clump together, more in the middle.

The conclusion from these analyses was startling: people from Western society, "including young children, are among the least representative populations one could find for generalizing about humans," the team wrote in 2010. They even came up with a catchy acronym to describe the phenomenon, naming our culture WEIRD, for Western, Educated, Industrialized, Rich, and Democratic societies.

Joe and his colleagues published a twenty-three-page paper titled "The Weirdest People in the World?" And in an instant, the ethnocentric view of psychology cracked. It wasn't so much that the emperor of psychology had no clothes. It was more that he was dancing around in Western garb pretending to represent all humanity.

WEIRD people are strange in more than a dozen ways, the study concluded, including the way we cooperate with others, dole out punishments, view fairness, think of the "self," value choice, and see three-dimensional space.

Take, for instance, the optical illusion that we just looked at on page 18.

In the 1950s and '60s, scientists tested out the Müller-Lyer illusion in at least fourteen cultures, including fishermen in Nigeria, foragers in the Kalahari Desert, and hunter-gatherers in rural Australia. They also tested the illusion on South Africans of European descent, as well as adults and kids in Evanston, Illinois.

The experiment was simple. The researchers showed people the illusion and asked how different the two lines appeared to be. What the researchers found was so surprising that some psychologists found it hard to believe, and they still debate the underlying cause of the results.

The Americans were quite susceptible to the illusion. On average, volunteers in Illinois thought line B was about 20 percent longer than line A. These findings lined up with previous studies. Nothing new here.

But when the researchers looked at the results from the *other* cultures, things got interesting. In some indigenous cultures, such as hunter-gatherers in southern Africa and farmers in the Ivory Coast, people weren't duped by the illusion at all. They saw the two lines as they were actually drawn—as equal in length. In all the other cultures, people's susceptibility to the illusion fell between the two extremes—between the duped Americans and the unfazed Africans. People from fourteen other cultures thought that the two lines were different in length, but not nearly as different as the Americans believed.

The researchers hypothesized that the illusion tricks Americans most effectively because we live among "carpentered environments," or right angles. That is, we're surrounded by boxes. Everywhere we look, there they are. We live in boxes (aka houses), sleep on boxes (aka beds), cook on boxes (aka stoves), commute in boxes (aka trains), and fill our homes with boxes (aka chests of drawers, desks, sofas, armoires, etc.).

Scientists hypothesize that all this exposure to boxes trains our brains to perceive the Müller-Lyer illusion in a peculiar way: When we see the two arrows, our brains take a shortcut. We subconsciously turn the two-dimensional lines on the page into the edges of three-dimensional boxes (or more specifically, drawings of edges). Why does this subconscious switch make us believe the top line is shorter than the bottom? Imagine that the two lines are the edges of buildings. The line on the bottom, with the arrowheads flipped outward, resembles an edge that recedes from our point of view—or one that's farther away from us. The line on the top, with the standard arrowheads, resembles an edge that points toward us— or one that's closer to us. Hence, the brain stretches out the line on the bottom because it's thought to be farther away from us than the line on the top, which is thought to be closer to us.

But in many cultures around the world, people aren't surrounded by boxes and right angles. Rather, they're surrounded by curved, smooth shapes. Homes and buildings often have dome-like designs, or they're made of more pliable materials like reeds or clay. And when people walk outside their homes, they don't stroll along sidewalks with lampposts (making right angles). They move through nature. Lots and lots of nature—trees, plants, animals, and terrain. And nature isn't so into right angles. Nature loves curves.

So when a San woman in the Kalahari Desert looks at the two lines of the Müller-Lyer illusion on a piece of paper, she isn't tricked by the arrowheads. Her brain doesn't automatically jump to the conclusion that these lines represent 3D edges of boxes. Instead, she simply sees what's actually drawn on the page: two lines of equal length.

By running the Müller-Lyer test on diverse cultures, the researchers exposed a massive fissure in psychology's foundation. Their findings showed that the culture and the environment you grow up in can profoundly shape basic brain functions, such as visual perception.

If that's true, then how else could culture change our brains? What other "human universals" or "general principles" in psychology are actually not universal at all, but rather unique to Western culture—consequences of living in and being raised in a particularly WEIRD environment?

Another way to put this idea: If being a member of a culture distorts something as simple as the way we view two black lines on a page, how might our culture be influencing more complex psychological processes? What could it be doing to our parenting philosophy or to the way we view children's behavior? What if some of the ideas we think of as "universals" when it comes to raising children are actually "optical illusions" created by our culture?

After returning home from the Maya village in the Yucatán, I felt so motivated and energized about parenting. For the first time in years I felt hopeful. I thought that—maybe, just maybe—I could figure out this parenting thing after all, that I could not only tame the wild hyena in our home, but also teach her to be helpful and respectful. The prospect made me giddy.

So I started to do what I do best: research. I wanted to learn as much as possible about the Maya parents' approach to raising children. I dug into the scientific literature, talked to scientists, and read academic books. I also took a long, hard look at contemporary parenting books.

I became frustrated almost immediately: I could barely find any information about Maya child-rearing in popular parenting books. As a matter of fact, I struggled to find any information at all about parenting styles in non-Western cultures. In rare cases when parenting books did mention practices from other cultures, they treated such knowledge more like an intellectual curiosity than as valuable information that could really help struggling moms and dads.

That's when I recognized the massive gap in parenting advice today. We hear almost exclusively from the Western perspective for guidance and instruction. So many voices and viewpoints are missing. And yet, when it comes to understanding what babies need to sleep, how young kids operate, and what to do when a toddler is lying facedown on the sidewalk (just asking for a friend), the Western world might not be the best place to look for answers.

For starters, Western culture is relatively new at raising children. On the world parenting stage, we're the ingenues. Many of our methods have been around for only a hundred years or so—in some cases, only a few decades. These practices have not, by any means, "stood the test of time." Oftentimes, our advice flip-flops so quickly from one generation to the next, it's dizzying. Take, for instance, the recommended sleep position for a baby. When my mom gave birth, doctors told her to place newborn Michaeleen on her belly for sleeping. Today that advice would be considered incredibly dangerous, even negligent, since putting newborns to sleep on their stomachs was eventually shown to increase the risk of sudden infant death syndrome (SIDS).

On top of that, when you compare Western parenting strategies to those found around the world—and across human history—many times what we do is quite WEIRD.

Long before Joe, Steve, and Ara published their landmark study, crowning the West the WEIRDest culture of the world, anthropologist David Lancy was wondering if the same was true about our parenting. Is our approach the exception? Are we the outliers?

David worked for decades to analyze anthropological data, ethnographic descriptions, and historical records, and concluded that the answer was a resounding *yes*! Many common practices—which we believe are essential or critical for raising children—aren't present in any other cultures around the world—or have begun to emerge only in recent times. "The list of differences is really, really long," David tells me. He summarizes these contrasts in his landmark book, *The Anthropology of Childhood: Cherubs, Chattel, Changelings*. "There may be forty to fifty things that we do that you don't see in other cultures."

For example, is praise the best way to motivate children? Is it the parents' job to constantly stimulate and entertain children? Are words the ideal way to communicate with young kids? Are verbal instructions truly the best to teach children? Many of these Western ideas actually make parenting harder, and they frequently go against the natural instincts of children, David said.

Take, for instance, the nuclear family. In Western culture, there's a general belief that the ideal family structure consists of one mom, one dad, and their young children, living together under one roof. And to make that structure even more ideal, some might say, the mom stays home and devotes her full attention to childcare. That is most "traditional," right?*

Not so in the slightest. If you look around the world—and investigate human history—you'll find that the nuclear family (and a mom whose sole job is parenting) is arguably one of the most nontraditional structures out there. For 99.9 percent of the time humans have been on earth, the nuclear family simply didn't exist. "It's a family structure that's been around for a tiny pinprick in human history," says historian John Gillis, at Rutgers University, who has been studying the evolution of Western families for more than thirty years. "It isn't old. It isn't traditional. It doesn't have any real roots in the past."

And it's definitely not how human children have evolved to be raised. The nuclear family lacks key teachers in a child's life. For hundreds of thousands of years, parenting was a multigenerational affair. Kids evolved to learn from a bunch of different people of all ages—great-grandparents, grandparents, uncles, aunts, family friends, neighbors, cousins, and all the children that tag along with them.

Over the past thousand years or so, the Western family has slowly shrunk down from a multigenerational smorgasbord to a tiny amuse-bouche, con-

---

* When you read this, depending on your background, you might think that the idea of a mom at home sounds antiquated. But even just a little more than fourteen years ago, 41 percent of people thought moms working outside the home was harmful to society, the Pew Research Center reported in 2007.

sisting solely of Ma, Pa, two kids, and maybe a dog or a cat. We not only lost Grandma, Grandpa, Auntie Fay, and Uncle Bill in the home, but also nanny Lena, cook Dan, and a whole slew of neighbors and visitors just hanging around the front porch or sleeping on the couch. Once these people disappeared from the home, most of the parenting burden fell on Mom and Dad.

As a result, for the first time in human history, moms and dads are suddenly doing this crazy-hard thing, called parenting, all by themselves (or even solo). "The idea of two people taking care of a child by themselves, it's just absurd. Totally absurd," John adds. "Two people are doing all the work of what multiple people are charged to do."

David Lancy likens this parenting approach to what happens when a blizzard traps a mom and a child in a house, alone. The isolation forces the mother to be the only playmate for the child—to be the only source of love, social connection, entertainment, and stimulation. These conditions can lead to tension and exhaustion. "There is every reason to believe that modern living conditions in which infants and toddlers are isolated from peers in single-parent or nuclear households produce a parallel effect," David wrote in his book.

All this isolation—this trapping our families in virtual blizzards—has probably not been so good for the mental health of parents and children. Many psychologists whom I spoke with think the erosion of the extended family is a root cause for the high rates of postpartum depression in the U.S., as well as the rising epidemic of anxiety and depression among children and teenagers. Moms, dads, and kids are simply lonely.

This isolation has yet another harmful repercussion: moms and dads have also lost *their* advisers. And we may have forgotten how important these advisers are.

In Western culture, we tend to think of motherhood as "an instinct that comes as naturally to women as the sex drive does to men," John Gillis writes in his book *A World of Their Own Making*. But in reality, parenting is a learned skill. And the traditional sources of knowledge are the women and men who have already raised a few whippersnappers themselves—the grandmas, grandpas, aunties, uncles, and nosy, helpful neighbors. Once the older generations disappeared from the home, so did their parenting knowledge and skills. New moms and dads are now left on their own to figure out the basics of parenting, such as how to help a baby to sleep through the night, soothe a toddler through a tantrum, and teach a big sister to love her new brother, not hit him.

The result today is a mom who's stuck between a rock and an UPPAbaby stroller: she bears more of the parenting duty now than ever before in history, and yet she is the least prepared for the job.

"Never have mothers been so burdened by motherhood," John concludes.

Little wonder, then, I'm exhausted on Sunday afternoons after spending the weekend with Rosy. For two days straight, I've been doing the job of about three to four people. I'm not just her mom, but also her grandma, a cousin, and an older sibling. And to top it all off, I'm pretty much winging it.

In other words, the creation of the nuclear family remodeled how we parent, but also how we learn to parent. Goodbye, Grandma. Goodbye, Aunt Carol. And goodbye parenting knowledge, skills, and extra arms for holding, cooking, and rubbing little backs at bedtime. Hello isolation, exhaustion, and stress.

Why am I such a WEIRD parent?

After learning about how WEIRD-ly I parent, I couldn't shake the idea that there must be an underlying reason. Of course, for something as complex as parenting, there are *many* reasons. But still I wondered if one keystone event may have triggered an avalanche of changes in Western culture—and, eventually, over hundreds of years, led us parents into the exhausted, stressed-out state we now call motherhood and fatherhood.

So for months, I called up countless historians and psychologists and asked them the same question: Why is our parenting so WEIRD?

Each person gave me a different answer: the Age of Enlightenment, capitalism, the Industrial Revolution, reduced child mortality, fewer children per family, our love of privacy.

Clearly the answer is multifaceted.

But then I called up Joe Henrich, one of the three psychologists who coined the term WEIRD. And boy, did his answer surprise me. "Well, I'm actually writing a book, called *WEIRD*, which tries to explain how Westerners became so psychologically strange," he said. "The key actually has to do with the Catholic Church."

"What? How?"

Over the next twenty minutes, Joe explained fascinating findings from his new study.

A few thousand years ago, families in Europe looked a lot like they do in many other cultures today: big, multigenerational, and close-knit. Families' homes were porous structures where relatives, servants, workers, regular old neighbors, and friends flowed in and out, without much fuss.

At the same time, kids enjoyed a huge amount of autonomy. The giant family structure formed a protective shell around toddlers and children. Mom and Dad didn't need to hover over them because some other adult—or a highly capable and caring older child—was always close by to help. As a result, children in the Middle Ages (and throughout most of Western history) lived largely free from adult instructions and directions, from about age six onward. They may have had obligations and responsibilities in the home, but by and large, they made up their own rules and decided for themselves what to do each day.

Yet parents still regulated one essential aspect of their children's lives: marriage. Although that idea might make you cringe a bit, bear with me for a moment, because the parents had a compelling reason for this involvement.

In many instances, parents strongly encouraged (or coaxed) their children to marry someone close to the family; for example, a distant cousin, a relative to an in-law, or a god-relative, Joe said. People considered these marriages "within a family," but in the majority of cases, there was no "biological" reason to prohibit these marriages. The bride and groom weren't related by blood or weren't closely related enough to cause health problems due to inbreeding.

These marriages served a crucial purpose. They formed a type of thread that held extended families together. With these yarns, families wove colorful—and strong—tapestries. The marriages kept land and property within the clan. Over time, the clan gained money, prestige, and power. And, perhaps more important for our purposes, the clan provided parents with plenty of help. Families stayed large, and children could be autonomous in a (relatively) safe way.

Then, sometime around 600 AD, the Catholic Church began tugging on this tapestry, and the tapestry began to fray.

"The Catholic Church became obsessed with incest," Joe said—or what it called "incest."

The church began regulating who could marry whom. To start, they prohibited first cousins from marrying each other, a reasonable restriction because first cousins share about 12 percent of genes and inbreeding can cause health problems.

But in the seventh century, the church extended the marriage ban to all "kinsmen," no matter how distantly related. Fifty years later, they tacked on marriages between god-relatives or in-laws. So for example, if your husband died, you could no longer marry his brother (which was actually a quite common—and biologically safe—choice for widows). The penalty for violating these laws was stiff: give us your property. By the eleventh century, popes and kings across Europe had implemented so many marriage restrictions that even sixth cousins couldn't wed. Keep in mind, sixth cousins are related through 128 great-great-great-great-great-grandparents. They share about 0.01 percent DNA. They are by no means "related" to each other, biologically.

Innumerable repercussions followed from these laws, Joe and colleagues reported in their 2019 study. The marriage laws shattered extended families into tiny pieces. By 1500 AD, the Western family began to look a bit like it does today. "At least in England and probably Germany, the dominant family form is likely the nuclear family," Joe said.

At this point, mothers and fathers still had a bunch of help raising children.

Wealthy and middle-class families hired live-in nannies, cooks, and cleaners. And poorer families continued to live in large, extended families for centuries. But by dividing up powerful families and clans, the church likely set off a chain reaction that shifted the way people think and what they value. In the study, Joe and his colleagues found that the longer a community had been exposed to the Catholic Church's marriage restrictions, the more likely people in that community thought like Westerners do—that is, they valued individualism, nonconformity, and other psychological traits unique to the West.

We don't know for sure that the Catholic Church is a key reason why Western parents are so WEIRD. Just because the two changes are linked together through time and space doesn't mean one caused the other. And some of our strangest parenting practices have actually arisen quite recently. But if you think about it, you can definitely see how shrinking down the extended family could play a large part in sowing the intense individualism we see in WEIRD societies—and radically change how we treat children.

When you grow up in a big, extended family, you have a bunch of obligations and responsibilities to others. You have to look after a younger sibling, help an ailing grandma, or fix meals for your cousins. You have to accommodate others' needs. And you have to go with the flow. Your individual needs take a back seat to socializing and cooperation. You're a little fish in a crowded, interconnected pond. When the family sits down to eat, everyone eats the same food, from the same pot. There's no other way.

Now, when we whittle down the family to two married adults and two kids, many of these obligations fly out the window. Cooperation isn't as necessary. Privacy abounds. We lose the skills required to deal with and accommodate others. We have time and room for individual needs and preferences. Eventually, over hundreds of years, you end up with a situation like the one we have at our house some nights: at the dinner table, everyone eats a different dish, with a different sauce to go on that dish, and everyone has a unique opinion about how that dish should be prepared and eaten. Individualism reigns supreme. And kids—holy cow!—can become really overbearing.

CHAPTER 2

Why Do We Parent the Way We Do?

When Rosy was about six months old, I brought her to the pediatrician with my husband, Matt, for her checkup and vaccines. At the end of the appointment, the doctor gave us this handy chart with a list of "action items" to help the little pork bun develop and grow. The chart included information about sleep training, feeding schedules, and how important it was to talk to the baby. "Narrate everything you do," the doctor told us. "For example, as I wash my hands, I tell Rosy, 'I am washing my hands now with soap and water.'"

"You'll be good at that," Matt said, looking at me. "You're a professional talker." And it's true—as a radio reporter, I can do some darn good talkin'.

When we got home, I put the handy chart on the refrigerator, and I set forth, like millions of moms and dads across the U.S., to parent with structure, routine, and a whole lot of talking. ("Now, Rosy, I am going to open the refrigerator door. Now I am going to bring out a bottle of wine and pour it in a glass. Now I am going to drink the wine.")

AGE	SLEEP	FEEDING
3-6 MONTHS	3 Naps 9-10 Hours at night	8-12 feedings per day
6-9 MONTHS	2 Naps 10-11 hours at night	5-6 feedings per day
9-12 MONTHS	2 naps 10-11 hours at night	Breastfeed before offering food; follow cues.

I got this, I thought to myself. Then I stepped back from the refrigerator and stared at the chart. Printed in black and white ink, on 8x11 paper, the chart reminded me of something that a Human Resources representative might hand me at the end of a required "training session." A little seed of doubt sprouted in my mind. I started to wonder: Where did this advice come from? Was it the best advice out there?

When I first became a mom, I had this sense that the way we parent today is the way we've always parented. That moms and dads have always talked to babies and young children like we do. That we've always stimulated and instructed children the way we do. We've always showered them with toys, trinkets, and praise. When a three-year-old takes her plate over to the kitchen sink after dinner, parents have always said, in a high-pitched voice, something like "Oh, fantastic! What a great helper you are."

In other words, I assumed that the advice on the pediatrician's chart was tried-and-true, handed down through the generations. That in a Macedonian village hundreds of years ago, great-great-great . . . great-grandmother Doucleff had held her baby and followed the same advice that's on the doctor's chart.

Sure, we parents have picked up a few new tips and tools from science and medicine over the years to make our lives easier and our children healthier. What those innovations may have lacked in historical precedence, they made up for with good scientific data backing them.

And so I believed that the advice coming from doctors and experts today was the best guidance parents have ever received. I believed that modern moms and dads were are all marching, en masse, toward an optimal parenting regime. One evening, a friend of mine even flat-out said this to me: "Michaeleen, we are optimizing the optimal."

Then about a year after I taped the doctor's chart to our refrigerator, I stumbled upon one of the most remarkable books I've ever read. I can't remember where I found it. It's not a bestseller. I think it's ranked about number 4,000 in Amazon's Baby & Toddler Parenting books. And it's quite dense—I spent months reading the entire book. But it was worth every minute. This book single-handedly shifted how I thought about "parenting advice"—and our culture's approach to dealing with children.

In the early 1980s, the British writer Christina Hardyment found herself in a difficult predicament: she had four children under the age of six. (Four under six? Is that even biologically possible? I shiver to imagine.) She felt overwhelmed by all the advice she heard from doctors, journalists, and book writers. And ultimately, she became suspicious of said advice. *Hmm*, she thought, just like me. *Where does this knowledge come from, anyway?*

So Christina undertook a massive project. She read and reviewed more than 650 parenting books and manuals, dating all the way back to the mid-1700s; around this time, "experts" began writing manuals for "intelligent parents," and the field of pediatrics began to emerge as a distinct discipline. The resulting book, called *Dream Babies*, traces the history of parenting advice from John Locke in the 1600s to the rise of Bill and Martha Sears in the 1990s.

The book's conclusion is a whopper: Much of the parenting advice out there today isn't based on "scientific or medical studies," or even on traditional knowledge passed down from grandmas to moms for centuries. Instead, a big chunk of it comes from centuries-old pamphlets—often written by male doctors—intended for foundling hospitals, where nurses cared for dozens, even hundreds, of abandoned babies, all at once. With these pamphlets, doctors were essentially trying to industrialize infant care. But their publications found another hungry audience: exhausted moms and dads. Over time, the size and scope of the doctors' pamphlets grew. Ultimately, they morphed into the advice books we have today, which are "swollen descendants of terse little booklets written by eighteenth-century doctors for the use of nurses in the foundling hospitals," Christina wrote. "Techniques of handling children have not made the steady progress toward improvement that some historians of childhood assert," but instead "they have always been tailored, sometimes attractively, sometimes unpleasantly, to suit the times."

Take, for instance, the idea that babies need to feed on a particular schedule—every two hours, as my pediatrician told me. That advice dates back at least to 1748, when Dr. William Cadogan penned an essay for the nurses at Coram's Foundling Hospital in London—a hospital that admitted nearly a hundred babies each day. Clearly, the staff at Coram couldn't feed (or even hug) so many babies whenever they cried (or "on demand," as we say). And so the doctor recommended four feedings a day, decreasing to two or three after three months. Initially a war doctor, William had turned to pediatrics after the birth of his daughter in 1746. And he came to the pediatric field with some misogynistic views of parenting: "It is with great Pleasure I see at last the Preservation of Children become the Care of Men of Sense. In my opinion, this Business has been too long fatally left to the management of Women, who cannot be supposed to have a proper Knowledge to fit them for the Task." (Never mind the fact that women had been fit for the task for millennia in Europe and two hundred thousand years elsewhere.)

A few decades after William published his recommendation for feeding schedules, doctors began offering up advice about babies' sleep—and their predilection for forming "bad habits." In 1848, Dr. John Ticker Conquest completely disregarded tens of thousands of years of history and warned mothers not to rock babies to sleep lest they become addicted to it. A rocker, he wrote, was an apparatus "contrived and at one time made use of to subdue furious lunatics." Experts also started recommending that babies physically separate from moms at night, and even stop nursing. "Although the baby's instinctive craving for its mother's presence was recognized, it was more important to ingrain it with the convenient habit of sleeping alone in a cot," Christina wrote.

And sleep training? Guess who proposed that unique technique? Why, a surgeon-turned-sportswriter, of course, who wrote under the pseudonym Stonehenge. If babies "are left to go to sleep in their cots, and allowed to find out that they do not get their way by crying, they at once become reconciled, and after a short time will go to bed even more readily in the cot than on the lap," Dr. John Henry Walsh wrote in his *Manual of Domestic Economy* in 1857. Besides doling out advice on infant sleep, John Henry also authored several books about guns, including *The Shot-Gun and Sporting Rifle* and *The Modern Sportsman's Gun and Rifle*. (And he lost a big chunk of his left hand one day when a gun exploded in his grasp.)

In the end, these doctors' advice books shifted how parents viewed children's sleep. For the first time, babies and kids no longer went to sleep when they were tired and woke up when they were rested. Instead, parents were now required to control, regulate, and time children's sleep, just like they did with a turkey roasting in the oven. Suddenly, there were all these rules and requirements about sleep, which didn't exist before. Parents became the sleep police. "Bedtime was now an opportunity to show who was boss," Christina wrote. Eventually, rules for sleep morphed into a moral issue: If your kids aren't sleeping at optimal times, for an optimal amount each day, then not only are you a bad parent, but look out! Your children are going to have problems later in life—problems in school, problems getting a job, problems . . . Well, just problems. Lots of problems.

I came away from reading Christina's book with a new perspective on the chart on the fridge. I no longer believe that Western parents today have the best advice, honed through centuries of experience and further refined by science. We are *not* executing optimal parenting. That idea couldn't be further from the truth. D'oh.

But rather, in many cases, we have the first advice printed on a page, no matter how ineffective that advice is. "Bedtime routines, bedtime routines, bedtime routines!" I hear from every direction, from my girlfriends to my pediatrician. But if bedtime routines work so well, then why does my home sound like a war zone at eight p.m. each night? And why has a book called *Go the F**k to Sleep* sold millions of copies in the past decade or so?

In fact, if you take a close look at many linchpins of modern Western parenting, you'll find surprisingly flimsy origin stories. These customs didn't catch on by proving to be effective or good for children, but rather because of timing and product placement.

––––––––

Over the past 150 years, Western parents have picked up three practices that have become cornerstones of our relationships with children. They are things that we think we *have* to do and also what we do *without* thinking. When you look at how these practices first came about, you find a repeating pattern.

No. 1: Thingamajig Apocalypse

Take, for instance, the plethora of pink, lime, and powder-blue thingamajigs piled up in the corner of our living room—those hundred or so plastic objects that I end up cleaning up each night. Yes, I am talking about toys (Legos and Magna-Tiles specifically). I give Rosy Legos because I think that they'll help her grow and develop cognitively, and because I want to keep her busy. But no scientific evidence has proven that children need these doodads. In fact, there's a strong possibility that Rosy would fare better in college, at her future job—heck, even in life, generally—without having a constant stream of new toys cluttering our home.

So why do I feel the need to provide Rosy with ABC train puzzles, fake tea sets, and wooden fruit she can "cut" with a fake wooden knife? Why do these items take up precious space in our cramped San Francisco condo?

The answer has more to do with the Industrial Revolution—and burgeoning consumerism—than it does with cognitive science or child development.

Back in the early 1800s, all kids in the U.S. pretty much played in the same way—no matter if they were rich, poor, or somewhere in between, they didn't have toys in their homes. Instead, they did what kids have done for two hundred thousand years: they created their own toys with objects they found around the house or outside. "A lack of store-bought toys was no disadvantage," historian Howard Chudacoff explained in his illuminating book *Children at Play: An American History*. "Even in wealthy families, informal playthings seemed more important than formal toys," he wrote. "Connecticut-born Caroline Stickney, daughter of a paper mill owner, cut up discarded bedsheets for doll clothes . . . [while] countless boys whittled toy boats and weapons from sticks and discarded pieces of wood, and they fashioned kites from paper, cloth, and string that they had collected."

In the mid-1800s, a new idea in psychology emerged and collided with the Industrial Revolution—and Western children have never played the same way again. Parenting experts began advocating for the "use of blocks, in school and at home, to teach values of order as well as building skills," and for the use of "board games to enhance powers of planning and order," Howard wrote.

A few decades later, the Industrial Revolution ushered in countless new ways to produce toys, dolls, puzzles, and books—in bulk. Never before were children's trinkets cheaper to produce or more appealing to children. Toys were more colorful; dolls were more lifelike; and both were more widely advertised to eager parents who had more disposable income in their pockets. At the same time, psychologists began to think that play was important for children's development. They advised parents to encourage children to play instead of helping with chores or the family business.

The end result was an explosion of toys in middle-class homes. "Good parents" no longer let children build their own toys from sheets and wood, but diligently showered them with the latest manufactured version of kites, weapons, dolls, and fake food. Toys, once thought to be completely unnecessary, were now deemed essential. And play, once considered the "devil's workshop," was now healthy and desirable.

Remarkably, you see this same pattern repeating again and again in key aspects of Western parenting. A practice comes along at the right time in history; it becomes overhyped by the media, psychologists, pediatricians, public health experts, or all four combined; and then its importance is amplified by a product you must buy or a scary self-help book you must read. The practice infiltrates our homes, schools, churches, and health facilities, and eventually becomes so baked into the fabric of parenting that we hardly even realize it exists.

Nothing could be more true than for the second "cornerstone" of parenting—what I think of as "Learn-a-palooza."

No. 2: Learn-a-palooza

This idea has been simmering in Western culture for about a century, but in the 1950s, it shot off like a rocket.

On October 4, 1957, the Soviet Union shocked the world by successfully launching Sputnik 1, the first artificial satellite, into Earth's orbit. The achievement hit "like a spitball in the eyes of American child-raising experts, educators, and Cold War propagandists," journalists Barbara Ehrenreich and Deirdre English wrote in their book, *For Her Own Good: Two Centuries of the Experts' Advice to Women*. A chorus of authorities blamed American parents for lacking the savvy of Soviet parents, who had clearly been raising their young to surpass American children in innovation and academics—"at least some of them [Russian children] were *more* creatively daring and imaginative than their American counterparts."

Sputnik 1 generated an almost instantaneous national mood of panic and alarm. American children were falling behind Russian kids, and if democracy and free will were to survive, gosh darn it, America's youth—from babies to teenagers—needed to learn faster, learn more, and learn earlier. "Johnny had *better* learn to read . . . or we may wind up in a world where no English is written anymore," a public service announcement asserted in *Newsweek* and *Reader's Digest* shortly after the satellite's launch.

And guess who suddenly bore the burden of teaching three-year-old

Johnny to read? The mother, of course. "It was her job to keep the child's sensory apparatus employed full-time," Barbara and Deirdre wrote. Mothers "were [now] supposed to keep the environment challenging, noisy, colorful, and ever-changing."

As a parent, it was no longer enough to make cookies with your four-year-old son, you also had to give him a math lesson on fractions. Every walk in the woods became a science exercise. Every story before bed became a chance to quiz the child on vocabulary. Every moment became a chance for mommy or daddy to stimulate the child; the more the better. And if you don't, not only will the Reds take over the world, but little Johnny won't get into college.

In the 1960s, parenting experts used guilt, shame, and fear to charge American parents with a new task: stimulate, instruct, and teach children, at every moment. This high-energy, high-talking approach stuck like superglue in American culture. We take the practice for granted. *Of course* that dad is giving that toddler a full physics lecture at the playground. *Of course* I started reading to Rosy when she was two months old and continue to now, when she's three years old. *Of course* we have 143 children's books in our house. That's not just normal. It's beneficial. It's optimal.

It's also exhausting (for moms, dads, and kids alike). And it's still not enough. Because on top of stimulation and lectures, we need to do something else—constantly.

No. 3: Praise. Praise. And More Praise

Toward the end of the twentieth century, society gave overworked parents yet another responsibility. And this one was a real doozy.

Praise is so ubiquitous around children today that you almost don't notice it. But if you pay attention (and even start to count it), it's almost unbelievable how much praise everyone showers on young children. We'll visit the post office and Rosy will put a stamp on a letter, and the man behind the counter will act as if she just negotiated peace in the Middle East. "Amazing! You put the stamp on the letter? What an incredible helper you are."

Truth is, I praise Rosy without even thinking about it. "Oh wow, you drew an *R*! Beautiful." "Good job putting that fork on the table." "You put your shoes on! Happy dance time." "You drew a heart! What an amazing artist you are!" The list goes on and on and on.

Why do I do this? Because in the 1980s and '90s, books, magazine articles, psychologists, and pediatricians began telling parents that if they didn't praise children, ad nauseam, something horrible would happen: we would hurt their budding self-esteem.

Defining the term "self-esteem" is a matter for another book. But let's just put it this way: Self-esteem is a cultural creation, not a human universal. The concept percolated through American popular culture during the 1960s, then took over our minds, schools, and homes with a rip-roaring vengeance a couple of decades later (when it became a keystone of the multibillion-dollar self-help industry). Western culture is likely the only place where the concept of "self-esteem" exists—and we are definitely the only culture that requires parents to maintain and cultivate it in their children. In America, parents are made to feel like they must nurture a "healthy" sense of self-esteem in their children, else their children could suffer from all types of social and emotional problems, including failure at school, alcohol and drug abuse, crime, violence, and even teenage pregnancy.

But when you actually look at the data connecting poor self-esteem with all these problems, the studies come up appallingly shorthanded. Causal connections are slim, shoddy, or nonexistent. Nevertheless, lack of evidence didn't stop experts from telling parents how to prevent such a dreadful future from befalling their children. They recommended a surprisingly simple measure: give children enormous praise and ignore their mistakes. "Parents were told to praise their young children at every opportunity, to criticize sparingly, to handle discipline with care lest self-esteem be damaged, to invite self-expression, and to encourage children to try new things," psychologists Peggy Miller and Grace Cho wrote in their mind-blowing book, *Self-Esteem in Time and Place*, published in 2017.

No one knows what effect all this praise—and erasure of criticism—has had on kids, the two wrote. The science is all over the map on the topic. In some instances, praise can motivate children to learn and behave. But in other situations, praise is demotivating. The result depends on a whole slew of circumstances—what actions you praise, how much the child feels they deserve the praise, how you dish it out, the age and personality of the children, the relationship you have with the child, et cetera.

And when praise greatly outweighs criticism—when parents ignore misdeeds and shortcomings—Miller and Cho worry that parents may be making their own lives harder in the long run. They may be teaching children to be self-centered and to compete with siblings for adult praise and attention. Children may become more vulnerable to depression and anxiety as they grow into adulthood.

In my experience, all the praise just makes Rosy more annoying—a bit more of a pain in the butt. She follows me around, literally seeking feedback and attention ("Look at me, Mama!"). Besides, constantly boosting Rosy's self-esteem is simply exhausting for me. As Miller and Cho point out, the approach requires that parents "spend a great deal of time and energy monitoring their children's behavior."

And when you look across cultures—and throughout history—our parenting approach (e.g., oodles of praise, little to no criticism, and constantly soliciting a child's preference) stands alone. One could argue that we're the only ones ever to act this way. In many cultures, parents praise very little—or not at all. Yet their children grow up exhibiting all signs of robust mental health, as well as great empathy. Furthermore, in the cultures we'll visit in this book, the children who receive little praise show more confidence and mental strength than their American counterparts, who are steeped in praise.

To be honest, after reading Miller and Cho's book, I felt a great sense of relief. For the first time since Rosy was born, I felt that I didn't need to praise her every action. That her self-esteem wasn't this fragile Fabergé egg that I would crush at any moment. I could let it all go and just be with her. I could just sit next

to her on the bus and not feel the need to tell her, "Good job!" (or lecture her about the physics of the bus's wheels). Our time together began to feel more like the time I spent with my grandfather as a little girl: calm, quiet, less pressure to perform.

And a funny thing happened. After a week or so with no praise, I noticed my words becoming more effective. When I did give her feedback, she was more likely to listen. The constant stream of praise and feedback had been drowning out what was actually important to me. Without the extra remarks, Rosy could more easily understand when I really needed her to listen or be cooperative. Even brushing her teeth at night became easier.

––––––––––

In his nonfiction megahit *Sapiens*, Yuval Noah Harari argued that progress in humanity is an illusion. And in many ways, technology and science have actually made our lives harder, not easier. Take, for example, email. The technology has certainly made communication faster, but at what cost? Has email made our lives more relaxed? "Sadly not," Yuval wrote. Now each day, hundreds of communications flood our inboxes (and our minds) from people who expect prompt replies. "We thought we were saving time [with new technologies]; instead we revved up the treadmill of life to ten times its former speed and made our days more anxious and agitated."

One could make the same arguments about parenting. As we've accumulated more technologies, more products, and more psychological insights, perhaps we've made our jobs much harder. We expect children to be busy at every moment, to promptly obey our every request, and to reach every milestone as early as possible. We've revved up the treadmill of parenting ten times, and indeed, we've become more anxious and agitated.

In other words, as we've devoted more and more resources to our children, have we become better parents, or simply more exhausted parents? Perhaps, in the process, we've lost critical parenting skills and knowledge our ancestors—or even our grandparents—once possessed. Skills that helped us to raise children more harmoniously, more calmly, and more effectively. Skills that made being a mom or dad much more enjoyable.

Now is our chance to recover those skills, and learn a few new ones in the process.

To do that, we're going to shift gears. We're going to expand our circle of parenting experts. Instead of relying solely on doctors, scientists, and surgeons-turned-sportswriters for parenting advice, we're going to learn from the world's superparents, whose tools and techniques boast what our modern tools lack: time and numbers. Their strategies have been tested and honed on millions of kids over thousands—sometimes tens of thousands—of years, making them about as "evidence-based" or "research-tested" as a parent could get.

Our first stop? Maria's house in the Yucatán, where we watched her preteen daughter, Angela, hop out of bed one morning and immediately start washing the dishes—all of her own accord.

But Wait! Can't Science Tell Me How to Parent?

When I first learned I was pregnant, I was over the moon. No, make that the Milky Way. Seriously. My husband and I had tried to have a baby for more than six years. And with the help of state-of-the-art science, we finally saw those two pink stripes on the pregnancy-test strip.

Eight months later and fifty pounds heavier, I really thought I was ready to be a mom—the best mom ever. I had just returned from reporting in the heart of an Ebola outbreak, during which I didn't once feel afraid or overwhelmed. *Being a parent couldn't possibly be harder than this,* I thought. (Oh, sweet child of summer.)

Plus, I had a foolproof strategy. I would solve any parenting problem the way I solved everything in my life: with science. Baby won't sleep? Not to worry. I'll find a research paper that will give me the optimal strategy. Toddler is flailing around on the sidewalk like a fish out of water? No reason to be concerned. I was sure psychologists had figured out an easy way to stop tantrums—and just as certain it was backed by plenty of high-quality data.

So before Rosy was born, I bought a bunch of parenting books and felt reassured by the oodles of references listed in the back. Science was going to be my saving grace. (Or was it a siren's song?)

Two months into motherhood, I suddenly started to hit roadblocks—serious roadblocks. Breastfeeding proved almost impossible. It took a herculean effort for both Rosy and me to survive the first six weeks of her life. After we fixed that issue, we ran smack into an even bigger problem: sleep. I couldn't get the little dumpling to stay asleep. Sure, she would drift off on my chest, my lap, even my back. But lay her down in the crib and, look out! Even our German shepherd started hiding her head under the bed to escape the din.

Time and again, the evidence-based strategies weren't of much help. Shocker, I know. Sometimes the strategies worked for a week or even a month, but the effect always faded, and we found ourselves back at step one.

And so I began to dig into the references in the back of the books I bought. Right away, alarm bells started blaring in my sleep-deprived brain. I may have slept for only about twenty hours in the past week, but my scientific brain wasn't complete mush. I could still see that many of these studies had major issues, from multiple directions. I started to question many of the findings and doubting that these parent strategies were actually going to work. *Can science really help me learn to be a better parent?* I wondered. Sure, science can help me to keep Rosy in good physical health with vaccines and antibiotics. But what about her mental and emotional health? Can science teach me how to get her to fall asleep more easily? How to stop her from throwing food at dinner? Or what to do when you awake one morning to see your two-year-old running down the sidewalk, buck naked? Can science tell me how to raise a kind, cooperative kid?

I posed those questions to psychologist Brian Nosek at the University of Virginia. He laughed a little, then made a statement I'll never forget: "Parenting questions are some of the hardest problems out there for science. Shooting a rocket to Mars is super easy compared to these questions." Parents are simply asking for too much from science when we want it to solve toddler tantrums or tell us how to get kids to be helpful, he said. Even in the twenty-first century, scientists just don't have the means to answer such complex questions.

Brian explained that parenting studies tend to have one major issue: they're what scientists call underpowered. This is exactly how I feel as a mom—underpowered. I am overstretched and trying to do more than my tools allow me to do. Many psychology experiments are left in the same state. They try to draw too many conclusions with too little information.

In many cases, researchers don't run the experiments on enough kids or families to know if an approach really works. Studies often involve only a few dozen kids, and even the "big" ones contain only a few hundred, not the thousands or tens of thousands needed to draw real conclusions about a parenting strategy. With too few kids in a study, you can't say with confidence whether or not the tool actually works or how well it's likely to work with *other* kids.[*]

Underpowered studies make the data look fuzzy. As Brian put it, "It's a bit like having an underpowered telescope to study the galaxy." Objects in the sky can blur together. Saturn's rings merge into the planet itself. Some of Jupiter's moons disappear. And the asteroid belt becomes a solid strip.

A researcher can write up and publish these descriptions. But what if somebody comes along with a more powerful scope? Oops. Looks like Jupiter does have moons and the asteroid belt isn't a belt at all, but more like a suspension of rocks. The initial study is completely wrong. And scientists completely reverse their initial conclusion.

The same happens with many, many parenting studies. The data supporting the recommendation are often so fuzzy that when another—more powerful—study comes along, scientists not only retract the initial recommendation, but even advocate the opposite behavior.

This flip-flopping can frustrate parents, and it can also lead to serious repercussions for children.

This is exactly what happened with peanut allergies. Back in 2000, the American Academy of Pediatrics advised parents not to give babies peanut butter because several small studies suggested that early exposure could increase the risk of developing a peanut allergy. But eventually larger, more powerful studies followed. These studies showed just the opposite: Exposure to peanuts, early on, *decreases* a child's risk for developing allergies. The original advice was wrong. Twenty years after the initial advice, the medical community made a complete about-face and now recommends that parents introduce peanut butter into a baby's diet as early as four to six months old.

In the end, the inaccurate recommendation likely contributed to the rise in peanut allergies in the past two decades. From 1999 to 2010, peanut allergies

---

[*] In the end, the research often ends up being what scientists call irreproducible. That is, if you ran the same experiment a second time, you would get a different answer or the findings wouldn't hold up. In 2015, Brian and his colleagues published evidence that only about 60 percent of psychology research is likely reproducible. And research in social psychology—which deals with relationships—looks even worse. They found that only about 20 percent of those studies were reproducible.

in children rose from about 0.4 percent to 2 percent, the National Institutes of Health reports.

Even when studies are sufficiently powered—and have strong evidence—many times they don't tell parents what we *really* want to know: whether the tool or strategy will work with our own children. Just because a tool works in a laboratory or with a small group of kids does not mean it will be useful for your kid, in your home. At best, studies tell you what might work, on average. So a tool could work amazingly well for a quarter of the families, not at all for others, and actually make some parents' lives even harder.

Therefore Brian recommends that moms and dads be wary of new ideas that arise from studies, especially when the evidence isn't very strong and the sample size is small. At the same time, influential figures like pediatricians, public health experts, journalists, and book writers (like yours truly) should also be more cautious about promoting these ideas. People need to understand the uncertainty in any scientific conclusion. Brian added: "With everything in science, humility is good."

SECTION 2

Maya Method

Togetherness
E
A
M

If a child misbehaves, they need more responsibilities.

CHAPTER 3

The Most Helpful Kids in the World

One June morning, Rosy and I hop on a plane in San Francisco and land six hours later in the sweltering heat of Cancún. I rent a brown Nissan sedan and we head west, toward the middle of the Yucatán Peninsula. After a few hours, we reach a stand selling pink plastic flamingos, about a dozen of them. I recognize them, like a line of friendly soldiers, from my last trip here. *Aha*, I think, *this is where we turn off the main road*.

We make a sharp left onto a pitted, gravel road and bump along at twenty miles per hour. We pass a few tidy homes with thatched roofs and chickens out front. We pass a stand selling Maya honey, and at one point, we stop to let a family of goats cross the road.

I glance behind me to find Rosy fast asleep in her car seat, holding a blue teddy bear. With her blond curls and pouty pink lips, she looks like an angel when she sleeps.

The road starts to narrow. Vines and branches scrape the car windows as we swerve to avoid big potholes in the road. With no houses in sight, I get nervous. *Did we make a wrong turn?*

Suddenly the road opens up into a big courtyard, about the size of the soccer pitch, and we come face-to-face with what looks like a double-necked brontosaurus. A pink brontosaurus. It's an eighteenth-century Spanish church with two spires, rising sixty feet high in the air, and painted entirely pink.

I feel a smile take over my face. *We're finally here*, I think. *And I love this place.*

We have arrived in the center of Chan Kajaal*—a tiny Maya village nestled in a tropical rainforest, not too far from the ancient pyramid of Chichén Itzá. The mercury tops one hundred degrees Fahrenheit, and the afternoon sun bears down like a hot oven. But it doesn't matter. The village is still bustling. On one corner, a butcher hacks up a freshly killed pig with a cleaver. Across the street, a girl, maybe six years old, carries a bag of corn to the tortilleria for selling. Several teenagers hang out by a shiny blue pickup truck. I see smartphones peeking out of their back pockets. I smell the faint scent of smoke in the air.

We are less than three hours away from the touristy hubbub of Cancún, but this community feels worlds away. There's no air-conditioning here. Little Wi-Fi. So life occurs largely outside. And with it comes this warm,

---

* To protect the privacy of the families in this book, I am using a pseudonym for the name of the village.

wondrous feeling that everyone around you is family—everyone has your
back.

Everywhere you look, there are people: mingling, moving, chatting.
Older sisters walk their younger sisters home from school, books in hand.
An *abuela*, with her gray hair tied up in a neat bun, spreads pumpkin seeds
on the sidewalk to dry. Young kids zigzag around on tricycles and bikes.
Older kids zip by on motorbikes. Interwoven among them, moms and
dads ride giant cargo tricycles, pushing a front platform filled with toddlers, groceries, and a few gallons of drinking water.

The village surrounds
an underground pool of
fresh water inside a lime-
stone sinkhole called a ce-
note. For centuries, Maya
families have scooped up
the water for themselves,
their animals, and their
gardens. The fresh water
also nourishes plants and
animals throughout the
village. Palm leaves grow

the size of elephant ears. Massive mango trees rise up in backyards like hot-
air balloons. And the birds—oh my goodness, there are so many birds—sing
their hearts out from every tree.

Most families' homes consist of little compounds, composed of several
small buildings. Kitchens are usually built with wooden sticks for the
walls and palm thatches for the roofs, while bedrooms can have cinder-
block walls. You'll often see a shed in the backyard to store corn; a pen for
chickens; and a scattering of fruit trees, including bananas, bitter oranges,
and guanabanas, which have white squishy flesh that tastes as tart as a
Sour Patch Kids.

After a few turns through the village, we make our way down a dark
street, shaded by a giant royal poinciana tree. I sense that we're getting close.
In one backyard, a young woman scrubs a pair of jeans in a bin of foamy

water. A turkey spreads its tail feathers at the fence. Then up ahead, I see it: a turquoise house with white-trimmed windows. My heart speeds up a bit.

"Wake up, Rosy. Wake up," I say. "There's what we have come three thousand miles for."

"What, Mama? What is it?" Rosy says.

"It's Maria's house," I answer. "She's going to teach me all about *acomedido*. And how to teach you to be *acomedido*. Are you ready?"

———————

For the past four decades, anthropologists have been coming to the village of Chan Kajaal to study how children learn from their families and their community. Parents here have figured out something that American parents (including this one) would give a pinky finger to know: how to get children to do chores voluntarily. Maya children—as well as children from other indigenous communities in Mexico—do an enormous amount of work around the house. They do the laundry, help prepare meals, wash dishes, and tend to gardens. They make tortillas to sell at the market on weekends; they butcher and cook pigs; they take care of older relatives and younger siblings. They are competent, self-sufficient, and remarkably helpful. And for the most part, they do these tasks without being asked, threatened, or lured with rewards. No gold stars. No allowances. No promises of ice cream.

Psychologist Lucia Alcalá has been at the forefront of this research, first as a graduate student at the University of California, Santa Cruz, and now as a professor at Cal State, Fullerton. In one study, Lucia and her colleagues interviewed nineteen mothers with heritage to another indigenous group in Mexico, called Nahua. The researchers asked the moms a series of questions about how their children, ages six to eight, help around the house. How often do the children do chores? What do they do? And how often do they pitch in voluntarily? The moms' responses are remarkable.

One mother told researchers that her eight-year-old daughter comes home from school and declares: "Mom, I'm going to help you do everything." Then she "picks up the entire house, voluntarily," the study reports.

As children grow older, their help becomes even more complex and comprehensive, the study found. "The mom comes home from work, and she's really tired," says Barbara Rogoff at the University of California,

Santa Cruz, who contributed to the study with Nahua-heritage moms in Guadalajara. "The mom just plops herself down on the couch. And the daughter says, 'Mom, you're really tired, but we need to clean up the house. How about I turn on the radio and I take care of the kitchen and you take care of the living room and we'll have it all cleaned up?'"

In general, these kids had already learned complex tasks, such as cooking meals and caring for siblings without adult supervision. And about three-quarters of the mothers said that their children routinely "take initiative" with housework. The child will simply see what needs to be done, hop up, and start doing it. They'll see dishes in the sink and start washing. They'll see a messy living room and start picking up. And should a younger sibling begin to cry, they'll walk over, pick the child up, and take the child out of the house to play—all without direction from their mother.

Lucia tells me that parents are teaching their children a skill that's way more complex than simply knowing how to wash dishes or do the laundry: they're teaching the children to pay attention to their surroundings, recognize when a specific chore needs to be done, and then do it.

"They're teaching children to be responsible family members. They want children to understand when somebody is in need of help, to be alert to what's happening, and then to help," Lucia says. And that skill also means knowing when not to help, she says. "So you don't interfere with the cohesion of the group or the group's direction."

"It's a lifelong skill to understand the situation around you and then know what to do," she adds.

This skill—of paying attention and then acting—is such an important value and goal for children that many families in Mexico have a term for it: it's being *acomedido*.

The idea is complex: It's not just doing a chore or task because someone told you to; it's knowing which kind of help is appropriate at a particular moment because you're paying attention.

In the same study, Lucia and her team also interviewed fourteen moms in Guadalajara who have more Western-like backgrounds. That is, they'd lived in the city for several generations and had few ties to indigenous communities. Guess how many of these moms reported that their children routinely "take initiative" around the house? Zero. These cosmopolitan kids not only do less housework and fewer complex tasks, but they also, in general, have to be asked to do them. Some moms said they go to great lengths to convince a child to help by negotiating with them or making chore charts. These moms also reported that their kids more often require rewards, allowances, or gifts to motivate them. (Parents from both back-grounds said that they sometimes have to pressure children to help by tak-ing away privileges, such as television time.)

But here's the part that really blows my mind: many times, the Maya and Nahua-heritage kids actually enjoy doing chores! Their parents haven't just taught them *acomedido*, they have also taught the children to value their work and feel proud of their contributions to the household. Helping with chores is a privilege.

Parents don't need to bribe or nag because their children already feel an internal motivation to contribute. They *want* to help their family and *want* to work together as a team.

And so that's why I've returned to Chan Kajaal, to find out how the parents motivate the children in this way. How do they tap into children's innate desire to help?

Over time, I came to realize their method to motivate children isn't unique to Maya and Nahua communities—not in the slightest. Rather, it's a fundamental method that parents, all over the world, use to transmit their cultures' key values to children.

The gumption to help around the house is a core value in the Maya communities, which moms and dads intentionally pass down to their kids. In Western culture, we also have this value, but, in many ways, parents have forgotten how to pass it down to our children. And that loss has made our lives a lot harder.

You see, when you transmit the value of helpfulness to a child, you get a whole bundle of fringe benefits. Kids become healthier mentally, and they also become less of a pain in the butt. Why? Because when kids learn to be helpful, they also learn to cooperate and to work together with you. So when Dad puts his jacket on in the morning and walks out the door, the child follows—no whining, no fussing.

CHAPTER 4

How to Teach Kids to Do Chores, Voluntarily

"From day one, when they are small, you start showing them how to help," Maria tells me.

Maria de los Angeles Tun Burgos is the perfect supermom to teach us how to raise helpful kids who also take pride in their work around the house. She has clearly done a superb job transmitting this value to her oldest daughter, Angela, who not only voluntarily washes dishes but also cleans the house while her mom's out running errands. Maria also has two younger daughters—ages five and nine—who are at different stages of the learning process, so we can see a glimpse of how she modifies the training as children grow.

Because here's the

thing about learning to do chores, voluntarily: it takes years to learn, Maria tells me. "You have to teach them slowly, little by little, and eventually they will understand."

In this way, teaching children to be helpful is a bit like teaching a child to read or do math. You can't just give a four-year-old verbal instructions, hang up a times table on the refrigerator, and expect the young child, right away, to know that $3 \times 3 = 9$ and $8 \times 4 = 32$.

Same goes for chores. You can't simply hang up a chore chart and expect a four-year-old to start washing the dishes on Tuesdays and Thursdays without you asking. As Maria says, you have to teach the child slowly. You have to train them. The child has to understand not just how to do the chores, but also when to do them, and why doing them is important and beneficial to the family—and themselves.

If you think about it, a chore chart might actually inhibit a child from learning *acomedido*. Why? Because the whole goal is for children to pay attention to the world around them and learn when particular chores are needed. If a chore chart tells a child to do the dishes on Tuesday, sweep on Wednesday, and take the garbage out on Friday, then a child may come to the conclusion that these tasks are the only ones they need to do. Then the child doesn't need to pay attention at other times, or they may even learn to ignore chores not on the chart. The chart ends up teaching the child the opposite of *acomedido*—that is, "Your responsibility is only what's on the chart."

Just as parents teach children to do math, Maria teaches her children to be *acomedido* with an intentional process. You could break this process into three key ingredients, or steps. As we'll see throughout the book, these three ingredients mixed together form an incredibly powerful recipe for transmitting values to children. Cultures all over the world, including Western culture, use this recipe to teach children essentially any desired skill or value.

Since these steps are so critical to parenting, we'll dedicate a chapter to each one and then circle back to go over what we've learned. We'll cover step one here, and tackle steps two and three in the next two chapters, respectively.

Okay, let's get going.

For a Western parent like me, the first step is counterintuitive. You have to do almost the exact opposite of what you think makes sense: you have to turn over tasks to the least competent family members in the home.

Step 1: Value Toddlers, Inc.

When I ask Maria directly how she raises such helpful kids, she introduces me to the concept that I've come to think of as Toddlers, Inc. Yes, I'm talking about fumbling, babbling, walk-like-you're-drunk kids between the ages of one and four. I'm talking about the same population of miniature humans who, we associate more with the term "terrible" than "helpful."

Maria says these clumsy little humans are key to raising helpful big humans. To explain what she means, she points to her youngest daughter, Alexa.

"No matter what I do, Alexa wants to do it, too," Maria says. "When I'm making tortillas, Alexa starts crying if I don't let her make tortillas. And afterward, she always wants the broom to sweep up."

"How do you respond?" I ask.

"I let her make the tortillas, and I give her the broom to sweep up," Maria says.

"And she actually sweeps and is helpful?"

"It doesn't matter. She wants to help somehow and so I permit her," she says, sitting on a hammock with her hands folded in her lap.

"Whenever she wants to help, you let her?" I ask, still not understanding. "Even if she makes a giant mess?"

"Yes. That is the way to teach children."

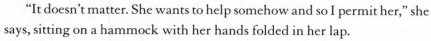

If you look at families around the world—whether they farm maize in the Yucatán, hunt zebras in Tanzania, or write books in Silicon Valley—their toddlers have two traits in common. The first is tantrums. Yes, toddler tantrums are pretty much unavoidable no matter where you live, the ethnographic record shows. But the second commonality is a bit more surprising. It's helpfulness. Toddlers everywhere are eager to be helpful—very eager.

Toddlers are born assistants. And they're hungry to get in there and get the job done "all by myself." Need to sweep up the kitchen? Rinse a dish? Or crack an egg? No worries. Toddlers, Inc., will be there on the double. Watch out! Here they come.

In one study, twenty-month-olds actually stopped playing with a new toy and walked across the room to help an adult pick up something from the floor. No one had to ask the toddler for their help, nor did the toddler need a reward for their assistance. In fact, the toddlers were less likely to help a second time if they were given a toy afterward, the study found. Now, that's *acomedido*!

No one understands exactly why toddlers feel so motivated to help (or why rewards appear to diminish the impulse). But it could stem from their strong drive to be around their family and connected to their parents, siblings, and other caregivers.

"I think this point is really key," says psychologist Rebeca Mejía-Arauz at ITESO University in Guadalajara. "Doing things with other people makes them happy and is important for their emotional development."

While I'm visiting Maria in the Yucatán, she emphasizes this same point. "When children are little, they like to do what the mother is doing. Alexa likes to play mom with her toys and dolls," she says.

In other words, toddlers are born with all the ingredients needed to become *acomedidos* all around the world, even here in the U.S. What differs is how the parents treat their little ones' *acomedido*. And that difference is critical—it's likely what determines whether the child continues to help voluntarily as they grow up or whether they "grow out of it," Rebeca says.

Many parents with Western backgrounds, including this San Francisco mom, often rebuff a toddler's offers to help. I mean, let's face it—toddlers may want to help, but they aren't very helpful. I know Rosy sure isn't. She is a destruction machine, and her involvement in chores slows me down and makes a giant mess for me to clean up. So I would rather her play in the living room or color on the kitchen floor next to me while I clean up the house. And I'm not alone.

Rebeca tells me, "We have mothers tell us things like 'I need to do a chore very quickly, and if my toddler tries to help, he makes a mess. So I'd rather do it myself than having them helping.'" In many instances, parents with Western backgrounds tell their toddlers to go and play while they do the chores. Or give their child a screen. If you think about it, we are telling the child *not* to pay attention, *not* to help. We are telling them, this chore is not for you. Without realizing it, we cut short a toddler's eagerness to help, and we segregate them from useful activities.

But indigenous moms in Mexico often do the opposite: "They welcome the help, and even ask for it," Rebeca says—even if the child acts rudely. If the child literally grabs the tools from the parent to take over a job (sound familiar?), the parent will still yield to the child, allowing the toddler to practice the task.

Take, for example, a two-year-old toddler who is eager to help her mom dig a maize field in a Mazahua community of northwest Mexico.

The mom begins weeding the garden. Right away, her daughter starts to mimic the mother's actions. Then the toddler demands to do the job all by herself. The mother lets her do this and waits. Soon the girl has taken over for the mother completely. When the mom tries to start again, the girl protests and demands that she be allowed to do it. All by herself! Again, the mom yields to the tiny, bossy human.

Rosy acts this way often. She demands my job. She grabs the fork while I'm trying to scramble eggs in the morning. She grabs the knife while I'm cutting onions for dinner. She grabs the dog bowl when I'm trying to feed the dog, the broom when I sweep, and my laptop when I'm trying to write (and then proceeds to punch every key as fast as possible).

Typically I respond to her grabbiness the way my parents responded to me as a little girl: I push her pudgy little hands away and say something accusatory, like "Don't grab from me!" And then I interpret her actions or behavior as demanding and controlling (I even hear my mom's voice in my head: "She wants to control you, Michaeleen").

But many indigenous parents are happy the grabby toddler jumped in to help. They're happy to see the toddler take initiative. They interpret the child's pushiness as a desire to contribute to the family. The only problem is that the child is too young to know, at first, how to help in the best way. The child just needs to learn. "One mom told us: 'When my toddler was doing the dishes, at the beginning, the water was all over the place, but I would allow my son to do the dishes because that's how he learned,'" Rebeca says, referring to her interviews with Nahua-heritage moms in Guadalajara.

Parents see this mess as an investment. If you encourage the incompetent toddler who really wants to do the dishes now, then over time, they'll turn into the competent nine-year-old who still wants to help—and who can really make a difference.

"For example, I talked to a family who had a business selling meat," Rebeca explains. One of the sons was interested in cooking pork very early. "The mother would hold the child while she was cooking." Sometimes she would even let him pick up pieces while cooking and move them to a plate. "She said it was risky because he could get burned. 'I was watching him carefully,' she told me." But over time the boy's abilities—and interest—in the family business grew and grew. By the time he was nine years old, he was making significant contributions to the family business. "He could even slaughter the animals," Rebeca adds.

Now, there are a few caveats here. Parents don't accept *every* offer from a child to help—or let the child do whatever they want, willy-nilly. If the task is too advanced for the child, the parent may ignore the child's request, or break the task into a smaller, more doable subtask. If the child begins to waste precious resources, the parent will guide the child into being more productive or tell them to leave.

In one Maya community in Chiapas, Mexico, parents *intentionally* reject young children's offers to help in order to increase their motivation in the task. For example, a two-year-old boy, Beto, wants to help his dad install a cement floor—a job that's way too difficult for the toddler. At first, the dad ignores Beto's pleas to participate. Then the father tells the boy that he needs to wait another year before he's ready for the task. This implicit rejection fuels the boy's desire to participate even more. Eventually, the boy grabs a tool and starts smoothing out the cement. Happy to see the boy so eager, the dad smiles. Then he watches Beto carefully and offers simple corrections, such as "Baby, not like that." When Beto makes a serious mistake and steps into the wet cement, the father states what the boy did wrong ("Baby, heeey, you stepped on it . . . you ruin it."), and he ends Beto's participation by telling him that his mom is looking for him.

Starting at a very early age, children are learning—and practicing—their place in the family. By including a toddler in a task, the parent is, in effect, telling the child, "You are a working member of the family who helps and contributes however they can."

Psychologists believe that the more a young child practices helping the family, even starting as a toddler, the more likely they will grow up to be a helpful teenager for whom chores are natural. Early involvement in chores sets the child on a trajectory that leads them to helping voluntarily later in life. It transforms their role in both the family and community. They become a responsible, contributing member.

On the flip side, if you constantly discourage a child from helping, they believe they have a different role in the family. Their role is to play or move out of the way. Another way to put it: If you tell a child enough times, "No, you're not involved in this chore," eventually the child will believe you and will stop wanting to help. Children will come to learn that helping is not their responsibility.

Psychologist Lucia Alcalá and her colleagues have documented this effect in the lab. In one experiment, she and her team gave pairs of siblings a task to perform collaboratively. They had to help each other pick out items at a model grocery store. With one set of European American brothers, the younger brother kept offering suggestions for groceries to buy. "He was trying to help," Lucia says, "but his older brother just pushed him away, over and over again. At one point, the older brother physically moves the little brother's arm away so he can't point to a grocery item."

After a few tries, the younger boy simply lost interest in the task. "The younger sibling goes under the table and, basically, gives up," Lucia recalls. "In another case, the younger brother goes away and doesn't want to continue because there's no room for him to be part of this activity."

Lucia thinks the same scenarios likely happen when parents tell children, over and over again, to go play while the parents do chores. This forms a pattern from which children learn that their role in the family is to play Legos or watch videos while their parent cooks and cleans.

Fortunately, all is not lost. Not in the slightest. Children of all ages (including a few adults I know) are incredibly malleable, and their desire to help is so strong that this pattern can easily shift. The key is for you, the parent, to shift how you think about the child. Encourage a child's involvement at any age, follow the ideas in the next chapter, and before you realize it, you'll turn a self-absorbed preteen into a dish-drying dynamo.

I put this idea to the test recently when I had the pleasure of taking care of a nine-year-old in our house for a week. She's a TikTok-loving preteen who walked around our home with her phone about three inches from her nose. On her first night with us, I asked her to come peel a potato, and she looked at me like I was from Mars. But I kept applying the strategies in the next chapter, and within a couple of days, she had already developed a keen desire to pitch in with household chores (and she served as a wonderful role model for Rosy). She volunteered to help me make the bed and ran into the kitchen at dinnertime to help chop vegetables.

By day five, she was following me around the house like a tween duckling. "What's next, Michaeleen?" she'd ask. She wasn't helping at every moment, but she was making real contributions to our family. And she and I were connecting in a genuine way. I could tell she enjoyed being part of our team and that she took pride helping and working together.*

So the first step to raising helpful kids can be summed up in a single phrase: Let them practice. Practice cleaning. Practice cooking. Practice washing. Let them grab the spoon from your hand and stir the pot. Let them grab the vacuum and start cleaning the rug. Let them make a bit

---

* The techniques in the next chapter also work on adults. With these tools and a little patience, I have trained several adults in my life to be much more helpful.

of a mess when they are little, slightly less of a mess as they grow, and by the time they're preteens, they will be helping to clean up your messes without you having to ask them—or even running your entire household.

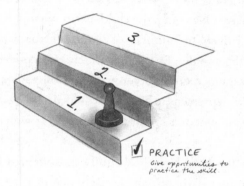

STEPS TO TRAINING
A CHILD

✓ PRACTICE
Give opportunities to
practice the skill.

It's never too early (or too late) to start inviting children to help, Rebeca says: "Children can really be involved in household chores way earlier and do way more than you realize." Western parents often underestimate what a child, at any age, is capable of when it comes to helping a family. So set your expectations high, and let the child show you what they can do, through their interests and their demands. ("But, Mom, I can do it!" Rosy tells me every day.)

Along the way, you will learn something about your kids and yourself. You will know how to work together, side by side, on common goals.

Try It 1: Train Helpfulness

The tiniest little staggerer has tasks to perform—to carry water, to borrow firebrands, to fetch leaves, to stuff the pig . . . learning to run errands tactfully is one of the first lessons of childhood.

———————

When it comes to requesting help around the house, Western culture has it backward. We tend to view toddlers and young children as being exempt from chores and pitching in. We often think they're incapable of really helping. That's certainly how I viewed Rosy. I thought I'd assign her chores as she got older, but while she was a toddler, I wouldn't ask for her help.

Yet in many hunter-gatherer cultures, parents take the opposite approach: as soon as a child starts to walk, parents begin requesting their help with tiny subtasks. Over time, the child learns what needs to be done around the house. And so, the number of requests actually *decreases* (not increases) as the child gets older. By the time the child is a preteen, adults no longer need to make many requests because the child already knows what's required. In fact, asking preteens to help out would almost be disrespectful. It would imply that they hadn't matured or learned. It would imply that they were childish.

Psychologist Sheina Lew-Levy beautifully documented this strategy with the BaYaka hunter-gatherers in the Republic of the Congo. First, Sheina learned to speak and understand the tribe's language. Then she followed children and their parents around for hours each day and counted how many times a parent or other adult in the community requested a child's help with such tasks as "Hold the water cup," "Come with me to find honey," "Carry these stakes for hunting," or "Help your sister get dressed."

What Sheina found was striking: the youngest children, ages three to four, received the most requests, while the older ones, kids in their teens, received the fewest. As the children grew older, they were expected to already know what to do. The small, easy requests, given early on, had taught children what's expected of them. Parents had successfully transmitted the value of helpfulness. "Children develop cooperative behaviors as they age," Sheina concludes. "Children are learning how to do tasks that are asked of them, and anticipating that they need to be done."

Another way to put that: Older children have already learned *acomedido*. They already know how to pay attention to the needs of others and what to do to help. So they don't need to be asked. Asking would be denigrating and embarrassing, and would earn you a big eye roll from a fourteen-year-old. ("Like really, Mom, I already know.")

So how do you start to bring the concept of *acomedido* into your family? It's actually not hard. When you're doing chores, and need help, ask for it. Or just make sure that the kids are around to watch. Here are a few ideas to get you started for babies to preteens.

Keep in mind, the age groups I'm suggesting are very approximate. Base your expectations on how much experience a child has doing a chore rather than how old they are. If a nine-year-old hasn't spent much time with you while you cook dinner or do laundry, don't expect them to already know how to do these tasks. Start off by giving them small subtasks (e.g., "Cut this onion" or "Put this shirt away") and work up from there. You may even want to start with the "Young Children" section on the next page. (That's what I do with adults who need to learn how to be helpful.)

Remember, the guidance here is intended simply to give you some ideas of what to try. See what the child wants to do or responds to. Let their interest and inclinations guide you.

Babies (0 to walking)

Think: *Watch and include*

"As early as the child can sit, sit him next to you while you're working, and he can see what you're doing," a Yucatec Maya mom told Lucia Alcalá and her colleagues.

With babes fresh from the oven, the primary way they can "practice" helping is by being close to a parent and watching their work. Toss out the idea that you have to "entertain" the baby with toys and other "enrichment" devices. Your daily chores are more than enough entertainment. Go about your business with the child in tow. When possible, let the baby see what you're doing. Prop her up in a seat so she can see you wash the dishes, cut vegetables, or fold laundry. Attach her to your stomach while you sweep, vacuum, or walk around the grocery store. Include babies in every task that helps you and other members of the family.

Young Children (from ages 1 to about 6)

Think: *Show, encourage, and request help*

"Once the child starts walking, you can begin to ask them to help you. . . . They can [for example] bring me my shoes from across the room," a Nahua-heritage mom told Rebeca Mejía-Arauz.

"When I wake up, I always clean and make breakfast—and the children are watching me. If you show them how to do it every day, they will eventually do it themselves," a Maya mom told me.

At this age, the goal is to fan the flames of a child's enthusiasm to help, not extinguish them. Here's how to do that:

Show

Just like with babies, make sure that young children have regular and predictable access to everyday chores. Avoid shooing them off to another room or outside to play. Instead, invite them to come over and be close to you while you work, so that they can learn by watching and occasionally pitching in.

"Many moms will say something like 'Come, my child. Help me while I wash the dishes,'" Rebeca tells me, referring to her interviews with Nahua-heritage moms. "The invitation is always for together, for doing the chore together."

Encourage

If a child asks to help, let them! If the task is simple, step back and let them have a shot at it. Don't start instructing; for small children, words are lectures—and confusing ones at that. Watch what the child does and try to build off their effort. If they start to make a big mess or big mistakes, gently guide them back into being productive. For example, in the Maya community in Chiapas, two-year-old Beto wants to help his grandma shell beans, but he's clumsy about it. The boy grabs a handful of whole beans and throws them in the trash. So his grandma corrects him and shows him the right way. She takes the beans out of the child's hand, before he can throw them away, and tells him that whole beans aren't to be thrown away. When Beto ignores her, she repeats the guidance.

If a task is too advanced—or too dangerous—for a child's skill level, relax. Stay calm. No need to scare them. Tell the child to watch while you do the task. For example, one Maya mom, while frying tortillas, tells her toddler, "Watch so you can learn." Or find some way that a toddler can participate that's safe. For example, Rosy holds the plate for me while I take chicken off the grill, or she adds salt and oil to a pot of pasta.

"Depending on the activity, sometimes children observe and other times they help," Lucia tells me. "Each mom knows whether a child can do a task or not." (And how do they know that? Guess what the mom has been doing while the child helps. Yup, watching. Watching. Watching. Are you detecting a theme here?)

Request Help

"A barely mobile toddler may be asked to carry a cup from its mother across an evening family circle to its father," writes David Lancy in The Anthropology of Childhood: Cherubs, Chattel, Changelings.

In the vast majority of cultures around the world (perhaps in all cultures, except a few WEIRD exceptions), parents will ask toddlers and young children to help them with a variety of tasks throughout the day. David calls this the "chore curriculum," but maybe in Western culture we should call it the "cooperation curriculum," because these tasks teach children to work together with their family. I'm not talking about tasks your children might already do for themselves, such as getting dressed or brushing their teeth. Instead, what you're folding in here are small, quick, easy tasks that help another person— or the whole family. These are requests performed alongside the parents for a common goal. They are often subtasks of a larger one (e.g., holding the door open while you take the garbage out). And they are often tiny—I mean *tiny*, tiny (e.g., putting away one pot in the cabinet that's across the kitchen, grabbing a bowl from the cabinet), but they are real. They really help.

There's no need to go overboard with the requests: three or four a day is probably enough. Just see what needs arise—say, when your hands are

full or your body is tired—and what the child shows interest in. Here are
a few tasks to try:

Go Fetch

> *"Run and fetch me" is one of the commonest phrases heard addressed to
> young children in Tikopia [Solomon Islands].*
>
> —Raymond Firth, anthropologist

Young children are great task rabbits. They can go fetch an item from the
car, garage, or yard. "Go upstairs to get toilet paper." "Go to the other room
to grab a pillow." "Go outside to pick some mint." Even simply walking
across the room to get your shoes is a great task for a toddler. Go, go, go.
Young kids *love* to go. Harness that energy while also teaching them to pay
attention to the needs of others.

Hold This

Holding objects while you work is another great job for kids—of all ages.
Not only does it encourage them to stick around so they can learn by
watching, it also frees up your hands. Here are some examples (notice the
pronoun usage; it's all about doing a task together):

- "Hold the light while we try to fix the stove."
- "Hold the plate while we take the pancakes out of the pan."
- "Hold the door while we take the garbage out."

Stir This

Young children are great sous-chefs. They can:

- Stir sauces, cake mixes, and dressings.
- Crack eggs.
- Marinate meat and fish.
- Tear herbs.
- Pound paste with a mortar and pestle.
- Start cutting or peeling vegetables. (We'll talk more about knives

later. But for now, you may want to start a toddler off with a steak knife or buy a small peeler.)

Carry This

Carrying can be a family endeavor. If your hands are full, then your children's hands can be full, too. After the grocery store, pack a small backpack or shoulder bag for children to carry to the car or into the house. Then work together to put the groceries away. With this activity, children will learn to organize the groceries in the kitchen and plan meals together with the family. While traveling, use a small suitcase so children can carry—and pack—their belongings. In our household, everybody carries something when we travel, shop, or go to school.

Tasks That Give Love

Young children love being "the mama," "the dada," or the "big brother or sister." Start training them to be kind to siblings by having them grab clean diapers, throw away dirty ones, pick up the baby's toys, entertain and feed the baby, and even work with you to prepare food and bottles. If the baby is crying, pause to see if the toddler or older child will help before you jump and pick up the baby.

Finally . . . Clean, Clean, Clean

Young children are the consummate cleaners. They can rinse dishes, pour soap into the dishwasher or washing machine, wipe tables, vacuum . . . you name it, toddlers will clean it. Whatever they lack in thoroughness, they make up for in interest and zest. It might not be super clean afterward, but they will try very hard to make it that way. Don't interfere with their actions. Give them the tools and let them go wild cleaning.

In general, any small task is great for young children. Again, see what the child shows interest in and welcome their help there. A few principles to keep in mind:

1. The task should be real, and it should make a real contribution to the family. The contribution doesn't have to be a large one, but it shouldn't be made up. For example, asking a child to "sweep the floor" after you've already swept it is not a real task. Nor is asking a child to cut up vegetables, only to throw them out. Maybe you retrim the vegetables a bit or help the child finish sweeping, but you want to be sure that the child's work contributes to the family.

Another pitfall is to give children "fake" tools, such as fake food, fake cooking equipment, or fake gardening equipment. Kids know the difference. They know they aren't learning the "real" tasks. And they can't contribute to a common goal when their part is "fake."

If a child is not ready for a task, such as cooking on a hot stove or sewing with sharp needles, no need to be alarmed if they want to help. Tell the child to watch you do the task. Or give the child a piece of the real equipment so they can practice on the side. For example, give an eager child extra cloth and thread while sewing, or a pot and spoon to practice stirring. While in the Yucatán, one mom gave Rosy a little ball of masa dough to practice tortilla making on the side (which is different than creating an artificial task for the child).

2. The tasks should be doable (or almost). The key is to give young children tasks that are suitable for their personal skill level. It's better to err on the side of too easy than too hard. If the job is too hard, the child will become frustrated and quickly lose interest (or they'll require too much instruction or oversight from you). But even the simplest task (e.g., carrying a loaf of bread out of the grocery store) can be exciting for a young child. For example, if I give Rosy a potato to cut up with a steak knife, she often becomes frustrated and walks away because the potato is too hard to cut with that knife (and if I give her a sharper knife, I'm so anxious about her cutting herself that neither of us can relax). But if I give her a banana to cut, she goes to town and asks for more work.

3. Never force a task. We'll talk more about this later. For now, just keep in mind that forcing a child to do a task can severely undermine their motivation. We'll learn many tricks for dealing with a stubborn, unhelpful child later on, but forcing a chore only hinders the teaching of *acomedido* and builds tension. If a child says no, or ignores you, leave it alone. Try again later. We're training the child to cooperate, not to obey the parent.

Part of working together is accepting a child's preference when they choose not to help.

Kids: Middle Childhood (from ages 6 to 12)

Think: *Encourage, activate, and let them take initiative*

"This is when you really teach them what is to be done," Maria says, referring to her nine-year-old daughter, Gelmy. "You will not give them the work of a mother, but rather something light. The first time they may not pay attention—and also the second and the third time, perhaps—but eventually they will understand."

As kids get a bit older, continue with the same guidelines as for younger children, encouraging their inclination to help and requesting help with subtasks. As the child's competency grows, the subtasks can become more complex, to keep pace with their expanding skill level. Pay attention to what they try to do or seem interested in trying. Anytime they show initiative, back away and let them go to town. Accepting children's contributions—without interference—lays the groundwork that will teach them to volunteer help.

1. Continue the focus on working together. Call children over to help with chores alongside you. Instead of "Put away your plate after dinner" or "Fold your laundry," you're framing the tasks as a communal activity, such as "Let's all work together to clean up the kitchen after dinner" or "Let's all help fold the laundry as a family."

"The invitation is for doing things together," Rebeca explains. "In Western culture, children often do work independently—one sibling does it on Thursday, one on Friday. But here it is 'Let's do the task together and we will finish sooner.'"

In our household before we go out and do something fun on Saturday, I'll call for a cleanup party. I'll call over Rosy and my husband, put some music on, and we'll clean up the downstairs together. Then I'll point out, "We really clean faster when we work together."

I take a similar strategy with the laundry on Sundays. After the clothes dry outside, I call both Rosy and Matt over and we all fold each other's clothes together. Again, I might observe that working together is quicker than doing it alone. Or I will note how nice—and important—it is to have clean clothes to wear next week.

2. Delegate subtasks. As children grow and become more competent, you can give the child a bigger portion of a task. For example, "Gelmy [age nine] right now is just rinsing the dishes while Angela [age twelve] washes them," Maria pointed out when I was in her home. "That's how I teach them—by having them do just part of the task. Eventually, Gelmy will learn the whole task."

3. Try activation. Instead of explicitly telling the child to do a task, "activate" their help by telling them you're starting a chore or by giving a hint that a chore is needed. In one of Lucia's studies, 50 percent of the Nahua-heritage moms said that they'll sometimes use this approach to prompt a child to help. "For example, a mother reported that she tells her daughter when she is beginning dinner," the study notes. Then the daughter knows it's time to start pitching in. "Mom, you want help?" the girl asks. "Yes, get me a tomato, get the things out, the onions or beans," the mom replies. "She already knows what to get ready for me."

Sometimes I'll say to Rosy, "Mango is hungry" or "Mango's bowl is empty," to teach her to pay attention to when the dog needs food. Or I'll say, "Time to take the garbage out," signaling to her that I need her to open and hold the doors for me. Or I'll say, "Grocery store time" so she'll know to go grab the reusable bags. Of course, she doesn't always do what I expect or want her to do. But she's learning, little by little, without nagging or fighting.

Okay, let's be honest here. At this point, you might be thinking, Holy cow (or even holy shit), this chore-training process sounds like *way* more work than simply shooing the kids away and getting those darn dishes finished in five minutes.

And it's true, this process requires quite a bit of patience with the small ones—more patience than I anticipated. When Rosy gets her little hands on the dishes or laundry, the whole process can slow way down. Sometimes she takes a whole minute or two to decide how to arrange a dinner plate in the dishwasher. Or after we fold and put away her clothes, she starts to yank everything out of the drawers and toss the clothes on the floor. "Let's do it again, Mama!" she shouts. "But—but—but . . . we just . . ." I say, grimacing.

A part of me wants to yell at her to leave the room. Another part of me wants to throw my hands up, and let the chaos unfold around me. But neither of those approaches would teach Rosy to be a helpful family member. So I take a deep breath, find more patience, and think back to the Maya grandma in Chiapas teaching the little boy not to throw away whole beans. *What would she do now*, I ask myself. *She would guide Rosy back on track.* So I gently take the clothes from Rosy's hands, put them back in the drawer, and tell her, calmly, "Folded clothes stay in the drawer. We'll fold them again next week." Then I leave the room.

That all said, there's another reason I'm motivated to stick with this approach (and build up my patience): it actually saves me an enormous amount of time. And I'm not just talking about saving myself time in the future when (if) Rosy becomes more helpful. I mean it saves me time right now, while she's still a tiny, clumsy tater tot.

I'll explain how this principle works in the next chapter, when we learn about step two of training helpful kids. It's a humdinger. After seeing it in action, I totally changed the way I thought about Rosy's role in the family. It not only teaches children to be more helpful, it's also vital to teaching them to be cooperative members of the family, including in their interactions with their siblings.

Summary for Chapter 4:
How to Raise Helpful Kids

Ideas to Remember (kids of all ages)

➤ Children have an innate desire to help their parents. They're born that way. It might not seem like it, but they genuinely have a built-in drive to belong to the family, and helping earns their place in the group.

➤ Oftentimes, they don't know how best to help. So they seem incapable or clumsy. The parents' job is to train them.

➤ When first starting to help with a task, a child may seem clumsy and perhaps make a mess. But with practice, they will learn quickly while still maintaining their love for helping.

➤ Never discourage a child, at any age, from helping a parent or family member. Shooing a child off can extinguish their motivation to pitch in and work together. If the task is too difficult or hazardous for them, tell them to watch. Or break the task into a doable subtask.

Do It Today

For younger kids (toddlers to about age six or seven):

➤ Request a child help you and the family throughout the day. Don't go overboard with requests. One an hour is plenty. Things to ask:
  • Go fetch something you need; carry a small bag of groceries; stir a pot on the stove; cut a vegetable; hold the door; turn on a hose.

➤ Be sure the requests are for:
  • Real jobs that make a real contribution to the family, not fake or mock work.
  • Working together as a team, not for the child doing it alone.

- Simple tasks that are easy for the child to understand and complete without your help (e.g., hand a child a book and tell them to put it on the bookshelf instead of asking them to go clean up the living room). You really can't make the task too easy.

_____

For older kids (> age seven):

➤ If a child isn't accustomed to helping, ease them into it. Try the tips above. And be patient. They might not help right away, but they'll eventually learn.

➤ If the child is already learning *acomedido*, increase the complexity of the task as their skill level increases. Let the child's interest and skills drive your requests.

➤ Instead of telling a child what to do directly, try activating them by indirectly alluding to a task (e.g., you could say, "The dog's bowl is empty" to remind a child to feed the dog, or "Time to make dinner" to remind a child to come over and start pulling ingredients from the refrigerator).

CHAPTER 5

How to Raise Flexible, Cooperative Kids

"In Maya culture, there's a belief that everybody has a purpose," psychologist Barbara Rogoff tells me.

"Even toddlers have a purpose?" I ask.

What is Rosy's purpose in our family?

"Well, yes. Everyone. And part of the goal of social interaction is to help everybody fulfill their purpose."

Hmm, I think to myself. *What is Rosy's purpose in our family?*

On the fourth night in Chan Kajaal, I'm so excited that I can't sleep. I toss and turn in the hammock. Stare at the circular fan. Listen to the dogs barking out on the street. It doesn't help that our room is about ninety-five degrees Fahrenheit, even at two o'clock in the morning.

Finally, around five a.m., before the first rooster calls, I hear a truck idling in our driveway.

I jump out of the hammock, throw on a pink sarong skirt, and give Rosy a kiss goodbye on her sticky forehead as she sleeps. Today, I'm going to see what I've been waiting more than a year for.

Whenever I tell friends and family back home about the Maya supermoms—about how little they argue with their children—many Americans have the same response: "Yeah, but you haven't seen the parents get kids ready for school in the morning. Go back and watch a parent do that, and I'm sure you will see conflict."

Well, today I'm going to go do just that: watch a Maya family handle the dreaded morning routine.

I hop into the pickup truck. Behind the steering wheel sits the person who's making this whole trip possible: Rodolfo Puch. In his early thirties, Rodolfo is a striking man with thick black eyebrows and shiny black hair combed up high into a wavy bouffant. He wears a crisp white shirt with the top buttons open and relaxed.

"*Días*," he says in greeting.

"*Días*," I respond.

"Are you ready to see Teresa shake the hammocks?" he asks with a big smile. Rodolfo has a great smile, one that involves not just his lips but also his cheeks, eyes, and forehead.

I tell him that I can't wait to visit Teresa's family, and I thank him again for setting up the interview. As we drive across the village, the sun's still tucked under the horizon, and the sky is a bright orange color, like the center of a ripe nectarine.

Rodolfo grew up in a village similar to Chan Kajaal, and today he runs a tourism company. I hired Rodolfo to set up interviews with families and interpret our conversations from Mayan to English. His help has been invaluable. No matter how cockamamie my ideas sound, he always responds in the same way: he nods his head and says, "Yes, we can. We can." And then he figures out a solution that's both possible and fulfills my needs.*

---

* As we'll learn in the next chapter, this method works incredibly well with young children, who often have crazy ideas. Instead of resisting these ideas with a statement like "No, no, no. We cannot do that," next time try simply nodding your head and saying, "We can, we can," and then listen to the child talking.

Today is no exception.

Rodolfo has convinced a couple in the village—Maria Teresa Caamal Itzá—who goes by Teresa—and Benito Kumul Chan—to let us come to their home in the wee hours and record audio while they get their children ready for school. That is, get a total of *four kids* dressed, fed, and out the door, all before seven a.m.

"If the kids don't make it to the gate by seven, they will not be allowed in school," Rodolfo adds.

Clearly, if I'm going to see power struggles and screaming, this will be the moment.

Rodolfo and I pull up at Teresa and Benito's home. The lights are off. It's dead silent. Everyone is still asleep—except Teresa. She's standing on the front porch, waiting for us. She's impeccably dressed. Wearing a mauve pencil skirt and pink lacy blouse, she looks like she's heading to a power lunch in Manhattan. Her long hair is tied up in a loose bun.

"*Días*," she says quietly with a nod of her head as we walk into her living room. "*Días*," Rodolfo and I respond in a whisper. Her three daughters are still sleeping in hammocks hanging across the living room. Right away, Teresa gets to work trying to wake them up. She tugs at the edge of one hammock. "Wake up. Wake up, Claudia. You need to go to school," Teresa says softly to her youngest, who's age six and still deeply asleep. "Wake up. Wake up. Ay-yai." Her voice remains quiet, but you can detect the tiniest smidge of frustration.

Aha! I think. *Here it comes: the mother-daughter power struggle.* I grip my microphone, ready to document how Teresa responds to disobedience.

But then Teresa pivots, literally. Instead of pushing little Claudia to wake up, she turns away and walks to the far edge of the room. Once there, she pauses for a beat before doing something I've never seen a Western mom try. Teresa basically transforms into a conductor—or better yet, a baseball manager, silently directing the team from the dugout. Rather than issuing a loud stream of instructions, threats, and explanations, she com-

---

Ninety percent of the time a child will move on and forget about it. Or they will ask again later. By then you may have figured out a good compromise.

municates through facial expressions and hand gestures. A twitch of the nose means "Start getting dressed"; a tug on the ear means "Brush your hair"; and a quick nod of the head means "You're doing a good job." If you don't pay close attention, you'll miss all the directions.

Teresa begins with the first baseman: her eleven-year-old son, Ernesto. He loves school and is already awake, dressed, and headed out the door. "Come back. Go find your shoes, Ernesto," Teresa says in a matter-of-fact manner. Ernesto doesn't respond and runs out the front door. Did he just ignore his mom? It's not clear. But Teresa doesn't seem to care. Unfazed, she turns to her MVP pitcher: Laura. She's sixteen and knows this game well.

"You need to comb the little girls' hair," Teresa tells her. Again her tone is all business. Although she conveys no urgency or stress, she doesn't sugarcoat the request, either. She doesn't sweeten her tone or preface her request with extra words, such as "Do you mind combing the girls' hair?" or "Do you want to comb the girls' hair?" or even "Could you please comb the girls' hair?" Instead, her request is direct: "You need to comb the little girls' hair." And it works.

Half asleep and walking like a zombie, Laura goes over to her littlest sister, gently wakes her up, and starts combing her hair. Teresa hands

Claudia her school uniform, and the little girl goes to the other room to get dressed. When Claudia returns, her older sister performs the sweetest act of sisterly kindness I've ever witnessed. Without being asked, the sixteen-year-old brings over a bowl of water and begins to wash her little sister's feet. Carefully and lovingly, Laura rubs off the brown dirt from Claudia's heels and toes, then dries them. Finally, Laura helps her sister put on shoes, all with the utmost tenderness.

The thought crosses my mind that perhaps Teresa's children are being so calm and kind with each other because Rodolfo and I are here watching. So I ask Teresa if our presence is changing their behavior. Teresa chuckles a bit, then says: "Well, Laura would be washing Claudia's feet faster if you were not here. She would be telling her sister not to move so she could finish more quickly."

Ernesto appears at the back door, still not wearing his school shoes. Teresa asks him, "Did you find your shoes? Where did you put them yesterday?" Again, Ernesto says nothing and walks out the front door.

Teresa then signals the girls over to eat breakfast. They come immediately and start eating. Standing there with my microphone in my hand, I'm struck by how incredibly peaceful everyone is. This entire time, Teresa has spoken just a handful of words. She has kept her energy so low. And the kids have followed her lead. While the girls eat, the room is so quiet that you can even hear the birds outside singing.

Then the silence is broken as Ernesto comes running in from the front yard, and he *still* doesn't have his shoes! *Argh*, I think, *Teresa has now asked him twice to find the shoes.* But she doesn't feel the need to escalate her response. She doesn't turn his disobedience into a conflict. She doesn't even remind him that she's already asked twice. Instead, she maintains her composure and simply reiterates her request in the same matter-of-fact tone: "Go find your shoes." (I also notice that she waits a full five minutes before repeating a request to a child. By comparison, I wait about ten seconds—if that.)

And Teresa's patience pays off. Ernesto goes back outside and quickly returns with his shoes!

Then Teresa gives another hand signal, and all four kids head out the front door. Laura climbs up onto the seat of the cargo tricycle, her younger siblings hop onto the platform in front, and Laura takes them to school. And that's that. The whole morning routine took about twenty minutes, from Teresa shaking the hammocks to the children walking out the door. It was smooth, easy, and uber calm. There was no drama. No back talk. No yelling. No tears. No resistance.

The morning madness was anything but madness. For the most part, Teresa's kids went with the flow. They listened and knew what to do. And when they didn't respond immediately to a command, Teresa never pressured them to move faster. She simply waited a few minutes and then asked again, with the same tone. She never triggered a conflict.

"The mornings are easy because the children help each other," Teresa says. And indeed, she couldn't be more right. The children were so cooperative. I could see that they not only wanted to help their mom, they also wanted to help each other.

But I sense something in the home that I've also felt with other families in Chan Kajaal. Beyond simply wanting to help each other, Teresa and her kids seem to understand each other at a deeper level than Rosy and I do. Teresa knew that pushing Ernesto harder wouldn't make him get his shoes faster. Teresa knew that Laura was more likely to get Claudia to wake up than she was. And Laura knew exactly how to comb her sister's hair so it wouldn't pull or hurt. Each family member understood how the other members work. As a result, their home had this wonderful sense of cohesion and coordination—a wonderful sense of "we," like "We are all in this together."

And then it hits me: Teresa has trained her family to work together like a World Series–champion team, while I have accomplished the opposite. I have trained a contrarian, a dissenter, or sometimes a full-out Hells Angels anarchist.

Why wasn't Rosy on my team?

If I could somehow recruit her onto my team, could I fix a whole bunch of our problems? Maybe the morning routine would be easier. Maybe leaving the park would be quicker. And maybe—just maybe—Rosy would go to bed without drama and tears. Could all these issues stem from one root problem?

Step 2: Give Kids Their Team Membership Cards

Before I met Teresa and Maria, I organized Rosy's schedule the way I thought all good parents should: when she wasn't in day care, I always had an "activity" planned for her to do.

When she was napping or sleeping at night, I would do all the chores. I'd clean the living room and kitchen, do the laundry, and make part of breakfast and lunch for the next day so we wouldn't be rushed in the morning.

On weekends, we'd go to the zoo, museums, and indoor play areas. We had playdates at parks, and we worked on crafts for Halloween and Easter. On rainy days, we filled our living room with toys, games, puzzles, and "learning tools." I felt good about these activities because I thought that they were enriching Rosy's life by exposing her to a variety of experiences. In practice, they also kept her busy, out of my way, and distracted so that she wouldn't drive me crazy.

But to be brutally honest with you, I never really enjoyed these activities. Saying it makes me feel like a bad mom, but it's true. At "kid-friendly" places, I was either completely bored or utterly overstimulated by the noise, lights, and chaos. I'd leave the children's science museum exhausted, on edge, and feeling like a small piece of my soul had died back at the snack bar after spending ten dollars on a piece of pepperoni pizza. (A slice of pizza that, by the by, I ended up eating after Rosy screamed in my face, "Yuck! I don't like this cheese!")

Playing at home with Rosy in the living room wasn't much better. Some afternoons I'd rather have stabbed my eyes out than play another session

What if there is an easier, more effective — and more enjoyable — way of being with a child?

of Princess Elsa and Anna. But I told myself, *This is what a good mother does. This is what Rosy needs and wants. This is good for her. This is helping her.*

Sound familiar?

Yet the time I spend with Maria and Teresa in Chan Kajaal leads me to reflect: What if all those preconceived ideas I'd been carrying around of "what a good mother does" are complete baloney? What if our jam-packed roster of activities is actually doing the opposite of what I intend, and instead of making Rosy happier and our lives smoother, they're actually making Rosy more poorly behaved and my life harder? Could these activities be eroding Rosy's internal motivation to be a cooperative member of the family—to be part of the team? Could they be eroding her confidence and her sense of self? Is there an easier, more effective, and more enjoyable way of spending time with a child?

Suzanne Gaskins has been studying Maya parenting for more than four decades. She's a psychological anthropologist at Northeastern Illinois University of Chicago. But every year, she spends several months living in Chan Kajaal, observing families, and interviewing parents. Suzanne knows the families in the village quite well. And they know her well, too.

When Suzanne lived here in the early 1980s, she was a new mom herself with a one-year-old boy. Right away, she noticed a striking difference between the Maya parents and her friends with kids back in Chicago. The Maya parents don't feel the need to constantly entertain or play with their children. They don't provide an endless stream of videos, toys, and treasure hunts to stimulate their kids and keep them busy. In other words, Maya parents are not on the floor playing princess games or spending weekends at kiddie museums, eating ten-dollar slices of pizza.

Suzanne calls these activities "child-centered." That is, they're activities solely for kids that parents would not do if they did not have children. Maya parents don't feel the need to schedule many, if any, of these activities, Suzanne finds.

Instead, the parents give their children an even richer experience, something that many Western kids do not get much of: real life. Maya parents welcome children into the adult world and give them full access to the adults' lives, including their work.

Adults go about their daily business—cleaning, cooking, feeding livestock, sewing, building homes, fixing bikes and cars, taking care of siblings—while the children play alongside them and observe the adults' activities. These real-life events are the "enrichment activities." They are the children's entertainment, and their tools for learning and growing, physically and emotionally.

Children are welcome to run over to watch and pitch in to help when they're needed. Over time, a child gradually learns to weave a hammock, raise a turkey, bake tamales in an underground oven, or repair a bike.

I see this type of learning all over Chan Kajaal. One afternoon at Maria's house, she begins washing corn in a bucket—a necessary step to making masa for tortillas. The process involves repeatedly rinsing the corn with fresh water. Bending over a blue bucket, Maria swirls dry yellow kernels in the cool, clear water. *Whoosh, whoosh.* Immediately, her two youngest daughters, Alexa and Gelmy, run over to watch. Maria dumps the water out and requests help from Gelmy. "Go turn the hose on," she tells the nine-year-old. Gelmy runs to the faucet to help her mom. All the while, little Alexa watches her mom and older sister.

"With a task like this, I tell the children to watch and learn," Maria tells me when she takes a break. "That is what I always tell them. 'This is important. Watch.'"

And so Maya parents—again, like the vast majority of parents around the world—organize children's schedules to provide opportunities for kids to be with or near the family as the adults go about their daily routines. Kids are nearby when adults work around the house, take care of the family business, or maintain the family garden—you name it, kids are welcome.

And young children actually love these activities. They crave them. Children don't see a difference between adult work and play, says psychologist Rebeca Mejía-Arauz. "Parents don't need to know how to play with kids. If we get kids involved in adult activities, that's play for kids." And then they associate chores with a fun, positive activity. They associate it with playing.

"Parents don't force children to do chores or work, but they organize their household and the context for children to develop those skills," says psychologist Lucia Alcalá. "It's a pretty sophisticated way to look at child development."

There's no doubt, welcoming children into the adult world makes learning to do chores much easier. If kids are near you when you make breakfast or do the laundry, they'll quickly pick up on how to scramble eggs or separate the whites from the darks.

But this approach has several other advantages. First, it gives parents a break. Instead of having to schedule, pay for, and participate in endless child-centered activities, parents can lead their normal lives—working or relaxing—while kids follow along, learning as they go. Rather than scheduling your life around your child, you can simply put your child into your schedule.

Moreover, humans likely evolved for children to learn by shadowing adults; it's the way they've been learning for at least two hundred thousand years (as we'll see in the next chapter). So for many kids, learning this way is easier and less stressful than learning through child-centered activities. And it generates less conflict and resistance.

And what a wonderful way to learn! There's no pressure to pick up a skill faster than you are able, no lectures, and no quiz at the end of the semester. Kids can simply learn at their own pace from being near adults, watching, and helping out.

But perhaps most important, this approach gives kids something missing in many American homes: their team membership card.

———————

Here in the West, we often employ two types of motivation: rewards (e.g., praise, gifts, stickers, allowances) and punishment (e.g., yelling, time-outs, groundings, threats). But in many other cultures, moms and dads tap into another type of motivation: a child's drive to fit in with their family and to work together as a team. To belong.

This motivation is powerful. Really powerful. Without it, moms and dads are pretty much raising children with both hands tied behind their backs. The motivation to belong not only prompts kids to hop up and do chores voluntarily, but it also helps them be more cooperative and flexible in general. It drives them to get ready for school in the morning, jump in the car when it's time to head home from the park, eat the food you put on their plate, and not delay when you ask them to come set the table!

Children do these tasks, with relative ease, because they have a commitment to their family. The family is washing the dishes, so a child washes them, too. The family is cleaning up the house, so the child cleans up, too.

Kids are wired for this type of cooperation. It's one of the traits that makes us human. It makes us feel good to work together and help the people who love us.

Children as young as eight or nine years old are fully conscious of this motivation, Lucia says. "We asked Maya children why they help around the house. Several kids said it's because they're part of the family, and it's a shared responsibility. Everyone helps." One child answered, "Well, I live there. Therefore, I should help." Another replied, "Because I also eat at home, I also need to help my dad."

But in order for moms and dads to tap into this natural motivation, there's one critical requirement: kids need to feel like they're full-fledged, contributing members of the family. They need to feel like their contributions genuinely make a difference and matter. For example, if a child is caring for a younger sibling, the child is *really* responsible for the well-being of their sibling.

Kids are acutely aware of their relationship to others—they know who's on their team and who isn't. Even young toddlers are aware of their interdependence and connections to others; they know who's helped them and whom they've helped.

They're also acutely aware of their role on that

team. Am I a catcher who is involved in almost every play out on the baseball field, or am I a right fielder who doesn't see much action? Or even more to the point, am I a VIP spectator way up in the box seats eating a hot dog and drinking an apple juice?

By welcoming children into the adult world, you confirm that they belong on the family's team. Metaphorically, you're giving them a membership card that they carry around in their back pockets. And that card offers full access to the benefits—and responsibilities—of the team. This card tells the child, *I do what these adults do because I'm part of this group. When the family does laundry, I do laundry. When the family cleans, I clean. When the family leaves the house in the morning, I leave with them. When the family . . .* You name it, the kid will follow.

Every time we include a child in an adult task—whether it's something as simple as taking the garbage out or something as complex as taking them to the Yucatán for a book project—we are telling that child that they are part of something bigger than themselves. They are part of a "we." And they are connected to the other members of this family. What they do helps or hurts others.

On the flip side, every time we choose an activity devoted to and centered around the child, we slowly take away that membership card. We tell children that they're different from the rest of the family, that they're a bit like a VIP, who's exempt from the family's work, from the adult activities. We erode their motivation to work as a team.

That's exactly what was happening with Rosy and me. I was teaching her that her role in our house was to play Legos, watch educational videos, and be served meals (specifically pasta-no-sauce and buttered toast). My role was to clean, cook, do her laundry, and shuttle her from one activity to the next. So why in the world would she put on her shoes when I ask in the mornings? Why would she eat the broccoli I cook? Or get in the bed when we're all exhausted?

In many ways, she was like the CEO of a tech company; I was her event manager. I was there to plan her days and ensure she was having a good time.

But after the morning with Teresa and my conversations with Suzanne about child-centered activities, I considered and reflected and, at the end of it, I found myself thinking: No longer. No longer! No longer will I buy a ten-dollar slice of cheese pizza at a toddler-packed snack stand and then eat it myself. No longer will I do the laundry while she watches the Berenstain Bears on YouTube. No longer will I cook her special dishes for dinner. Those times in the Doucleff family are over.

I decided to stop being Rosy's event manager and start welcoming her into my world. I decided to stop entertaining her and learn to simply be with her.

After I got home from the Chan Kajaal village, I made three huge transformations in the Doucleff household:

1. I totally revamped Rosy's schedule. I realized that weekends and afternoons after preschool were precious moments for Rosy to gain her family membership card—for her to be around the inner workings of our household and immersed in the adult world. So I scrapped almost all the child-centered activities. No more kiddie museums, zoos, and play centers. I even cut out the birthday parties, except the ones being held by family friends with whom Matt and I want to spend time. Same goes for playdates: if I don't want to spend time with the mom or dad, we don't do them. Or I just drop her off at the playdate and give her some time alone with another family. What I found is that Rosy actually really enjoys taking a break from Matt and me. Even when she was just 2.5, she didn't mind having playdates without me. As long as she felt connected to another adult, she was good.

When we do have free time, we choose activities that the whole family will enjoy, ones that we used to do before Rosy arrived. Sometimes we have to modify the activity a bit so she can join in (e.g., cut a hike short, modify a bike route, skip the second round of drinks at dinner). But the activities are not focused on her, not for her, and not "kid only." They're the activities of the adult world, and she's a full participant.

And here's the big shift: Instead of waiting to do chores while Rosy naps and sleeps, we do them when she's around. Saturday mornings we cook something fun for breakfast and clean the house—all together, with neither Matt nor me skipping out. Sunday mornings we do the laundry— again, all together—and in the afternoon, we go to the grocery store. Sunday evenings we work in the garden, walk the dog, or visit friends.

What do I do now when she sleeps and naps? Well, gosh darn it, I relax! I read a book, take a walk, watch a bit of Netflix, or have long, gloriously uninterrupted conversations with my husband. And sometimes I take a long, long, long bath, or lie down for a nap myself.

2. I totally changed the way I thought about her zest to help. Even if she made a huge mess, broke something, or came over and grabbed a utensil from my hand, I'd remind myself, *She is trying to help but doesn't know how. I need to teach her. And that can take time.* I would step back, let her perform the tasks as she wanted to, and try to minimize instructions or comments. And I would encourage any interest in doing chores, even when it seemed like she was only playing or joking around.

3. I gave her as much autonomy as I could. We'll learn more about this later in the book, when we visit the Hadzabe. For now, I want to emphasize that respecting a kid's autonomy—that is, minimizing bossiness—is necessary for this system to work.

Try It 2: Train Cooperation

In Western culture, we go to extra efforts to draw a line between the kid world and the adult world. Kids go to school; parents go to work. Kids go to bed early; parents go to bed late. Kids eat kid food; parents eat "adult food" (as my seven-year-old niece told me last summer). The separation is sharp. But it doesn't have to be this way. Your job is to find opportunities to merge the two worlds. And there are many, many opportunities. You just have to learn how to spot them.

Keep in mind that some kids may need time to adjust to their new environment—especially older children who haven't had much experience in the adult world. They might not know how to behave quite right at first. And you may need to slowly introduce them to new experiences over the course of several weeks and months.

"The trouble, I think, is that children have been brought up only in childproof places," says Barbara Rogoff. "Then when they enter a place that runs by different rules, like an adult setting in a middle-class society, sometimes they're disruptive. Other people get angry. And then the parents give up."

But don't give up! Be a little patient. Remember, you are *training* the child to learn a new skill.

With time and practice, children can learn to behave properly in adult settings, Barbara says. "If you start out early, or wean an older child into a situation, they can learn. Kids are really good at distinguishing between the adult world and child world." They're also good at figuring out which rules apply to different locations.

Come to think of it, how do we expect children to learn to act maturely if we never expose them to mature adults on a regular basis? If Rosy spends all her time playing with other three-year-olds, how could I expect her to act more mature than a three-year-old?

Exposure to the adult world makes great training for school, too. It teaches kids how to be patient, quiet, and respectful, as well as how to watch and listen.

Here's how to get started.

Dip Your Toe

• **Make Saturday or Sunday your family membership day.** On this day, everyone in the family is treated similarly and invited to all the

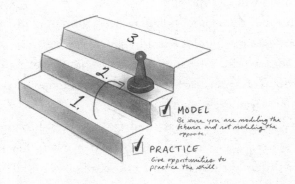

STEPS TO TRAINING
A CHILD

✓ MODEL
Be sure you are modeling the
behavior and not modeling the
opposite.

✓ PRACTICE
Give opportunities to
practice the skill.

same activities. Replace child-centered activities and child-only enter-tainment (including child-centered TV, YouTube, and games) with family-centered and adult activities. Focus on immersing the child in the adult world. Do chores around the house, in the yard, or at the of-fice. Go grocery shopping together. Go to a park and have a picnic with family and friends. Go fishing. Go to the beach and read or work while your children play. Have a dinner party and get the children involved in the planning—picking out napkins, the menu, drinks, and all the good stuff. Go to a church activity designed for all ages. Or volunteer where children are welcome, such as a food bank, soup kitchen, community garden, or trail maintenance group. Throughout the day, try thinking to yourself, *It's not my job to entertain the children. It's their job to be part of the team.*

• **Take a daily time-out from entertaining and instructing your child.** You'll want to start out small, say just five minutes at a time. Then work your way up to where you can do this for a whole Saturday and Sunday.

During these time-outs, just let the children be. Don't instruct them, explain stuff to them, or give them toys (or screens) to play with. Let them figure it all out for themselves. Just go about your business and let them tag along with you. Do chores. Do work. Do nothing. Lie on the sofa and read a magazine. At first, it might be easier to try this outside of the house. So take the kids to a park and bring a book or some work to do. Sit on a bench and be quiet. If the children whine or complain that they're bored, just ignore it. They'll figure out a way to stimulate and entertain themselves, without you or a screen. And as their skills mature, life will become easier, quieter, and more peaceful.

If it helps, think 20-20-20: For 20 minutes each day, I'm at least 20 feet from my children, and for 20 minutes, I'm silent.

20 20 20

minutes each day   feet away   minutes of silence

Jump In

- **Minimize (maybe even scrap?) all the child-centered activities.** Don't worry, your child will still partake in plenty of these activities at school and with friends and family. But make it a goal to say no to as many birthday parties, zoo trips, playdates, and "enrichment outings" as possible. Young children really don't need these activities.

For older children, help them take responsibility for their own child-centered activities. Teach them to plan, organize, and execute their own activities. Let them set up their own playdates and visits with friends. Show them how to sign up for sports, music classes, and other after-school activities. Teach them to bike, walk, or take the bus to the activity. If that's not possible, help the child set up a car pool with other families. The goal here is to minimize your involvement in child-centered activities and maximize their autonomy.

Remember, child-centered activities are the ones that parents do only for the child; the parent wouldn't be there if the child wasn't around, and the parent doesn't really enjoy the activity. Exactly what falls into that category will vary from parent to parent, activity to activity. For example, team sports are often designed only for kids, but they often involve many family members and close friends. Many families come together to cheer and support each other. So only you can decide what counts as "child-centered."

Personally, I ask myself whether or not I'd attend an activity if Rosy was sick. For example, her preschool class has weekly dinners with the other families. I truly enjoy these nights. The other parents have become friends, as well as a part of our family's support network. I want to value and strengthen those connections. So even though the dinners are for her school, they count as "family-centered" in my mind and we still go. I also really love playgrounds, if you can believe it. I love watching the birds, reading a book, or writing in a notebook. I love that playgrounds bring together kids of all ages. But I don't like playing on a playground. That turns the activity from family-centered to child-centered, in my mind. So Rosy and I go to the playground often, but I work while she plays. Period.

Another great litmus test is how your child behaves after an activity.

Are they calmer and more cooperative, or agitated and more antagonistic? If it's the latter, drop the activity. It's eroding their team motivation. And if the activity somehow triggers conflict, arguments or resistance, ditch it. An activity isn't worth conflict. Children need less conflict, not more.

On the flip side, after an afternoon of working together around the house, is your child more agreeable, more cooperative, and more capable of entertaining themselves? What about the stress level in the home? Is there less conflict and resistance?

Personally, I find that Rosy experiences a sort of unpleasant "hangover" after intense kid-focused activities. She'll behave poorly for about an hour or so as she transitions back to family-centered life, where she has to follow the routine and be cooperative. I also think that the child-centered activities are stressful for her because they leave her disconnected from the family and often make her overstimulated, to boot. Child-centered activities are often about "I," and what she really needs—and craves—are more "we" activities.

• **Maximize exposure in the adult world.** Take children to places that aren't typically thought of as "kid-friendly" but can show kids how the adult world works. Take them to the grocery store, the doctor's office, the dentist's office, the bank, the post office, the hardware store, the copy store—basically any place you need to go for work and family business.

Don't expect them to behave perfectly at the beginning. You need to train them, slowly, over time. Start small—say fifteen minutes or so—and build up over time. Or let the child lead you. Observe and see how much time they can handle in an adult place. Rosy is very good at letting me know when she has reached her limits in the adult world. Conversely, sometimes she surprises me with how patient and calm she can be. Just last week, Rosy spent three hours (!) at an eye appointment with very little fussing and chaos.

But when she acts up, I remind her: "This is not a place to play. It is a privilege to be here, and if you aren't a big enough girl yet, you will have to leave." When she touches or plays with a piece of equipment, I remind her: "These aren't toys. This is a big girl's place where we don't play."

- **Throw out toys and all other child-centered objects.** Okay, so you don't have to throw out *all* of them. But you can definitely prune the supply down to a few books, pencils, crayons, and maybe a set of Legos (or a toy the child regularly plays with). And you can definitely stop buying new toys. Remember that kids spent two hundred thousand years without these items. They don't need them at all. Besides, relatives and friends will provide more than enough gifts to keep your house filled with pink plastic objects and blue fuzzy bears.

There are oodles of advantages to having fewer toys—and caring less about toys, in general. You will save time cleaning up and managing these items. You will have more space and less clutter in your house. Your house will look less juvenile (for example, if you have a playroom, you can use it for an adult-centered activity, like sewing or woodworking). And once you start viewing toys as unnecessary and dispensable, you can use them to train your child in other skills, such as helping and sharing.

- **Use toys to teach *acomedido*.** If toys and games are no longer essential in the home (but a privilege for the child to have), then it is no longer a parent's job to clean them up—at least not by yourself. Now you can set some useful rules about these objects. Show a child how to clean up their toys or work together to do it. And if they don't participate or fail to pick them up on a regular basis, simply throw the toys away or give them to charity. This idea comes from a Nahua-heritage mom in one of Lucia's studies. When her son won't clean up his toys, the mom threatens to "sweep the toys away." Immediately, the child picks up the toys.

If I have to ask Rosy more than three times to clean up a toy (or I find myself picking it up over and over again), I throw the toy away. Or I put it in a box, and at the end of the week we take the box to Goodwill. Sometimes I warn her with a statement like "Last chance to clean this up or it's going in the trash!" Other times I just throw it away. Not once has she asked for one of the discarded items. Quickly, we've pruned the toys down to ones she really cares about, and she's become better at cleaning up.

- **Use toys to teach sharing.** When you go visit friends, ask your child to pick out a toy or book to give to the other family. Or go through the toys together each month and set aside half for charity. I bet you my right pinky finger that your kids will really enjoy sharing with friends and charities, and will start doing it voluntarily after a few weeks.

• **Reconsider your role as a parent and your child's role in the family.** Is your role to keep the child busy and entertained? Or is it to show them life skills and teach them how to work together with others?

Now think about your child's role in the home. Is she the beneficiary of endless entertainment or does she have a greater purpose—to help and cooperate? To work together as a team? How does she contribute or want to contribute?

Expect children to help with routine tasks like making meals, cleaning up, helping with laundry, and taking care of pets. Ask them to watch or pitch in—or just make sure they're around while the work is being accomplished. If they resist, remind them that they're part of the family and families work together.

When you invite the child to help, remember the invitation is always to work together. You're not asking the child to perform the task alone. You can say something like "Let's all fold this laundry together and we'll get it finished faster." Every task becomes an opportunity to work together and reinforce the child's membership in the family. (Also, remember, the invitation to help is not an order. The child can say no if they want.)

• **Start training a coworker.** If you really want your child to feel like a full-fledged member of the family, get them involved in your career or job.

• Regularly bring them to your office or place of employment (as much as management will allow, but ideally a few hours a week). Let them hang out while you work. They can color, draw, or read. If they show interest in your work, offer up small tasks that are easy and feasible for kids to do. For example, Rosy loves making beautiful thank-you cards to give to people we've interviewed. She also staples contracts, scans documents, and puts stamps on letters.

• At home on the weekends, if you need to work, invite a child to be near you while you do it. You don't need to tell them what to do. Simply say something like "Now we're working and we need to be quiet." Rosy loves sitting next to me while I write, even though all I do is stare at the screen. She lies next to me and rests. Or she colors and "reads."

- Be creative. Look for ways to include your kids in your job that our culture doesn't usually encourage. For example, take your child on a business trip with you, or to a business dinner or party. Ask for your child's advice or opinion about a business problem or task. Discuss work at dinner or while driving in the car and seek their input. Or simply show them your work—show them your slide-show presentations, your project reviews, your accounting tables. Show them on a map where you work and where your clients or customers work. Show them everything you can. Bring them into your world.

With Rosy, I often interview her for radio stories, even when the piece isn't about parenting. Why? She loves being recorded and hearing her voice played on tape. But also, she often has an interesting take on topics. She's really good at summarizing ideas. And eventually, I want her to help me transcribe interviews and edit pieces, so I need her involved as early as possible.

So when I got home from Chan Kajaal and put these changes into place, did everything switch to amazing right away? Well, no. It took me months of practice to stop entertaining Rosy, to quit being her event manager. I still find myself setting up "activities" for her every now and then, or turning our walk in the park into her biology lesson. But overall, this new approach has made our lives much less stressful. My husband and I aren't rushing around from child-centered activity to child-centered activity each weekend. We have way more time for our own hobbies and interests, such as hiking, gardening, reading, and being completely lazy at the beach for three hours on a Saturday afternoon. And Rosy loves learning about our interests. Whatever we get excited about, she gets excited about, too! And it turns into an opportunity to boost our collaboration skills.

And I haven't eaten a ten-dollar slice of cheese pizza since.

Introduction to TEAM Parenting: A Better Way to Be Together

It's seven a.m. on a hot, sticky day in July 1954. School is out for the summer in Alton, Illinois, a small Midwestern town on the Mississippi River. Nine-year-old Mickey Doucleff is already up, dressed, and ready to work. A few minutes ago, his dad gave him "the call."

"All he had to say was 'Mickey' in his deep voice, and I knew what it meant. I was wide awake," he later recalls.

Young Mickey runs a comb through his military buzz haircut and barrels down the stairs. The scent of cinnamon sugar wafts through the air.

Mickey's dad stands at a worktable, rolling out cinnamon rolls and placing them on baking trays. A giant mixer, the size of a mailbox, whips around thirty pounds of sourdough. The white dough hits the sides of the mixer every few seconds with a loud, rhythmic *bam, bam, bam*.

"Morning, Dad," Mickey says. He walks past his father and into the front of the shop. A glass showcase displays chocolate-glazed donuts, blueberry muffins, and apricot Danishes. Behind the counter, loaves of whole wheat, rye, and babka bread are stacked on a shelf. Several customers are already lined up, waiting to pick up orders.

Mickey grabs a white apron, ties it around his skinny waist, and gets to work.

"Good morning," he says. "How can I help you? Did you see the donuts are on sale for ten cents a dozen?"

If you look around the world today, on all six livable continents, you will find a common way of parenting. It's a way of relating to children that moms and dads have turned to over and over again, across wildly different climates and societies, from hunter-gatherers in the Kalahari Desert and pastoralists in Kenya to farmers in the Amazon and bakers along the Mississippi River. The approach has likely been around for tens of thousands of years, probably even hundreds of thousands of years. And not that long ago, many American parents practiced it, too. But in the past fifty to one hundred years, someone convinced moms and dads in the U.S. that we needed to go off script. And the approach began to disappear in many American communities.

Now we're going to learn how to bring it back.

This approach consists of four core elements that provide the foundation for the parent-child relationship: togetherness, encouragement, autonomy, and minimal interference. I came up with a simple acronym, TEAM, so that when I'm struggling with Rosy (or all hell breaks loose in the Doucleff home), I can easily remember the core elements and use them to rein in the chaos.

We'll be diving into each of the four letters in this book. Let's start with *T*, which stands for "togetherness."

Western society focuses heavily on teaching children to be independent—to get dressed in the morning by yourself, clean up your own room by yourself, complete your homework by yourself. The list goes on. But that line of thinking likely goes against hundreds of thousands of years of evolution. We humans have an extraordinary drive to be with and help others—it's one of the key characteristics that separates us from other primates. And it's likely one of the reasons we *Homo sapiens* survived for the past two hundred thousand years while (at least) seven other *Homo* species did not.

"Apart from language . . . the last outstanding distinction between us and other apes involves a curious packet of hypersocial attributes that allow us to monitor the mental states and feelings of others," the evolutionary biologist Sarah Blaffer Hrdy writes in *Mothers and Others: The Evolutionary Origins of Mutual Understanding*.

What's more, this drive to help appears early in life. In one study, toddlers voluntarily helped an adult with four completely different tasks: they fetched an item the adult couldn't reach, opened a cabinet when the adult's hands were full, corrected an adult's mistake, and cleared away an obstacle in a person's way. To be helpful in such diverse ways, toddlers must already possess an extraordinary amount of empathy, mind-reading skills, and motivation to cooperate.

The drive to help each other is woven into our DNA. As Lady Gaga says, we are "born this way."

So when parents insist that young children work alone, we're fighting their innate desire—even need—to be together and collaborate. We end up building tension and stress between us and our children, setting ourselves up for struggle and conflict.

Think about trigger points for tantrums or anxiety. Many of them involve points in the day in which a child is separating from their caretaker, such as "drop-off" at day care (why do we call it drop-off? Rosy thought we were really going to drop her!), naps and bedtime, or when a parent leaves for a work trip.

To understand better what I'm trying to say, consider for a moment our dog, Mango. She's a twelve-year-old German shepherd, and she's a sweet, wonderful dog. But geez Louise, she is loud! She barks at everything: when the doorbell rings, when people walk into our house, when people hug, when people dance—you get the picture. Her default response is to bark. At first, we tried to train her out of all the barking, which took an enormous amount of effort. And any solution proved only short-lived. Eventually I realized that barking was hardwired into her genes. She had been bred to bark. And besides that, barking is her way of protecting us, helping us, and showing us love. And so I decided to work with the barking instead of fighting it so much.

Kids and togetherness are the same. Young children have, in many ways, been bred to be around people and work together with them. It's their default mode and their way of loving us. It not only helps them build deep connections with the adults they love, but it also helps them develop cognitively and emotionally. They need to work together to be healthy.

So around the world you see that supermoms and superdads don't fight this instinct, but rather they harness it. They know that doing tasks "together" is just as valuable—if not even more important—than doing something alone. If a child needs help or is asking for it, the mom and dad will swing in to assist. For example, if a five-year-old needs help getting dressed in the morning, then the parents help, and they help willingly—even if the child is fully capable of getting dressed on their own. The parents don't constantly force the child to be independent or accelerate the process of becoming independent. Instead, parents give kids the room and time to develop at their own speeds.

If you think about it, how can we expect a child to help us if we aren't helping them when they're in need? (Or expect that child to help a sibling?)

Conversely, the supermoms and superdads aren't shy about asking children, even young toddlers, for their help when they need it. Around the house, this could take the form of requests like "Go fetch a cup of water," "Go get a firebrand from the neighbor," "Come turn on the hose while we water the garden," "Come help us shuck the corn," or even "Go figure out if Aunt Mary is having an affair with neighbor Bob"—yes, among the Ese'Eja hunter-gatherer tribe in the Bolivian Amazon, children are the gossip columnists for adults because the little ones can hang around houses undetected while the adults talk.

Okay, time for another confession: When I first read about the importance of togetherness, it sounded like a new type of hell. I found being with Rosy exhausting. Some evenings after dinner I would secretly crawl across the kitchen floor to the bathroom and lock the door, just to have a few minutes of peace and quiet. The last thing I wanted was to be stuck together like two pieces of Velcro for hours upon hours each day.

But in Chan Kajaal, I have the opportunity to watch Maria and Teresa practice togetherness, and I see that I'm doing it all wrong. For starters, I'm

TOGETHERNESS

ANYONE can do it.   No need to make special   Peaceful coexistence.
Grandma, uncle, cousin, plans (or entertain).   Calm. Easy. Relaxing
neighbor, nanny.   Do your thing and let   QUIET
                         the kid be with you.

making it too hard. Way too hard. That's why I cannot sustain it for more than an hour or two. And I'm making it way too much about me. I have the *who* and *what* of togetherness all backward.

- **Who:** Togetherness is by no means the exclusive domain of the mom and dad. In many instances, the parent isn't involved at all. Anyone who loves the child can provide togetherness. Everywhere you look in traditional communities, such as Chan Kajaal and Kugaaruk, you'll see someone besides a child's mom or dad offering togetherness: grandma, grandpa, aunt, uncle, sibling, neighbor, babysitter, friend. You name it. Togetherness is big sister Laura helping little sister Claudia get dressed. It's Grandma Sally taking three-year-old Tessa out to pick berries on the tundra. It's nanny Lena taking Rosy to Golden Gate Park. A big brother sleeping with his little brother. A neighbor holding a baby. A friend holding a hand. Togetherness is a circle of love that surrounds the child, no matter where they go.

As we'll continue to see, having these other caretakers is a core component of TEAM parenting. And it makes raising children so much easier (and less exhausting for mom and dad).

- **What:** While being together with children, the parents and other caretakers don't constantly give instructions, commands, and warnings. Nor do they constantly stimulate children by playing with them or giving them educational lessons. Togetherness is the opposite of this dynamic. And I think you'll find it's a far less demanding (and exhausting) mode of parenting.

Togetherness means letting the child hang out or tag along with you, whatever you need or want to do. You welcome the child on an errand or chore, then simply let the child do their thing. If they come over and want to help or watch, they're allowed. But if not, that's okay, too. The child's in your world doing their own activities. Two individuals—the caregiver and the child—are coexisting together in the same space, but not demanding attention from each other. Later on we'll learn more about how you train a demanding child to learn this skill. For now just realize the less you demand of a child's attention—through orders, directions, and corrections—the less the child will demand your attention.

Togetherness is easy. It's relaxing. It flows. It's what happens when we all stop trying to control each other's actions and simply let each other be. Inuit supermom Elizabeth Tegumiar sums up this idea for me one evening at a drum dance in Kugaaruk. I keep trying to tell Rosy what to do while she's playing with other kids. Elizabeth turns to me and says, "Let her be. She isn't cranky. She's fine."

Rosy and I see this easy, relaxed togetherness everywhere we travel for this book. In Chan Kajaal, Maya moms feed chickens or weave hammocks while the children climb trees nearby. Up in the Arctic town of Kugaaruk, Inuit moms and dads go to check fishing nets on the river, and the kids come along to play on the rocks. On another day, two moms butcher a narwhal on the front lawn while Rosy and a bunch of young kids ride bikes and play in a stream nearby. Every now and again, a kid stops by to take a look at the muktuk (whale meat). But parents never give any instructions, unless the child shows interest—or if the parent needs genuine help. Parents and children simply coexist together.

At the same time, you can see that the kids are taking it all in. "This is how it's done. This is how we do things." They're learning.

Not that long ago, adults in the U.S. still used togetherness as the primary way to teach kids all sorts of skills. It's how my grandpa learned to grow peanuts in Georgia, as well as carpenter skills to build furniture. It's how my grandmother learned to bake, cook, knit, and sew. And how my own mom learned to fry chicken and sew on a button. It's also how Mickey Doucleff learned to be a baker.

———————

Mickey is my father-in-law. When I tell him about how Maya parents in Chan Kajaal teach children to do chores, he immediately knows exactly what I'm talking about. "That's a lot like how I grew up," he says. "That's how I learned everything at the bakery."

Mickey's father was an immigrant from Macedonia. And in 1951, his father opened Duke Bakery in Alton, Illinois (near the site where Abraham Lincoln debated Stephen Douglas before the Civil War).

From the bakery's opening day, Mickey's family expected him to contribute to the family business. His first job, at age four, was folding pie boxes. "I was supposed to get paid a penny a box. I don't think I ever received any compensation. That was the lure," he says, chuckling.

He spent almost all of his free time at the bakery. "We played inside, outside, and around the bakery every single day," Mickey says. He and his brother had no nannies, camps, or karate lessons. After school, on the weekends, and during the summer, the children's entertainment was being together, at the bakery, while the family worked.

"My brother and I were always welcomed in the bakery, and I hung out there daily—except when the weather was really nice and the neighbor kids wanted to play."

Over those years, Mickey learned how to make everything the bakery sold, from a Mississippi mud pie to babka bread. And he learned with two simple tools: watching and experimenting. "Hands-on work," Mickey says. "Just trying out different tasks."

Mickey's dad was a man of few words, and like Teresa, he chose those words carefully. Instead of offering a full lecture on how something should be made, he'd offer small course corrections. Like: "There's too much sugar on the cinnamon bread," or "You kneaded the sourdough too much," or "Did you remember to proof the bread?" But generally, he let Mickey and his brother make mistakes—imperfect pastries and misshapen pies.

And he let his sons simply hang around. "There was never any pressure to work. No pressure," Mickey says. "Nobody ever yelled or got upset if we just watched."

By the time Mickey turned nine, he'd learned enough skills to make significant contributions to the family business. "I was mostly working in the front, taking care of customers," he says. But he was also honing his baking skills.

It was around this time, he remembers, that his uncle Nick asked Mickey to make him a loaf of cinnamon bread. "I could barely reach the workbench, but I felt honored that he would want me to make something for him. So I told him, 'Of course.'"

The next day, when Mickey got home from school, his dad asked him, "Mickey, do you remember what you promised Uncle Nick?"

"So right away I went back in the bakery, and my dad had set aside a piece of dough that was already mixed, just for me. He had also placed a crate under the table so I could reach the bench."

Mickey rolled out the dough, added cinnamon sugar, shaped it into a loaf, and put it into the oven.

"I wasn't very proud of the way it looked. And I had forgotten to proof it. It could have been much better, but for my age I think it was okay. And Uncle Nick was thrilled. He was happy, and he said he enjoyed it."

All of this prepared Mickey to take over the bakery after college. He worked there for nearly fifty years until he retired, in 2019. But being a full-fledged member of the bakery staff next to his family gave him an even bigger gift growing up: a sense of pride about work and contributing to the family. "Immensely," the seventy-four-year-old says with tears in his eyes. "My dad never turned down anyone who wanted to work, even a small child."

———————

Now we can start to see a glimpse of a new dimension of parenting—one that doesn't involve control. We can start to see a way of collaborating with the child that involves merging our agendas with theirs and going after a common goal. Lucia calls this sophisticated form of collaboration "fluid," and in the next few chapters, we'll learn more about how this collaboration works. We'll see how to minimize resistance with children while opening up channels for communication and love.

Summary for Chapter 5:
How to Raise Cooperative Kids

Ideas to Remember

➤ Children have a strong natural motivation to work as a team and
to cooperate. Think of it as "peer pressure," but with their family
instead of their peers.

➤ Child-centered activities, designed only for kids, erode this team
motivation and give a child the impression that they're exempt
from family responsibilities.

➤ On the flip side, when we include children in adult activities, we
amplify a child's motivation to cooperate and do what the family is
doing. The child feels like a full-fledged member of the team, with
both benefits and responsibilities.

➤ Children will often misbehave when they have to move from the
child's world (including child entertainment) to the adult world.

➤ In the vast majority of cultures around the world, parents do not
constantly stimulate and entertain children. This mode of parenting
can be exhausting and stressful for both a child and a parent.

➤ Children do not need this entertainment or stimulation. They are
fully equipped to self-entertain and occupy themselves. They can
do all of that on their own with very little input from a parent or
devices in the home.

Do It Today

For all children:

➤ Minimize child-centered activities. Be sure children have access
to your life and work. Be sure they're around while you do chores
or other adult activities. Your activities are more than enough
entertainment and stimulation.

➤ Minimize distractions such as screens and toys. The fewer "entertainment" items a child has, the more attractive your world becomes and the more likely they'll be interested in helping and being with you.

➤ Maximize exposure to the adult world. Go about your business and bring the child with you. Take them on errands, appointments, visits with friends, and even to your workplace, as much as possible.

➤ On the weekends, choose activities that you want to do—activities you would do even if you didn't have children. Go fishing, hiking, or biking. Work in the garden. Go to the beach or park. Visit friends.

For older kids (> age seven):

➤ Let an older child plan and organize their own child-centered activities (e.g., sports, music and art classes, other after-school activities, playdates). Encourage them to handle the logistics themselves, such as sign-ups, transportation, et cetera.

➤ Slowly ramp up a child's responsibilities in the house, including increasing the care of younger siblings and contributions to cooking and cleaning. Think of ways they can help you at work.

➤ If an older child has had little exposure to the adult world, introduce them by degrees. Go about your business and bring the child with you. If the child misbehaves, explain to them how they need to act in the adult world.

➤ If the child is still disruptive, be patient. Don't give up. Try again later. They'll learn.

CHAPTER 6

Master Motivators: What's Better Than Praise?

Each day around noon, when you walk by Maria's house, you'll hear a sound coming from the kitchen. *Tap, tap, tap. Tap, tap, tap.* Then there's a pause for about twenty seconds. And again. *Tap, tap, tap. Tap, tap, tap.*

Is she hanging up something on the wall? Building a piece of furniture?

Tap, tap, tap. Tap, tap, tap. It goes on for fifteen minutes, maybe longer.

As I walk closer to her door, the scent hits my nose: sweet, buttery corn, caramelizing as it toasts above a coal fire.

Maria sits at her kitchen table with a big mountain of pale yellow masa in front of her. She pinches off a little ball of dough, about the size of a walnut, and with her fingertips, flattens the ball into a perfect disk. *Tap, tap, tap. Tap, tap, tap.* Then she gently lays the disk on a hot skillet for a minute or so, until it puffs up like a puffer fish, and she flips it to the other side. These tortillas taste like heaven—warm, creamy, and soft. I will never eat a better tortilla in my life.

Then Maria's five-year-old daughter, Alexa, comes over to help, and what I witness is a master class in motivating children. Alexa's little fingers are clumsy, slow, and just barely getting the job done. But Maria doesn't stop her. She doesn't swoop in and grab the child's hand and show her how to make the tortillas better. Instead, she steps back and lets Alexa make misshapen ones, however Alexa feels is best. She lets her daughter practice. And when the little girl tires of the task, Maria doesn't force her to stay and finish. Alexa hops up and goes outside, while Maria continues working.

Next Gelmy, Maria's middle daughter, comes to the table. She's nine years old and has been playing outside with a friend. Now she wants to help. Compared to her little sister, Gelmy is a pro at making the tortillas. But she still has a lot to learn. Making tortillas like Maria's is incredibly difficult. It takes years of practice.

So most of Gelmy's tortillas end up a bit misshapen. She tries over and over again to make a perfect one. Then, voilà! Gelmy does it! She makes a beauty: a perfect little disk, even in thickness, and round as the moon.

Guess what Maria does? Or more to the point: What she doesn't do?

———————

In the 1970s, an American psychologist named Edward Deci set his sights on an ambitious goal: to figure out what motivates a person to act voluntarily. Up to that point, psychologists had focused on a different type of motivation, one shaped and controlled by external forces, such as rewards (e.g., money), punishments (e.g., time-outs), and recognition. But Ed wanted to know what makes people act without the spur of such outside forces. What naturally motivates a person to seek out a new challenge or to step up to help others when there's no obvious reward on the horizon? What makes a person do something when no one is watching? What fuels their inner fire?

For example, when I first started writing this book, all the effort I was putting in seemed foolish. I was basically doubling my workload each week, and the travel completely drained my bank account. At the same time, I didn't know if anyone would ever care about this story or if I would recover any of the money. All the same, in my free time, I still found myself writing and researching. Why? Because I really enjoyed it. I loved meeting the people in this book and learning from them. And I felt like I was growing as a writer and journalist through the process.

I had what Ed calls "intrinsic" motivation—the drive to write came from inside me, and not from an external reward. With intrinsic motivation, the activity is enjoyable on its own; it is "internally rewarding."

Intrinsic motivation makes a person dance in their living room at night when no one is watching. It makes Rosy immediately start coloring in the morning when she wakes up. And it makes Gelmy come in from playing with her friends to help Maria with the tortillas.

In many ways, intrinsic motivation is magical. It allows people to grow, learn, and work without (much) struggle or resistance. And it likely lasts longer than its counterpart, extrinsic motivation.

External influences, such as rewards and punishments, can actually weaken intrinsic motivation. Sticker charts, promises of ice cream, timeouts, threats of punishment or other consequences often "undermine this type of motivation."

In other words, if you were to give Gelmy ten pesos—or a gold star on a chart—for each tortilla she makes perfectly, over time she might stop making tortillas voluntarily. Yet with no reward, the little girl willingly comes to the table to help her mom, day after day. Why? What fuels intrinsic motivation?

To date, psychologists have published at least 1,500 studies about this type of question. And it's possible to draw remarkable parallels between the findings of these studies and how parents treat children in Maya communities, such as Chan Kajaal. Western psychology finds that three ingredients are needed to spark intrinsic motivation. The first one, we've already talked about: connectedness.

Ingredient 1: Sense of connectedness. Connectedness is the feeling of being related to others, of belonging to a team or family. Studies show that when a child feels connected to a teacher, they'll want to work hard in that class. The same goes for parents. The more connected a child feels with their family, the more they will want to work with us on family goals and chores. A great way to connect with our kids is to give them their membership card—welcome them into our world and come together as a family to accomplish common goals, like making tortillas for lunch. Working together is more enjoyable and often faster.

Ingredient 2: Sense of autonomy. I've mentioned autonomy before, and it's so important (so very important) that we'll devote a whole chapter to it later. But in the situation I describe earlier, you can see this ingredient at work in Maria's interactions with her daughters. By not forcing Alexa or Gelmy to come help make tortillas—and by not forcing them to stay after they'd lost interest—Maria was honoring her children's autonomy.

Ingredient 3: Sense of competency. In order to stay motivated at a task, a child needs to have a sense that they're competent enough to do the job. Nobody wants to keep working at something when they feel constantly frustrated or like they aren't making any progress. On the other hand, an easy task may become too boring to continue. So there's a sweet spot: the task is challenging enough to keep you interested, but also easy enough that you feel competent doing it. This sweet spot is where intrinsic motivation likely occurs.

INGREDIENTS FOR MOTIVATION

1. CONNECTEDNESS
Does the child feel a part of a TEAM?

2. AUTONOMY
Does the child feel like they are making the decision to act?

3. COMPETENCY
Does the child feel like they are capable of doing the task?

Maria and other Maya parents have several tricks up their sleeves to help children feel a sense of competency while doing chores and other adult tasks. We'll talk all about those tools in just a second. But first a word about a tool they *don't* use. That's praise.

During my entire stay in Chan Kajaal, I never hear a parent praise a child, and I definitely never hear lavish praise—e.g., "Oh, Angela, that's amazing how you did the dishes without being asked. You are a wonderful daughter!"—even though the children often behave in ways that would make me squeal with joy.

The parents don't say, "Good job," or other phrases like that. "Sometimes they may use facial expressions to show their approval. And these nonverbal expressions are important. They are clear signs of approval," says psychologist Rebeca Mejía-Arauz. While Maria and I are talking, I notice her using these signals with me. She lifts her eyebrows to acknowledge that I'm getting the hang of what she's telling me. Or she nods her head and says, "Hmm."

When it comes to no praise, Maya parents aren't alone. In all my travels outside of the U.S., I've never heard parents praise their children. And I've definitely never heard a constant stream of praise like the one that comes out of my mouth on a daily basis. (Heck, sometimes I even praise Rosy when she makes a mistake—"Oh, good job for trying." What's that all about?)

I hear so little praise on my trips around the world that I have become suspicious of it. I am starting to think that praise causes more trouble for parents than it's worth.

Praise is a tricky beast. It can fizzle with a kid for many reasons, especially when the praise doesn't feel genuine, doesn't seem justified for the accomplishment, or is simply ever present. When a child's every positive action garners a "Good job" or "Nice," then praise can undermine their intrinsic motivation, making children less likely to do a task in the future.

Praise has another pitfall—a big one. It can cause strife among siblings, because praise breeds competition. Psychologists have found that when young children grow up hearing frequent praise, they learn, from an early age, to compete with siblings for approval and attention from their parents. The lack of praise may be one reason Maya siblings work well together (and fight less than American siblings). They don't need to compete with one another for verbal kudos.

So if Maya parents don't use praise as a tool, then what are they calling on? Turns out, they have quite a few alternatives. The first one is so beautiful that once I really understood how to use it, my relationship with Rosy blossomed like a magnolia tree in the spring.

That tool is "acknowledgment."

Step 3: Acknowledge A Child's Contribution

Instead of praising children, Maya parents acknowledge or accept the child's idea or contribution to an activity—no matter how inconsequential, ridiculous, or misshapen that contribution (or tortilla) might be.

Maya parents let the child make a meaningful contribution to the daily tasks, and they don't tend to fuss with that contribution in order to meet the expectations you would have as an adult. Parents value a child's version of sweeping, the child's misshapen tortilla, or the ideas a child brings forward. They value a child's vision. And they respect that vision.

Acknowledgment from parents fuels the child's interest in a task, says psychologist Lucia Alcalá. "I think that it gives the child motivation to help more. A child sees that their contribution matters and they're helping the family. That's more powerful than any praise."

For example, when Alexa makes a misshapen tortilla, Maria may fix it slightly before putting it on the skillet. But she doesn't try to force Alexa to make a better one. She doesn't lecture Alexa about how to do it. And she doesn't grab the little girl's hands to help her.

Instead, Maria acknowledges and values Alexa's contribution to lunch by accepting the tortillas as she made them. Maria has confidence that, eventually, Alexa will master tortilla making through practice and watching. Why rush the process? (Rushing would only cause conflict and stress.) Until Alexa has more experience, Maria quietly bolsters her sense of competency, which in turn likely boosts the girl's motivation to practice making tortillas again tomorrow.

The reverse is also true. If a parent resists a child's idea or contribution, it can erode a child's sense of competency and demotivate them. Parental resistance can come in many flavors, such as ignoring an idea, rejecting it outright (by saying something like "No, no, we can't do that," or "No, we don't do it like that. We do it like this"), or giving a lesson on the "proper" way a task is done. Parents can also resist by not using the child's work, completely redoing it, or grabbing a tool from a child and doing the work oneself.

Maya and other indigenous parents tend not to resist like this—they don't get in a child's way while the child is helping. "The moms don't stop the child from doing something, even if it's wrong," Rebeca says, referring to the Nahua-heritage moms. Instead—and this is key!—the parent pays attention to what the child is doing, and then builds off the child's idea. As a result, the parent sets up a beautiful cycle of collaboration, wherein the child or parent contributes an idea and the other takes the idea and expands it. Lucia calls this "fluid collaboration." It's when two people are working seamlessly together, like a single organism with four arms. In those moments, there's minimal talking, minimal resistance, and minimal conflict.

In a way, the Maya parents treat the child as a copartner in the activity. Parents believe that knowledge isn't one-directional, flowing only from the parent to the child. Rather, they recognize knowledge is bidirectional. Information and ideas can come from the children, too.

KNOWLEDGE FLOW

ADULT to CHILD
How we think
knowledge flows.

FLUID COLLABORATION
a more
respectful way

After our conversation, Rebeca's words echo in my head for days, even weeks afterward: *They don't stop the child from doing something, even if it's wrong.* I repeat that phrase to myself over and over again, while trying to collaborate with Rosy. Quickly, I realize that I have been doing just the opposite. I interfere with her contributions—not just once in a while, but all the time. I resist her ideas, and I even flat-out ignore them. And I definitely haven't believed that I could learn from Rosy, especially in the kitchen. I think knowledge flows only from me to her and not the reverse.

There are so many examples of this, it's hard to choose. But one instance sticks out in my mind, perhaps because it happened just before I started writing this chapter. To be honest, I'm embarrassed to tell you about it—it makes me look silly and childish. But I'll share it anyway, as it's a vivid example of what a big difference my acknowledgment—and my valuing Rosy's ideas—could make in our relationship.

One Sunday afternoon, Rosy's coloring in the living room, and I'm making kebabs for a dinner party. It's a perfect task for a three-year-old: all you do is push chunks of chicken and vegetables—zucchini, mushrooms, and peppers—onto skewers. So I invite Rosy over to help: "Come, my love. Come help me make the kebabs for dinner."

She runs over and takes her place on a step stool next to me. I continue to make the kebabs. Immediately, she veers off course. She insists on making an "all-chicken" skewer. My knee-jerk reaction is to stop her. To change her trajectory. To force her creations to conform to the expectations I have for the kebabs. "But that's not what we're making," I say. "We'll run out of chicken and won't have enough for the other kebabs."

A big argument erupts. In the end, Rosy starts crying and runs away, quite upset, and returns to coloring in the living room.

Well, that was a miserable failure, I think. And I finish the kebabs myself. I decide to move on and forget about the argument. It's not the first time that my attempt at collaborating with her has ended in tears. At least this time, I'm not crying as well.

A few weeks later, when I sit down to write this chapter, I relisten to my interviews with Maria, Teresa, Rebeca, and Lucia. And I begin to see the error of my ways. I thought Rosy was having a hard time collaborating with me, but in reality, *the problem is me*. I'm not collaborating with her. I resist her ideas and don't value them. Many times, I don't listen to what she's trying to tell me.

So I decide to give myself another shot at collaborating with Rosy. I go back to the store, buy more kebab ingredients, and set up the exact same scenario: Sunday afternoon, me making kebabs, Rosy coloring in the living room. Again, I call her over: "Rosy, my love, come and help with the kebabs." This time, however, she doesn't get up. In fact, she doesn't even look up from coloring. *Hmm, not very motivated*, I think. So I acknowledge my mistake from last time: "You can make whatever design you think is best—even an all-chicken one."

She rushes over. "I can?"

"Yes."

She hops on her step stool and gets right to work. She makes a giant chicken-and-pepper kebab, with about eight chunks of chicken all smashed together. I don't stop her, but instead acknowledge her contribution—not with words, but through my actions. I take her finished kebab and place it on the plate next to the others. And, the acknowledgment works. Rosy smiles at me and begins working on another kebab. *Oh no*, I think, *we are going to run out of chicken*. But that doesn't happen. To my utmost  surprise, she changes course—and she starts collaborating. She pays attention to what I'm doing and joins me. She makes kebabs that look more like mine, using zucchini and mushrooms, too. We begin to work in a way that's fluid and organic, like the one organism with many limbs. I help her push some mushrooms onto her skewer and she passes me a piece of chicken when I clearly need one. Working together is smooth, easy, and fun, until she gets tired, runs off, and starts coloring again. But this time no one is crying. In fact, we both feel really good.

I even feel a tiny grin on my face. Valuing her input and acknowledging her ideas had really made a difference, shifting how the entire experience felt.

And guess what? That chicken-and-pepper kebab, the one she made, tasted really good. Next time we'll make a bunch of those, as well as the mixed veggies.

Try It 3: Learn to Motivate Children

As a parent, there are many ways to acknowledge a child's ideas without actually doing what they ask. Sometimes a simple comment like "That's a good idea" is all a child needs to feel included and motivated to stay involved, even if you don't use their idea at all. A Maya parent could say, "*uts xan*," which literally translates to "also good." An adult would interpret this statement to mean, "I don't agree." But to a child, it seems like acceptance.

As I've mentioned, the interpreter Rodolfo Puch used this strategy with me while setting up interviews in Chan Kajaal. I would come up with crazy ideas—"Can Rosy and I move in with Teresa for the rest of the summer?"—and Rodolfo never outright rejected them. He never rolled his eyes or informed me, "No way, you crazy gringa lady! We cannot do those intrusive things" (which he had every right to do). Instead, he would acknowledge the idea. He would nod his head and say, "Yes, we can. We can." Then he would let the idea go for a while, until I brought it back up again. By that point, he had usually figured out how to satisfy my request in a feasible and respectful way.

Nahua-heritage parents sometimes acknowledge children's work with small, casual gifts (otherwise they don't generally give rewards for specific tasks, Lucia and her colleagues find). But the gifts aren't tied to a particular task, such as "If you help me do the dishes, I'll buy you ice cream." Instead, the parent rewards the child for their general helpfulness, "as being a contributing member of the family," as Lucia and her colleagues write. And these treats are typically small, such as "cooking a special meal or buying the child something necessary like underpants."

In many cultures, parents acknowledge contributions by connecting them to maturity, growing up, and starting to learn. For example, one mom told Lucia and her colleagues how she acknowledges her son's help around the house: "When he does something good, and what he needs to do, I just tell him, 'Oh my son, you've already learned [to work],' and he gets very happy." Other moms say they "congratulate" a child on "growing up" as the child contributes more to the work around the house. One mom says she gives the child a hug and acknowledges their "mature family role." (I tried this last night with Rosy after she voluntarily started sweeping the living room, and she loved it!)

Recognizing a child's overall helpfulness provides more information to a child than praising a specific task. Instead of focusing on a one-off accomplishment, you're helping the child to learn an overarching value.

Anthropologist Jean Briggs has documented a similar type of acknowledgment used by some Inuit parents. In one case, she describes how parents acknowledge a five-year-old girl who is learning to be generous by sharing her candy with a sibling: "A five-year-old is already savvy and she knows she's supposed to give most of it [the candy], if not all of it, to her three-year-old sister, so she does and [the adults] say, 'Look at that, she gave it. How generous she is.'"

Many parents around the world take this idea one step further by associating cooperative behavior with being a "big girl" or "big boy." Up in the Arctic, one Inuit mom connects hitting a younger sibling to being "a baby," whereas being kind and generous to the sibling is associated with "not being a baby." This tool is so powerful in our home that we'll discuss it again in the next section.

Here's how to start trying these approaches at home with kids of all ages, from toddlers to teens.

Dip Your Toe

• **Point out helpfulness (and unhelpfulness).** Instead of praising children for helping with a request, switch to acknowledging overall helpfulness. Don't overdo it or do it too frequently. A simple statement like "That's helpful" is all you need when a child shows *acomedido* or voluntarily helps. You might even wait until the end of the week to acknowledge the child's overall effort. Focus on the learning aspect or the contribution to the family: "You are really starting to learn to be helpful," or "You are starting to be a big girl and contribute to the family's work."

To help your child better understand what "helpfulness" means, point it out in others. This also helps communicate to your child that you value this trait and that it's important to you. When you acknowledge helping, focus on how working together makes everyone's life easier. For example, one morning on the way to school with Rosy, I said: "Dada was really *acomedido* this morning. He was paying attention and pitching in when needed."

"Yeah, and so am I," she responded without missing a beat.

- **Acknowledge unhelpful behavior as well.** Don't be afraid to point out when the child *isn't* being helpful. "Parents often say sarcastically, 'Don't be too *acomedido*,' or 'Don't help too much,'" Lucia says. "That signals to the child to help."

You can also acknowledge when someone else fails to show *acomedido*. This will help the child learn what *not* to do. And focus on why that behavior isn't valued. Again, use simple statements so it's clear. For example, one afternoon, a friend of Rosy's didn't help us pick up toys in our living room. So I said, "That wasn't very *acomedido*. If she had helped us, we could have all finished faster."

- **Stop punishments and rewards for specific chores.** These tools simply don't work when it comes to teaching children to do chores (or really, anything) voluntarily. In many cases, they actively undermine children's own drive to help.

In place of punishments and rewards, try these motivational tools:

- **Explain the value the task holds for the entire family.** Try explaining to the child why helping out is so important—or essential—in the home. One Nahua-heritage mom told Lucia that she never punishes her daughter: "But I do get upset and admonish her." When her daughter doesn't clean up her toys, she tells the girl, "You need to try harder." The mother explained to Lucia, "I tell her that so she sees that we're also trying hard with the little that we can give her, so she should try hard, too."

This approach works well with Rosy, especially when she can see I'm tired and overworked. I tell her, "Rosy, your father and I are working hard to make this house nice for everyone. We are trying our best. As a family member, you need to work hard and try your best."

- **Connect the helpfulness to maturity.** If a child takes initiative and does a chore voluntarily, acknowledge their growth and progress by saying something like "Oh, you're starting to learn how to contribute," or "You cleaned up your toys because you're a big girl."

I also tell Rosy when she acts like a baby. For example, if she doesn't clean up her toys or help with the dishes, I say, "Oh, you didn't do it because you're a baby?" And that comment often leads to a whole discussion about what big girls do versus what babies can do. For example, "Do babies get to ride a bike?" "Do babies get to eat ice cream?" Eventually, Rosy wants to be a big girl and goes and cleans up.

• **Let the child have fun with the chore.** I'm not a big fan of making chores "fun" or turning them into a game. I cannot sustain that energy for very long, and I don't enjoy acting like a three-year-old. But if Rosy comes up with her own way to make the chore more playful, I don't stop her. Instead, I pay attention to her idea or contribution and try to build upon it. For example, one afternoon while hanging the clothes on the line to dry, she starts throwing the clothes all over the porch. So I decide to incorporate her "play" into the chore. I tell her, "Stand by the clothesline and I will throw you the clothes to hang up." She loves it! She wants to keep throwing the clothes back and forth. Eventually, we get the job done. It takes a little longer, but her motivation for doing laundry skyrocketed. Now she runs over when I call (sometimes), and we have incorporated the "throwing" idea into several other chores, such as cleaning up Legos and putting away books. I tell her, "Rosy, stand over by the bookshelf and I'll throw you the books." That totally gets her helping!

• **Threaten natural consequences.** If you need to use a threat, try to make the punishment as close to a natural consequence as possible. For example, sometimes I tell Rosy, "If we don't clean up the kitchen, ants will come and take over the counters. Do you want ants in our food?" Or I say, "If we don't wash your lunch box, you will have to eat from a dirty, stinky box tomorrow. Do you want that?"

• **Point out when you help them.** With Rosy, I find that pointing out reciprocal responsibility works well to boost her motivation. For example, one night she doesn't help with the dishes. When I ask her to come help, she says, "I'm tired," and runs away. Ten minutes later, she comes back and asks me to help her find her lovie. Then I say something like "Wait, did you help me with the dishes just a few minutes ago?"

Jump In

- **Learn to value a child's contribution.** When a child comes over to help with a task, listen to their idea. Acknowledge it in some way, either by trying it, incorporating it into your activity, nodding your head, or saying, "We can." If the child takes action, don't stop them. Instead, pay attention and see how they're trying to contribute. Then think of a way to build off that contribution or a way to improve their work slightly.

  Whatever you do, suppress the urge to resist. Refrain from interfering with the child or changing their course. If you step back and let a child "take over" a task, the child will be way more motivated to help out again in the future than if you reject, minimize, or ignore their ideas and contributions.

- **Measure how much you praise your children (and how much you resist them).** Your smartphone is a great device for analyzing your parenting habits—and gaining a fresh perspective. One evening, put your phone on the kitchen counter or dining room table and set it to record in the background for thirty to sixty minutes while you interact with your children. Then, later that evening, listen carefully to the recording. How many times do you praise the child for an inconsequential task or something they should just be doing without the need for praise? How many times do you resist their ideas? Or just ignore them when they're trying to contribute? How many times do you interfere with their actions and try to change their course?

I accidentally ran this experiment one night when I left my radio mic running on the kitchen counter for two hours while Rosy and I made dinner. Listening to the tape afterward was really difficult. It actually made me cry. As I played back our conversation, I realized that not only was I resisting Rosy's ideas and contributions, but I wasn't listening to her words at all. Many times she was trying to tell me *X*, while I was so certain *Y* was correct that I could not hear her. I really thought that I knew the answer and didn't need to listen to her. She kept trying so hard to get her ideas across that *she* would start crying. And the pleading and pain in her voice was so sad that it broke my heart. I realized I needed to stop talking so much (including praising her) and make a real effort to pay attention to her words and actions. (Psychological anthropologist Suzanne Gaskins had given me similar advice a few months earlier. "American parents need to stop talking so much and listen more to their children," she said.)

- **Have praise-free days.** Once you realize how much you praise your child, try pruning it back. Start small: Set a timer for fifteen minutes and try not to verbally praise the child until the timer goes off. Work your way up to two hours, and eventually, entire days. Assess how you feel after these praise-free moments. Is parenting less stressful, less tiring? How does your child act? Do they seek your attention less? Are they less demanding? Is your time together a little bit more relaxing? Does your child fight less with their siblings?

———————

We now have the three ingredients, or steps, needed to support children's helpfulness. As we'll see in the next two sections, parents can use these three steps to transmit any value they want to a child. Across the globe, cultures use this "formula" to transmit all kinds of values, such as generosity, respect, and patience.

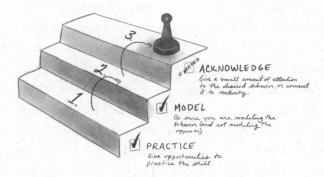

STEPS TO TRAINING
A CHILD

ACKNOWLEDGE
Give a small amount of attention to the desired behavior, or connect it to maturity.

MODEL
Be sure you are modeling the behavior (and not modeling the opposite)

PRACTICE
Give opportunities to practice the skill.

The steps are: Practice, Model, Acknowledge

1. Practice. Give kids oodles of practice helping out around the house and working together, especially the young ones. Assign tasks, invite them over to watch, and encourage their desire to participate.

2. Model. Give children their membership cards. Immerse them in your day-to-day life so they can gradually learn chores by watching and can feel like full-fledged members of the family.

3. Acknowledge. When a child tries to help, accept their contributions and value their ideas. Respect their vision. Tell the child when they are learning the value. Point out the presence of the value (or its absence) in others' actions. Connect their learning to "growing up" or maturing.

Summary for Chapter 6:
How to Motivate Children

Ideas to Remember

➤ To motivate a child without bribes or threats, the child needs to feel:
- Connected to you or another person close to the child.
- Like they are making the choice to do the task and no one is forcing them.
- Like they are competent and that their contribution will be valued.

➤ Praise can undermine motivation and generate competition (and strife) between siblings.

➤ Parents can learn quite a lot from a child. Knowledge can flow in both directions. Don't assume your approach or vision is the best. When you pay attention to a child's vision or ideas, you'll likely find the child often has valuable and useful information.

➤ Accepting a child's knowledge, idea, or contribution is a potent way to motivate the child.

Do It Today

For children of all ages:

➤ Resist the urge to correct a child, especially when they're pitching in or helping the family. Step back and let a child perform a task without interfering, even if the child isn't executing the task as you wish or taking the optimal approach.

➤ If a child is resisting a request (e.g., to help with the dishes), you're likely forcing the issue too hard. The child knows what you want. Stop asking. Wait and let the child take the lead.

➤ Pay close attention to how a child is trying to contribute and then build off their ideas instead of resisting them.

➤ Help a child learn a task by letting them practice that task instead of lecturing or explaining the task to them. Offer simple course corrections, sparingly, while the child takes action.

➤ Accept a child's contribution to an activity even if it isn't what you expect or want.

➤ Use praise very sparingly. When you do praise, attach it to learning an overall value (e.g., "You are starting to learn to be helpful") or to maturity (e.g., "You are really becoming a big girl").

Inuit Emotional Intelligence

T
Encourage
A
M

If a child misbehaves, they need more calmness and more touch.

CHAPTER 7

Never in Anger

On the surface, the tiny Arctic village of Kugaaruk looks like a town you might find along the New England coast. A handful of wooden houses—painted red, green, and tan—sit perched atop stilts only a few yards from a pebbly beach. A motorboat or two sit in the front yard of each home. Kiddie bikes lean against front steps. Front doors are never locked, and you can see kids running in and out of neighbors' and relatives' homes, grabbing peanut butter sandwiches and glasses of Tang for lunch.

But when you sniff the air, you can detect a unique smell here—like seaweed mixed with beef stew. In one backyard, a full rack of caribou ribs hangs up from a shed door, drying in the salty breeze. Across the street, three polar bear skulls sit on a bench in a family's front yard, their white, shiny canines longer than a thumb. And if you go into someone's kitchen and open up the freezer, you might find a big chunk of seal for future dinners.

This isn't New England—it's far, far away. So far, that back in the early 1960s, when a young anthropology student from Harvard University ventured near here, many thought the trip would kill her.

"I really wanted to go to the most remote and uncontacted place in the north that I could find," Jean Briggs later said, "so that I could find people who were as little influenced by our culture as possible."

This desire brought her to the top of the world, past the Arctic Circle and about 250 miles north of the Hudson Bay. Here the land fractures into hundreds of pieces, making it difficult to tell on a map what's an island and what's the sea. This vast swath of land is Inuit country, and it has been for a millennium.

For a Western anthropology student, the trip was risky. For a female anthropologist in the 1960s, the trip seemed mad and foolish to many of her colleagues. Winter temperatures can easily drop below minus thirty degrees Fahrenheit. There were no roads, no electrical heating systems, no grocery stores. Jean could easily have died.

But her risk paid off. During her seventeen-month-long sojourn in the region, Jean performed groundbreaking fieldwork that would eventually transform how Western psychology understood emotions—especially anger.

About a thousand years ago, a unique tribe of people lived along the Alaska-Russia border. The group, called Inuit, had developed extraordinary technologies that enabled them to thrive in one of the harshest environments on earth. They bred dogs specifically to pull sleds, designed waterproof pants out of seal skins, and built sleek sea kayaks from which they could bring down the biggest animals on earth. The tribe was so strong, so skilled, that families could travel hundreds of miles across the Arctic Circle. Over the next few centuries, Inuit settled a vast territory, spanning about three thousand miles, from the Bering Strait to Greenland.

In the 1960s, many Inuit families lived like their ancestors had centuries before, as nomadic hunter-gatherers. The sea was their grocery store; the tundra their garden. Families moved from camp to camp in pursuit of animals. They harpooned seals through the ice in the winter, speared Arctic char swimming upriver in the spring, and tracked down migrating caribou in the summer. Animal skins and hides gave them boots, parkas, bedding, and tents. Whale and seal blubber fueled lamps for cooking and heating their homes.

In August 1963, a service plane dropped Jean off on top of a granite bluff overlooking the white-water rapids of an Arctic river. Several families had camped along the river for the summer. At first, Jean's life in the camp seemed pretty easy. Blueberries were plentiful across the rust-colored tundra, and silver trout crowded the river below the camp. "Often twenty and occasionally as many as forty trout, each weighing between ten and forty pounds, may be caught by one fisherman in a day's jigging," Jean wrote. But by early October, the river began to freeze. Snow fell daily. Winter was approaching quickly. Jean realized that, in order to survive, she needed the help of an Inuit family. She convinced one of the couples at the camp, Allaq and Inuttiaq, to "adopt her" and "try to keep her alive."

Allaq and Inuttiaq were extraordinarily kind and generous to Jean. They taught her to speak a dialect of Inuit language, Inuktitut. They showed her how to catch fish and shared their winter supply of food. They also allowed her to sleep inside the family's igloo, huddled under the warm caribou blankets side by side with their two younger daughters, Raigili, age six, and Saarak, age three. (Their teenage daughter was away at boarding school.)

At first Jean had intended to study shamanism. But after a few weeks of living with Allaq and Inuttiaq, she realized something even more remarkable was going on with this family and the whole community.

"They never acted in anger toward me, although they were angry with me an awful lot," she recalled later.

She observed that Allaq and Inuttiaq had an astonishing ability to control their emotions. They never lost their temper, boiled over, or expressed so much as mild frustration, despite living in a tiny igloo in minus thirty degree temperatures with two young children and now an American grad student, to boot (who later admitted to being "difficult" at times).

"Indeed, the maintenance of equanimity under trying circumstances is *the* essential sign of maturity, of adulthood," Jean would write in *Never in Anger*, her book about her time with Allaq and Inuttiaq's family.

Inside their home, small mistakes were ignored. Petty grievances or complaints didn't exist. Even major setbacks prompted little response. Once, for example, Allaq's brother tripped over a stove and knocked a boiling pot of tea across the igloo floor. No one flinched. No one even looked up from what they were doing, despite the fact that the hot water was now melting the igloo floor. Instead, the young man quietly remarked, "Too bad," and then went about cleaning up the mess and mending the floor. "I felt no unusual intensity even in the general murmur of laughter," Jean wrote.

Another time, Allaq, the wife and mother of the family, had spent days braiding a fishing line with caribou sinew. When her husband used the line for the first time, the sinew broke instantly. No one showed a hint of frustration with the setback. Instead of acting emotionally, Allaq and Inuttiaq focused on being productive. In Jean's portrayal, Allaq laughed a little, and her husband handed her back the line "with no sign of reproach," saying only, "Sew it together."

Reading this, I marveled. What would living in such a calm, anger-free household be like?

When an adult did lapse a little and failed to restrain their emotions, other adults lightly mocked the behavior. Take, for example, a time when Inuttiaq "shot impulsively at a bird" who flew past. Watching from a distance, Allaq commented, "Like a child." Meaning: a lack of patience is the province of kids, not adults.

Despite trying very hard to tamp down her own emotions, Jean seemed like a wild child compared to Allaq and Inuttiaq. She could never live up to Inuit's standards of self-regulation. Adults considered even small expressions of irritation or grumpiness—too minor for Westerners to even notice—as signs of immaturity. "My ways were so much cruder, less considerate and more impulsive," she later said. "[I was] often impulsive in an antisocial sort of way. I would sulk or I would snap or I would do something that they never did."

In Jean's recounting, Allaq especially comes across as a pinnacle of calm and aplomb—even in childbirth. As impossible as it sounds, many Inuit women do not scream, or really make any sort of fuss, during childbirth. Allaq gave birth to her fourth child while Jean was living with the family. And her description is almost comical in what a nonevent the birth was:

Allaq had spent the evening frying bannock [bread] for our household. . . . [She] shared in the feast, had joked with her sisters as usual when they came in to share the bannock, had nursed Saarak tenderly to sleep at her breast as always, blown out the lamp, and apparently settled down to sleep. That was 11:30. At 1:30 I woke to hear the wavering cry of a newborn baby.

While giving birth, Allaq had remained so silent that Jean hadn't even registered her labor.

Then, after the birth, a serious problem arose. The placenta was stuck—putting Allaq at risk for a fatal hemorrhage. Inuttiaq, the only other adult present, made a few terse "exhortations" at the placenta, but he never yelled or cried. There was no ER-medical drama. Instead Inuttiaq lit a pipe, said a prayer, and eventually the placenta emerged.

Okay, at this point, while reading Jean's book, I honestly started to find her observations hard to believe. No screaming during childbirth? No yelling for months while crammed into an igloo with small children? In San Francisco, I'm yelled at on a daily basis—inside our home, outside our home, on Twitter. And I yell at Rosy—oh goodness, I'm too embarrassed to say how much I yell at Rosy. Surely, Jean had exaggerated in her depiction of the family's self-control.

And if she did report accurately, how did Allaq manage it? I'm curious not only about how Allaq and the other Inuit moms maintain their composure under such trying conditions but also how they pass that calmness along to their children. How do these parents take a tantrum-ridden, hot-tempered three-year-old and turn them into an easygoing and peaceful six-year-old? Could they help me tame my mini shrew?

And so, nearly six decades after Jean's trip, Rosy packs her *Frozen* suitcase accordingly and we fly up to the town of Kugaaruk, Canada, just across the peninsula from where Jean stayed.

———————

Arriving in Kugaaruk feels like landing inside a postcard. "A setting built for an emperor," I can hear one of my Japanese friends say. The landscape is utterly gorgeous.

With about two hundred homes, Kugaaruk is nestled between two spectacular bodies of water: the *kuuk* (or river), which runs so crystal clear that you can kneel down and have a drink anytime you're thirsty, and a blue-gray bay that glistens with ripples in the summer's low-lying sun. Several islands rise up from the bay like the backs of green giants bending over to fish.

Behind the town, the tundra spreads east as far as you can see. In late July, blueberries and blackberries carpet the gray tundra with tiny fruit about the size of peas. The bushes grow so small—just an inch or two above the ground—you have to kneel down and essentially kiss the reindeer moss while you pick their fruit. But it's worth the effort. The berries are tart and yummy.

During our first few days in Kugaaruk, Rosy and I find ourselves in a similar situation to young Jean Briggs: We don't have a great place to stay. The one hotel in Kugaaruk has a leaky roof, and it's expensive. So I start to ask around for a room to rent.

My hopes quickly dwindle, though, as I grow acutely aware of our notoriety in the town. Everywhere we go, Rosy makes it a priority to show off her tantrum skills. On a trip to the grocery store, she throws a box of granola bars in my face, and as we walk back to the hotel, she lies down on her back in the middle of a dirt road (while a family, butchering a whale, looks on), and screams, "Mama, Mama!" over and over again as I try to ask a kind lady if she knows about another place to stay in town.

Kugaaruk is only about three blocks wide and a few dozen blocks long. The town has one grocery store, one playground, one coffee shop. Everyone either walks or rides ATVs everywhere. Everyone knows everyone. Everyone sees everything. On top of that, almost everyone is Inuit. With my pale white skin and Rosy's blond hair, we stick out like sore thumbs.

As we make our way around town, I can't hide my inability to handle

Rosy's tantrums—and my angry responses to them. It's on full display. Even in the hotel room, the walls are so thin, I know the women who run the place can hear me trying to coax Rosy to sleep. Hear me losing my temper. Hear me yelling, "Stop! Just lie down and go to bed!"

By contrast, everywhere Rosy and I go, the moms appear completely unflappable. They never seem to lose their temper or even become flustered. Children are everywhere, lots of them. And yet there's never any urgency to the parents' responses to them. Parents never make quick actions to quell a child's energy or movements. They make no loud demands or insist a child stop what they're doing or act a certain way. No matter what, the adults just radiate calmness: ubiquitous, pervasive calmness. I can feel this calmness everywhere: at the grocery store, at the playground, in my brain, in my bones, in my heart. To be honest, I love it.

I see you walk by with your little girl each day
—always alone—
and I really want to help you.

And this calmness appears contagious. Because even the kids are remarkably chill—for the most part. I don't see children arguing or negotiating with their parents at the grocery store, or whining and crying when it's time to go home from the playground. On the second day in town, I realize that despite all the kids around, I haven't seen a single toddler tantrum (besides Rosy's) and I haven't heard one baby crying.

That second night, Rosy and I linger around outside by a little stream. My worries are sky-high, and my nerves frayed. Just then a young mom named Tracy rides up on an ATV. No older than twenty-five, she's sandwiched on the ATV between three children. In front of her, a toddler snuggles against her chest; behind her, a child who's about five years old wraps his arms around her waist; and a baby peeks out of the hood of her jacket in a baby carrier called an *amauti*. When she talks, her black hair, cut in a cute pixie style, bobs around her heart-shaped face. Tracy's words are soft, and her smile gentle. I can feel my heart rate calming from its erratic thumping as she shares her experiences as a mom. *This trip is going to be okay, Michaeleen*, I think for the first time.

Tracy's life isn't easy, by any measure. In addition to raising her three kids, she cleans rooms at the hotel full-time and also helps her husband and father-in-law prepare for hunts. I ask her if being a working mother of young children is stressful, and she answers, "No, I love being a mom. They keep me busy, but I love it."

Oh my goodness, I think to myself. *I must look like a complete hot mess of a mother to this young woman—and all the parents in Kugaaruk.* I have gray hairs, a PhD in chemistry, but I can barely handle one kid. I feel embarrassed and ashamed, and yet I don't get the sense that Tracy is judging me at all. In fact, I feel like I've found a friend—someone Rosy and I can call on if we need help.

When you yell at children
they stop listening.

This pattern occurs over and over again in Kugaaruk. Other moms and dads don't judge my poor parenting skills—at least not to my face or with the side glances and comments I'd get in San Francisco—but rather, they want to help me. And they aren't shy about reaching out.

Several women who see Rosy and me walking around town can't believe their eyes: "You are alone? Taking care of your daughter alone? Without help?" they ask. At the grocery store, another woman stops me by the apples. "Kids aren't supposed to be around one person, every hour of the day," she says with a slight tone of pity.

They aren't? I think. *Interesting point.*

Another woman, spying us from her living room window, comes running out. Wearing a pink camouflage jacket, she offers to take Rosy for a few hours so I can have a break. "I see you walk by with your little girl each day—always alone—and I really want to help you," she says.

I'm so accustomed to thinking of childcare as a one-woman show that, feeling shy about accepting her help, I say something ridiculous like "Oh, thank you, but I can do it by myself."

Then on the third day in Kugaaruk, Rosy and I meet Maria Kukkuvak and her daughter Sally—and I learn a useful way to think about little humans.

"Your daughter must be sick of you. That is why she is misbehaving," Sally tells me as we're having a cup of tea at her mother's kitchen table. "Rosy needs to be around other kids. You need a break."

Well, I know I need a break from Rosy. I'm sick of her. But it had never occurred to me that Rosy might get sick of me, too, and that might be why we argue so much.

> Your daughter must be sick of you.
> That is why she is misbehaving.
>
> — SALLY KUKKUVAK

"You travel with your husband for a few days and you both get sick of each other, right?" Sally says. "It doesn't mean you don't love each other. You just need a break."

It's not an exaggeration when I say that Sally is one of the most wonderful people I have met. She's a mental health outreach worker at the clinic, and her face radiates warmth and friendliness while she talks. "I smile with my eyes," she tells me as she brushes her bangs to the side. And it's true, every time Sally smiles, her eyes form thin lines that curve upward, like an effortless grin.

We are the same age: forty-two. But Sally has already raised three children, helped her siblings raise another seven or eight, and now regularly looks after four young grandchildren. As a parent, Sally is a world expert. She has seen it all. Although she never flaunts her expertise to me, she can see that I'm struggling with Rosy and makes a generous offer. "My mom is going out camping soon. She says you can stay in her room while she is gone. Then our family can help with Rosy. You need the help." Truer words have never been spoken.

The next night Rosy and I move from the hotel into Maria's home. And boy, are we lucky. Her family is so full of love that sometimes, even now back in San Francisco, I'll find myself crying at night longing to be back with them. I want to be back in Maria's living room, sharing raw caribou or playing bingo. I want to be back in the free-floating peace of their home.

I feel it the moment Rosy and I walk in the door. Dressed in gray jeans and a black T-shirt, Sally stirs a big pot of spaghetti with meat sauce. "Come on in and have some dinner," she says. There are at least a half dozen kids hanging out in the living room, playing video games and cards. As Rosy and I pass through with our suitcases, Sally is serving up pasta, filling up bowls and passing them out to the kids.

"Thank you so much for letting us stay with you, Sally, and for the dinner. We are so hungry," I tell her after we stow away our bags.

"There is always plenty of food. Eat as much as you would like," Sally says as she hands Rosy and me bowls of pasta. "Having you two is no problem at all. We have so many kids in this house all the time that one more won't make a difference at all."

And it's true—this living room is the social center for the Kukkuvak family. Only two children technically live in the house, but that doesn't matter. At any given moment, you can find aunts, uncles, cousins, nieces, and nephews visiting. Family and friends flow in and out freely, at all hours of the day.

Tonight is no exception. As we eat pasta, I count ten people in the living room, including a five-month-old baby, an eighteen-month-old toddler, a three-year-old girl, a six-year-old boy, two thirteen-year-old girls, and two fifteen-year-old boys.

These kids go out of their way to make room for Rosy, scooping her up (literally) and taking her under their wings. One of the thirteen-year-old girls, Susan, immediately starts brushing and braiding Rosy's hair (which hadn't been brushed in three or four days because Rosy won't let me touch it). Then Rebecca, age nine, comes into the living room, gently takes Rosy's hand, and says, "Let's go play outside." Two other small kids follow them out, and that's that: Rosy is officially one of the gang. I can feel my body relax, as if the burden of solo parenting is something I've been carrying on my back for days, months, even years.

———————

Parenting books often mention a concept from psychology and neuroscience called executive function. Basically, it's a suite of mental processes that help you act thoughtfully, instead of impulsively. It's the voice in your head that makes you pause before you react, asking, *What repercussions will follow my action? Is there a better approach?* Executive function helps you to control your emotions and behavior, or to change direction when needed. Studies suggest that better executive function as a child predicts a number of better outcomes later in life—better performance in school, better mental health, better relationships, higher chances of finding and keeping a job, et cetera.

In Kugaaruk, the children are dripping with executive function: they can see another child's point of view, remain flexible when situations change, and adapt to the needs of others. They exhibit way more emotional maturity than many children older than them in the U.S.—in many ways they are more emotionally mature than me. Even the little children often act patiently, empathetically, and generously. And they're excellent at sharing—toys, food, clothes, you name it. Objects seem to present as an opportunity to cooperate and play together instead of argue and compete.

For the rest of our time in the Arctic, Rosy plays with these children for hours upon hours each day, with basically no supervision needed from me or the other moms. Problems rarely arise. The older kids already know the rules well, and they help the little ones learn them, too. The teenage girls want to mother Rosy, and the younger kids want to play with her. If Rosy becomes upset, the older kids figure out the problem, fix it, or simply yield to her. They take the high road.

The first night in Sally's living room, I watch the kids play together for about two hours. And I don't see one argument, one tense moment, one cry of "That's mine!" (except Rosy). And the adults don't referee or constantly issue commands. Instead they relax, texting on their phones and talking about an upcoming hunt.

That evening, watching this scene unfold, I realize that this Inuit family is going to teach me way more than I expected. I arrived in Kugaaruk with one goal: to figure out how to teach Rosy to control her anger and act with kindness to her family and friends. But these Inuit parents were going to school me on so much more, including how to control my own reactive and angry parenting style.

CHAPTER 8

How to Teach Children to Control Their Anger

Ten days into our stay in the Arctic, I witness an incredible scene.

It's a typical afternoon at Maria's house. Uncle Gordon reads on the couch. Sally's son, Tusi, sits next to him, looking at his phone, while two of Sally's grandkids play Dance Dance Revolution in front of the big flat-screen TV. Everyone, from age three to forty-five, is just "doing their own thing," amiably coexisting.

Then Rosy and her new BFF, Samantha, join the scene, and I brace for all hell to break loose. Both girls wear princess dresses with tulle skirts, Rosy's in light yellow, Samantha's in bright red.

Together the pair pretty much terrifies me. Their energy is so strong. Like Rosy, Samantha is smart, talkative, and adventurous. Beneath her wild and frizzy black hair, the look on her face is pure joy. "We are giving Missy a bath," she says, smiling. Missy is the family's tiny Yorkshire terrier. She couldn't weigh more than seven pounds. And both Samantha and Rosy want to force her to jump in a bucket of soapy water. Right now, poor Missy hides underneath a side table in the living room.

"I got her," Rosy screams as she lunges for the dog.

Bam! Rosy's arm hits a mug of steaming coffee sitting at the edge of the table, knocking it across the room. The brown liquid arcs through the air and comes spattering down on Sally's white rug. Hot coffee spreads and pools across the antique table. My heart sinks. *Jesus, Rosy!* I want to scream. *We are guests in this home. Why can't you be a little more careful?*

But when I look around, I see that nobody else is reacting. Zip. Zero. Nada. Gordon and Tusi haven't looked up from their reading. The kids are still dance, dance, dancing. Nobody seems to have noticed that hot coffee just flew across the room and made a tremendous mess.

Emerging from the kitchen with a towel in her hand, Sally lays it on the rug, slowly and gingerly, as if she's laying out a yoga mat and preparing for a meditation. Rosy had essentially replicated the scene from Jean Briggs's book, in which the young man knocked a pot of boiling tea across the igloo and no one reacted.

But most surprising is Sally's response. She doesn't yell or reprimand Rosy. Instead, she turns to Tusi and calmly says, "Your coffee was in the wrong place."

Over the past several years, I've interviewed more than a hundred Inuit parents in the Arctic, from Alaska to eastern Canada. I've sat with elders in their eighties and nineties while they lunched on "country food"—stewed seal, frozen beluga whale, and raw caribou. I've talked with moms selling hand-sewn sealskin jackets at a high school craft fair. I attended a parenting class in which day care instructors were taught how their ancestors raised small children hundreds (perhaps even thousands) of years ago.

Across the board, all the moms and dads mention one golden rule of Inuit parenting: "Never yell at a child," says seventy-four-year-old Sidonie Nirlungayuk, who was born in a sod house not far from Kugaaruk. "Our parents never yelled at us, never, ever."

Even when Sidonie's mother gave birth, she didn't yell, just like Allaq in Jean Briggs's *Never in Anger.* "I got up in the middle of the night and heard what sounded like a puppy," Sidonie explained. "'Can somebody let the puppy out?' I said. But then I look over at my mother. She's kneeling down and had just given birth. The 'puppy' was a baby. My mother didn't make a sound."

When Sidonie became a mom herself, she continued this no-yell policy. "We weren't allowed to yell at our own children," she says. "Everything I said to them, I would say in a calm, calm voice."

Really? Everything was in a calm voice? Even if a child slaps you across the face? Slams the front door and locks you out of the house? Or insists on intentionally "pushing your buttons"?

"Yes," says Lisa Ipeelie with a giggle that seems to emphasize how silly she finds my question. "When children are little, it doesn't help to raise your voice, or get angry at them. It will just make your own heart rate go up."

> Getting angry at a child has no purpose.
> It only stops communication between
> the child and the mom.
> — MARTHA TIKIVIK

Lisa, a radio producer and mom, lives in the Arctic town of Iqaluit, Canada. She grew up with twelve siblings. "With little kids, you often think they're pushing your buttons, but that's not what's going on. They're upset about something, and you have to figure out what it is."

Inuit view yelling at a small child as demeaning, elders tell me. The adult is basically stooping to the level of the child—or throwing a grown-up version of a tantrum. Same goes for scolding or talking to children in an angry voice.

"Getting angry at a child has no purpose," says eighty-three-year-old Martha Tikivik. Born in an igloo on Baffin Island, she has raised six children. "Getting angry isn't going to solve your problem. It only stops communication between the child and the mom."

Elder Levi Illuitok of Kugaaruk agrees. He was born on an island near Kugaaruk and learned how to hunt seals and caribou around age seven. "I never, ever remember my dad being rude or loud to me," the seventy-nine-year-old says. But that didn't make his parents pushovers. "My mom was strict. She wouldn't allow us to stay up late, and she made us get up together in the morning. But she never yelled," he says.

When you yell at children,
they stop listening.

— SIDONIE NIRLUNGAYUK

Traditional Inuit parenting is incredibly nurturing and tender. If you took all the parenting styles around the world and ranked them by their gentleness, Inuit approach would likely rank near the top. In one family we visit, the moms and aunts feel so much love for the babies and toddlers present that they cry out from across the room, "I love her! I love her!" Inuit even have a special kiss for kids, called a *kunik*, where you put your nose against the cheek and sniff the skin.

Even mild punishments, such as time-outs, are seen as inappropriate, says Goota Jaw, who teaches an Inuit parenting class at the Nunavut Arctic College in Iqaluit. These types of punishments prove unproductive and only isolate the child. "Shouting, 'Think about what you just did. Go to your room!' I disagree with that. That's not how we teach our children. Instead, you are just teaching children to run away."

And that's not all you're teaching them. "When you yell at children, they stop listening," observes Sidonie. In fact, she thinks that American kids don't listen because their parents are always shouting. "You can tell when a parent yells at a child because the child doesn't listen anymore."

Over and over again, Inuit parents repeat this same idea, that yelling and shouting makes parenting harder because kids stop listening to you. They block you out. As seventy-one-year-old Theresa Sikkuark puts it, "I think that's why white children don't listen. Parents have yelled at the children too much."

Turns out, many Western scientists agree with these Inuit elders. When I return to San Francisco, I call Laura Markham, a clinical psychologist who authored the book *Peaceful Parent, Happy Kids*. I ask her if yelling at kids has a negative impact, and she responds in an uncanny echo of Sidonie.

"When we yell at children, we are training them not to listen," she tells me. "A lot of times, parents will say, 'But he won't listen until I raise my voice,' and I say, 'Okay. Raise your voice to get him to listen and then you'll always have to raise your voice.'"

She maintains that Western parents simply shoot themselves in the foot when they yell. Because, in the end, yelling doesn't teach children to behave. Instead, it teaches them to get angry. "We are training them to yell when they get upset and that yelling solves problems," she says.

Think back to the formula—to train a child to behave in a certain way, we need two main ingredients, and a dash of a third: practice, modeling, and, if necessary, acknowledging. When we yell and get angry at children, we *model* being angry. Since children often yell back at us, we give them oodles of *practice* at yelling and getting angry at us. And then if we yell back, again, after they yell at us, we *acknowledge* and accept their anger.

By contrast, parents who control their own anger—both around and toward their children—help their kids learn to do the same. "Kids learn emotional regulation from us," Laura says. Every time you stop yourself from acting in anger, your child sees a calm way to deal with frustrations. They learn to stay composed when anger arises. So to help a child learn emotional regulation, the number one thing parents can do is learn to regulate their own emotions.

Some of this might already sound familiar to you. Maybe you've read one of the many books out there devoted to "positive parenting." There are a slew of them, and many are bestsellers. Because clearly, given our druthers, all of us parents would rather scream less, scold less, and just feel less angry. But how do you remain a positive parent at, say, 5:30 p.m. on a weekday when you've worked all day, still have a deadline in three hours, and your kid sprawls out on the floor at the grocery store, screaming, because you will buy only one box of popsicles instead of two?

On such matters, many of the available books fall short. I feel like they're missing two key pieces: how to reduce your own anger toward your children, and how to discipline or change your child's bad behavior without anger. After all, once you stop being angry, you still need to teach your child to be grateful for one freakin' box of popsicles, or even better, to share the popsicles with the whole family.

Over the next few chapters, I'll give you the tools to handle everything from the hot-button moments when children have tantrums to your run-of-the-mill, everyday misbehavior. In the end, we'll learn tools for changing behavior over the long term while also transmitting values such as respect and gratitude. Let's begin with how you can stop being so angry yourself.

CHAPTER 9

How to Stop Being Angry at Your Child

Personally, my go-to parenting approach, on a daily basis, centers around yelling—or more specifically, nagging and *then* yelling. Sometimes the episode caps off with me screaming some ridiculously ironic statement, such as "ROSY, STOP SCREAMING! JUST *STOP*!"

So when I arrive in the Arctic, anger-free parenting seems a bit like a mirage—or come to think of it, like the Paleo diet. I know I shouldn't eat so many carbohydrates and sugars, but when nobody's looking, I down a whole bowl of pasta. Doesn't everyone? Doesn't everyone yell at their kids when nobody's looking?

Nope. Not Sally, nor her mom, Maria, her sister Nellie, nor any of the host of parents in the family. They all make the anger-free parenting method look easy. One night, for example, Sally watches three of her grandkids, aged from eighteen months up to six years, while I watch Rosy. The house is complete mayhem. Entropy is taking over. One toddler, a little boy named Caleb, is especially a handful. At one point, he even draws blood on Sally's face. But she never loses her cool. Not once.

Watching her in action, I'm so impressed—not only because she stays so calm, but also because she never lets the children walk all over her. She uses other techniques to discipline and change behavior that don't involve yelling—and oftentimes don't involve words at all.

Watching the parent-child interactions around Kugaaruk, for the first time in my life, I see a way to parent that doesn't involve anger—or yelling. It's transformative. First, I notice how relaxed and calm the adults are. I also see the profound impact this calmness has on the kids in the house, including Rosy. The result is pretty much immediate. Under Sally's and Maria's calm wings, Rosy's fiery belly cools. Her angst eases. One night, she becomes upset because she wants milk, which we don't have. She starts to have a tantrum, but when she realizes this behavior is not having an effect on any adults in the room, she literally falls to the ground like the Wicked Witch of the West and cries, "Nooooooo!"

Observing this shift in Rosy raises a mirror up to my own anger. It makes me realize how when I raise my voice and scold her, I actually trigger her tantrums and meltdowns. We get caught in a feedback loop that's as terrible as it is predictable. I start screaming; Rosy yells back. I yell more and make some flimsy threats. Then she lies on the ground, kicking and screaming. I go to pick her up and try to calm her down. But it's too late. She's angry. And to show it, she might lash out with a slap or pull my hair—which escalates my anger even more.

WHAT OUR ANGER TEACHES

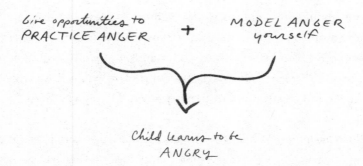

But somehow Sally and Maria never fall into this toddler-parent emotional trap—this anger do-si-do. They never engage in power struggles with children. And over the time I spend with them, I work hard to reverse engineer how they do it.

From what I can tell, it's a two-step process:

1. **Stop talking.** Just stay quiet. Don't say anything.

2. **Learn to have less—or even no anger toward children.** (Note: I'm not talking about *controlling* your anger when it arises, but rather *generating less anger* in the first place.)

On the surface, these steps may look suspiciously like the positive-parenting trap. But hear me out. And clearly, this isn't an easy process. The second step is especially difficult. But lord knows, if I can change (or at least make a big improvement), anyone can. Remember, I grew up in a viciously angry home. When I first got to college, I remember being stunned by the silence in my dorm room at night. Where was all the yelling and screaming? Why was everyone so quiet?

But I didn't want Rosy to grow up in an angry home. I wanted her to learn other ways of coping with frustration and annoyances. And to be honest, as I eased into my forties, I thought it was a good time for me to learn a more nuanced way of communicating, not just with Rosy, but also with my husband, colleagues, and, well, everyone. First, no more yelling.

Step 1: Stop talking

It took me about three months to stop yelling at Rosy, and then another three more months to stop talking entirely when I felt angry. I still slip up from time to time and start issuing commands, demands, and scoldings. But in general, I've learned the art of staying silent when Rosy triggers a rush of anger and frustration through my blood. Here's what I do:

- **Close my mouth.** When Rosy angers me, I always seem to erupt with a volcano of verbiage: "Rosemary, please stop that." "Why are you crying

now?" "What is wrong?" "Do you need?" "Do you want?" All of these questions and statements are doing the opposite of what I want them to do. They convey a sense of urgency and stress. And they worsen Rosy's tantrums. Even when I try to remain calm, the words always give away my emotion.

But Sally and Maria always seem to do the opposite. Whenever I see them in an exasperating situation with a child, they pause, say nothing, and observe. They almost look like a stone-faced therapist listening to their fifth overly emotional client of the day. If Sally and Maria say anything at all, the words are quiet and calm. And I mean *very* quiet. So quiet that, if I'm not next to them, I can't hear what they say. As we'll explore in the next section, remaining quiet and calm helps the child do the same. While, conversely, a volcano of verbiage—even if it sounds friendly—simply raises the energy level—and anger level—of the child.

So following Sally and Maria's lead, I've flipped my strategy. Now when I feel anger toward Rosy, I simply close my mouth. I press my two lips together and hold. I think, *Hold still like a rock, Michaeleen. Be a rock. Be a rock.* And then I just watch Rosy for a beat. So I can assess the situation.

- **Walk away.** For a few minutes, even a few seconds, I just walk away. You can leave the room. Get out of the car. Walk down the sidewalk. Walk across the park. Or simply turn your back on the child. Maria told me this strategy, straight up, on the first day we met, while chatting at her kitchen table. "When I feel anger coming, I leave the children or grandchildren alone," she said. "I just leave them alone."*

The desire to yell and talk will dissipate with the additional space, so you can return to help the child. As we'll learn in the next chapter, this

---

* Look at the first part of Maria's sentence: *When I feel anger coming*. Maria doesn't wait until anger has already struck to leave the room. Instead, she removes herself from the situation when she first detects signs of incoming anger. I think one of my problems was that I used to ignore the early signals of anger. By the time I acted, the emotion was so intense, I couldn't control it. But recently, I have been paying more attention to the tiny inklings of frustration or annoyance that precede anger. Dealing with those milder emotions (e.g., by leaving the room) is much easier than wrangling in anger itself.

distancing can also help communicate to the child in a calm way that their behavior, at that moment, is unacceptable. Ignoring children makes a powerful tool for disciplining.

Simply doing these two things—staying quiet and walking away—has a great immediate impact on my relationship with Rosy. Right away the channel of communication begins to open up between us.

But Rosy can still feel that I'm angry. She's like a canary in an emotional coal mine, she can sense my emotion before it comes out of my mouth. And when I finally do speak to her again (eventually, I have to say something), I often resort to a threat with clenched teeth or wide eyes: "If you don't listen to me, I'm going to . . . take away all your dresses!" (Yes, I've actually made that ridiculous threat before. And even more ridiculous ones.)

So I set about on what seems like an impossible goal: to stop being angry at Rosy—or at least be a lot less angry at her.

Now, full disclosure: If I hadn't seen how profoundly Sally and Maria's parenting calmed my daughter, I might not have been so motivated to work on this. Truth is, before staying with Sally and Maria, I genuinely believed that in order for Rosy to learn—to learn respect and gratitude—I had to be firm and strong. And I had to reprimand and scold. My parents had raised me this way, and I thought that's what all good parents do. I didn't think that a tender, gentle approach could really work. But Maria and Sally convinced me it not only works, it is actually more effective, especially with a child like Rosy.

And so with a hefty dose of skepticism, I try to do the impossible: stop feeling so angry at my daughter.

Step 2: Learn to have less—or even no anger

Now, before we dive in, I need to be clear: I'm not talking about *suppressing* anger. And I am not talking about letting anger pass or soften with time. Indeed, if you walk away and wait long enough, your anger will eventually go away; I guarantee you. Problem is, with a small child, in a small condo, I often do not have the privilege of time and separation. When Rosy gets upset, she follows me around the house, pins me in a corner, or even grabs on to my leg like a giant oyster mushroom latched to a tree.

What Inuit moms and dads show me is how to have less anger in the first place, not just toward Rosy but toward all little humans. How to get punched in the stomach at seven o'clock in the morning by a three-year-old and not feel a smidge of ire.

How do you do that? After talking to moms, dads, grandmas, and grandpas, I start to see the key: these parents take a different view of young children's actions than we do in Western culture. Inuit parents interpret children's motivations differently. For example, in Western culture, we tend to think children are "pushing buttons" or "testing boundaries," or even being manipulative. When Rosy was just a baby, my older sister said to me on the phone, "It's amazing how young kids learn to manipulate us so early. You'll see."

But what if this idea is completely wrong? Do we really know if toddlers and young children "manipulate" us the way that adults manipulate? That children push our buttons the way that adults push buttons? There's no scientific evidence that suggests either of these statements is true. There are no brain scans in which the "manipulating" circuitry lights up when toddlers misbehave. There are no psychological studies in which two-year-olds "come clean" and admit, yes, all they want to do is enrage Mom and Dad.

Truth is, these ideas about children are cultural constructions. In a way, they are folktales that we Western parents tell ourselves to help us navigate behavior we don't understand. And in other cultures, including among Inuit, parents tell themselves other tales—tales that make it easier to keep a cool head around little children and to have less anger toward them. Tales that strengthen the parent-child relationship instead of straining it. Tales that make parenting easier.

So, what if we throw out the window the Western way of thinking and come up with better narratives for understanding the ways of young children? Instead of characterizing young children as manipulative button-pushers trying to make us angry, what if we think of them as illogical, newbie citizens trying to figure out the proper behavior? What if we assume their motivations are kind and good, and it's just that their execution needs some improvement?

In other words, if I want to feel less anger toward Rosy, I need to shift the way I interpret her actions and misbehavior.

Over and over again, Inuit elders offer three rules to help parents keep a cool head when children lose theirs:

- **Expect children to misbehave.** Expect them to be rude, violent, and bossy. Expect them to make a mess, do tasks improperly, and sometimes be an overall pain in the butt. Don't take it personally (or think you're a bad parent). It's just how children are made. And it's your job, as the parent, to teach them how to behave acceptably and control their emotions.

If the child doesn't listen, it's because she is too young to understand. She is not ready for the lesson.

—DOLOROSA NARTOK

If the child can't meet expectations in the moment, try to change the environment, not the kid.

One afternoon, I sit in a booth at Kugaaruk's only restaurant, having afternoon coffee with Dolorosa Nartok. She explains how her family, when she was little, kept their igloo warm with a seal lamp, while Rosy does her best to thwart the interview. She keeps grabbing the microphone and swinging it around like a jump rope.

Dolorosa can see me getting frustrated. I plead with Rosy to stop: "Rosy, please stop grabbing the microphone. How many times do I have to ask? Why won't you listen?"

Dolorosa looks at me with a slight expression of pity and says simply, "If a little child doesn't listen, it's because she is too young to understand. She is not ready for the lesson."

It's an insight I'll never forget. Dolorosa goes on to explain how Inuit par-

ents view young kids' misbehavior. "Little children don't
have understanding yet," she
says. "They don't understand
what's right and wrong, what
respect is, how to listen. Parents must teach them."

This perspective is anal-
ogous to the way Western
parents think about reading
or math. For example, Rosy,
at age three, is too young to
know that 2+2 = 4. If she

says 5 or 6, I'd never get angry at her because I don't expect her to understand math. I expect that I'll have to teach her, at some point. And if she's
too young to grasp a concept, I wouldn't lose my temper and get frustrated,
but wait and try again later. Inuit parents take a similar approach to teaching emotional skills to young children.

Here in the U.S., we overestimate children's emotional abilities. We
expect children at a very young age—even eighteen months to two years
old—to have well-developed executive function and to understand sophisticated emotional concepts such as respect, generosity, and self-control.
And when they don't demonstrate these qualities, we become frustrated
and lose patience with them.

Many Inuit parents view children from an opposing perspective. They
expect children to have poor executive function and poor emotional control,
and they see it as their job to teach children these skills. Basically, when a
child doesn't listen or behave, the reason is simple: The child hasn't learned
that particular skill yet. And perhaps, they aren't quite ready to learn it. So
there's no reason for a parent to get upset or angry.

Several anthropologists have documented this same parenting philosophy in communities across the Arctic Circle. So the idea is likely ancient,
dating back at least a thousand years, before Inuit migrated into what is
today northern Canada. In *Never in Anger*, Jean Briggs writes:

The Utku [Inuit] expect little children to be easily angered (urulu, qiquq, ningaq) . . . and to cry easily when disturbed (huqu), because they have no ihuma: no mind, thought, reason, or understanding. Adults say they are not concerned (huqu, naklik) by a child's irrational fears and rages, because they know there is nothing really wrong. . . . Because children are unreasoning beings, unable to understand that their distresses are illusory, people are at pains to reassure them. . . .

In the Utku view, growing up is very largely a process of acquiring ihuma since it is primarily the use of ihuma that distinguishes mature, adult behavior from that of a child, an idiot, a very sick or an insane person.

About 1,500 miles east of the Utku, the anthropologist Richard Condon made a similar observation while staying with Inuit on the tiny island of Ulukhaktok in the Northwest Territories, Canada. He writes:

Kids are considered to be extremely bossy. Since they have not yet incorporated the culturally valued norms of patience, generosity, and self-restraint, kids often make excessive demands of others and become greatly upset if these are not forthcoming. Children are also viewed as being overly aggressive, stingy, and exhibitionist, all behaviors viewed as antithetical to ideal behavioral norms.

And so there's no reason to get angry when a small child is rude, screams in your face, or strikes out. It's not a reflection of a parent's skills, but a mere reflection of the way that children are made.

•   **Stop arguing with small children.** Sidonie Nirlungayuk, age seventy-four, puts it quite eloquently: "Even when a child mistreats you, you don't fight back with a young child," she says. "Just leave the point alone. Whatever is wrong . . . eventually the behavior will get better."

Several elders give me similar advice during interviews. But it's Elizabeth Tegumiar who helps me understand just how seriously parents take this idea. Rosy and I meet Elizabeth on our first night in Kugaaruk, at the hotel restaurant where she works as a cook. After we eat dinner, she comes out of the kitchen wearing a yellow apron tied around her waist and holding a big plate of extra french fries for Rosy. Elizabeth has a petite frame and a smooth, wrinkle-free face, which makes it hard to tell her age, but I think she's in her mid-forties. She has short, reddish-brown hair, gray eyes, and she typically wears black sweatpants and a gray hoodie.

Right away, Elizabeth is interested in my work, and we strike up a conversation about parenting. When I tell her about common practices in the U.S., she purses her lips and widens her eyes in disbelief.

Elizabeth was born and raised "out on the land," as she says. She has a deep understanding of Inuit culture, history, and parenting. And she graciously shares her knowledge. So I ask her if she would like to work with me on the project. I hire her to set up interviews with elders and interpret them from Inuktitut into English. Her advice has been incredibly valuable, not just for my reporting, but also personally. She has helped me to have less anger toward Rosy and taught me to view Rosy's motivations and actions with more kindness and love.

Inuit see arguing with children as silly and a waste of time, Elizabeth tells me, because children are pretty much illogical beings. When an adult argues with a child, the adult stoops to the child's level.

"I remember one time I was arguing with my uncle. I was talking back to him and he got angry," she recalls. The argument was such a rare event that it had stuck in her memory for forty years. "My dad and my aunts just laughed at him because he was arguing with a child."

During my three visits to the Arctic, I never once witness a parent argue with a child. I never see a power struggle. I never hear nagging or negotiating. Never. The same is true in the Yucatán and Tanzania. Parents simply don't argue with children. Instead, they make a request and wait, silently, for the child to comply. And if the child refuses, the parents may make a comment, walk away, or turn their attention elsewhere.*

And you can, too. Next time you find yourself nagging, negotiating, or

---

* Remember Teresa getting her four kids ready for school? When Ernesto didn't get his shoes, she never turned the request into an argument. She waited for about five minutes and asked again, calmly.

getting into a back-and-forth with your child, just stop. Close your mouth. Close your eyes if you need to. Wait for a beat. Touch the child's shoulders lightly and walk away. Or employ one of the tools discussed in the next chapter. But do not argue. Ever. *It will never end well.*[*]

Okay, now we have two rules for reducing our anger toward children: expect misbehavior and never argue. What about the third? Well, that turns out to be a core element of the universal parenting approach.

---

[*] Come to think about it, every time you negotiate with a child, you simply train them to negotiate with you. Remember the first ingredient for passing along a value or trait: practice.

Encourage, Never Force

Forcing a child will never help. Tell them about their mistakes, honestly. Eventually they will learn.

—Theresa Sikkuark, age seventy-one, from Kugaaruk

While interviewing parents for this book, I hear one piece of advice the most. I hear it from moms, dads, grandmas, and grandpas, but I also hear it over and over again from psychologists and anthropologists who study hunter-gatherer communities all over the globe.

This advice, in theory, sounds so simple and so easy. But man-o-man, it's so hard for me to actually implement. It goes against every parenting bone in my body.

The big idea? Never force a child to do something.

Instead of forcing, you *encourage.* And the *E* in TEAM parenting stands for "encouragement."

In many hunter-gatherer cultures, parents rarely scold or punish a child. They rarely insist that a child comply with a request or behave in a certain way. They believe that trying to control a child prevents their development and simply stresses the parent-child relationship.

This idea is so prevalent among hunter-gatherer cultures worldwide that there's little doubt it's an ancient way of treating children. If we could go back in time and interview parents fifty thousand years ago, we would (very) likely hear the same advice.

Forcing children causes three problems: First, it undermines their intrinsic motivation—that is, it erodes a children's natural drive to voluntarily do a task (see chapter 6). Second, it can damage your relationship with your child. When you force a child to do something, you run the risk of starting fights and creating anger on both sides. You can build walls. Third, you remove the opportunity for the child to learn and make decisions on their own.

ENCOURAGE

Use tools other than threats, bribes, and punishments to motivate.

Treat children like small adults; talk to them calmly and with respect.

Forcing a child to do something turns you into a child's enemy.

Sally's mom, Maria, eloquently sums up this idea over tea one afternoon in her kitchen. "Parenting is a two-way street," she says. Adults don't like being forced to do something or act a certain way; children feel the same way. "When you force children to do things, they grow up angry and mad. Children won't have respect for parents and elders," Maria says.

But if you treat your child like a small adult and talk to them calmly and respectfully, they will do the same with you—eventually.

"You talk to little kids and toddlers this way, too?" I ask.

"Yes, even with the little ones," she answers.

Maya parents have a similar philosophy, says psychologist Lucia Alcalá. "Parents told me, 'You can't force children to do something. You can guide them and help them see why something is important for them to do and to learn. But you can't impose learning,'" Lucia says. Forcing children doesn't just create conflict; it also breaks up the overall cohesion of the family. "You don't want to have your own children as your enemy," she adds.

Aha, I think as Lucia talks. *So this explains why Rosy and I have become enemies. I force Rosy to do things all the time.* I force her to take her plate into the kitchen; I force her to stop yelling at bedtime; I force her to eat green beans. To brush her teeth. To hold my hand when we cross the street. To stop hitting the dog. I even force the words that come out of her mouth ("Say thank you!").

And over time, this need to control her has built up resentment and conflict between us.

Of course, not forcing children doesn't mean you throw your hands up and give up on sculpting their behavior. Not at all! (I still need Rosy to do many things, like brush her teeth, help clean up after dinner, and respect me and her father.) But what it means is you don't use control and punishment to get the job done. You are more skilled and nuanced than that.

Around the world, parents wield a whole slew of tools to encourage a child to listen, learn, and behave properly. The tools also show children how to be good family members that respect each other. We've already heard about several of these tools (group motivation, opportunities to practice, and acknowledging contributions), and we'll hear about many more in the following chapters, including dramas, storytelling, questions, consequences, and physical touch.

Just note: encouragement and training sometimes take time. These aren't quick fixes, but they are steps toward deep changes that will persist as the child grows. Along the way, you'll give your child a gift that helps them throughout their lifetime—strong executive function.

Try It 4: Learn to Have Less Anger Toward Children

The next time a child does something that totally enrages you or even simply triggers a rising sense of irritation in your body, do the following:

1. Close your mouth. Just say nothing. If you need to, close your eyes.
2. Walk away for a few seconds or a few minutes until the anger passes.

3. Think about the misbehavior from a different perspective or put it in a different context. Think: "She is not pushing my buttons. She is not manipulating me. She is an illogical, irrational being. And she doesn't yet know the proper way to behave. It's my job to teach her rationality and logic." (If those thoughts don't resonate, you can also try a different track and think about the child's strong drive to help. Think to yourself: "She wants to help. She wants to contribute and work together. But she doesn't know how. I have to show her the best way.")

4. Then with the calmest voice you can muster, simply say to the child the mistake she is making or the consequences of her actions. For example, if she hits the dog, try: "Ouch, that hurts the dog." Or if she hits you, try: "Ouch, that hurts me. Ouch. You don't want to hurt me."

5. Then leave it all alone. Just let it go. Let the misbehavior pass.

6. And if needed, use one of the parenting tools described in the next chapter to encourage the proper behavior.

Summary for Chapters 8 and 9:
How to Teach a Child to Control Their Anger

Ideas to Remember

Anger

> ➤ Anger toward a child is unproductive. It generates conflict, builds tension, and stops communication.
> ➤ When a parent frequently yells and screams at a child, the child will eventually stop listening to the parent.
> ➤ Parents and children can easily fall into a cycle of anger, in which the parent's anger generates anger in the child, which in turn triggers more anger in the parent.
> ➤ You can stop this cycle by responding to the child with kindness and calmness.

Anger control

> ➤ We often overestimate children's emotional intelligence.
> ➤ Anger control is a skill children learn over time with practice and modeling.
> ➤ To help a child learn anger control, the best thing you can do is control your own anger in front of the child.
> ➤ Every time we yell at a child, we teach them to yell and act in anger when they're upset or have a problem. The child practices being angry and yelling.
> ➤ Every time we respond to an upset child with calmness and quiet, we give the child the opportunity to find that response in themselves. We give the child an opportunity to practice settling themselves down.
> ➤ Over time, this practice teaches the child to regulate their emotions and respond to problems in a calm, productive way.

Tips and Tools

➤ When you feel anger toward a child, stay quiet and wait for the anger to pass. If you speak, a child will feel your anger. So, best to stay silent.

➤ If you can't control your anger, walk away or distance yourself from the child. Return when you are calm.

➤ Teach yourself to have less (or even no) anger toward children.

- **Change how you view children's behavior.** Expect young children to misbehave and cause problems. They aren't pushing your buttons or trying to manipulate you. They're simply irrational beings who haven't learned proper behavior yet. You have to teach them. (Their misbehavior doesn't mean you're a bad parent.)

- **Never argue (or even negotiate) with a child.** Arguing gives the child practice at arguing while you model the behavior yourself. If you start arguing with a child, stop talking and walk away.

- **Stop forcing children to do things.** Forcing causes conflict, erodes communication, and builds anger (on both sides). Use the tools in the next chapter to encourage proper behavior instead of forcing it.

CHAPTER 10

Introduction to Parenting Tools

Parenting books often tell me not to yell and scold, but they don't give me many tools to use in place of anger. They tell me to validate the child's feelings (e.g., "You feel really upset right now." Or "Oh, you feel so mad. It really upset you when your brother took your toy"). But they don't tell me how to *change* the child's behavior. How to help the child move beyond the emotion and address the problem that is causing their tantrum or argument in the first place. If we constantly validate a child's emotions, how does the child learn a more productive way to handle frustration or problems?

It's like we are all carpenters, working tirelessly to build a strong, beautiful house. Then some "expert" comes along, swipes away the only tool we have—a

loud, angry hammer—and then leaves without handing us any replacement tools. No drills, no saws, no level, no screws. What do we do next?

During my stays in Kugaaruk and in the Yucatán, I witnessed moms and dads use a dazzling array of parenting tools. And these tools don't just modulate kids' behavior or keep them safe—they're far more sophisticated than that. They also teach children how to think before acting and how to cope with disappointment and change. In other words, these tools allow children to develop fantastic skills of executive function.

One word about these tools before we get started. At first, I made the mistake of taking these tools too literally. When you move an idea from one culture to another, the idea can change meaning. What I describe in these chapters will work best if you tailor them for your own child, family, and daily life. For example, one tool uses questions to help your child think through their behavior. The specific questions that Inuit parents used in the central Arctic in the 1960s, or fifty years later, might not be the best for an American preteen in New York City in the 2020s. Be creative. Use your imagination. Watch how your child responds, listen to the words your child uses, then adapt the tools for them.

For example, to help children and toddlers learn to share with a new baby sibling, some Maya parents will tap into the child's desire to be a "big sister" or "big brother" and to take care of younger children. "It's your younger sibling, the poor thing. Give him a little," the parent will say, implying that the child needs to help the baby sibling.

But when I tried this with Rosy, I saw little progress. She'd look at me like I was speaking another language. *Well, that doesn't work*, I thought. But then one day I watched her play "Mama" with her teddy bear, Einstein. "Einstein, shhh shhh. You don't need to cry, Einstein, because Mama is here," she said, rocking the bear like a baby.

In that instant, I realized that Rosy was telling me how to help her learn to share. She doesn't want to be the big sister (she doesn't really have a good role model for this). She wants to be the mama! So the next time a little toddler at the playground waddled over in his diaper, wanting a piece of Rosy's cookie, I said, "The poor thing, he needs his *mama* to share some of the food. Are you the mama, Rosy?" Instantaneously, I saw the lights go on in her mind. Her eyes got wide, her mouth curved up in a tiny grin, and a few seconds later, she was sharing her food.

I'll introduce these tools in three sets. The first set will help you with tantrums and moments when the child has lost control of their emotions. The second set is a great resource for everyday misbehaviors like whining, complaining, and demanding. And the third set changes behavior over the long term, as well as transmits key values. That third set we'll cover in chapters 9 and 10.

I: Tools for Tantrums

A few days into our trip to Kugaaruk, I finally start to understand how to help Rosy during tantrums—and how to get those tantrums to decrease in intensity and frequency. I have one person to thank for this wisdom: interpreter Elizabeth Tegumiar.

One afternoon, Elizabeth, Rosy, and I go to the grocery store to buy potato chips, deli turkey, and crackers for lunch. While we wait in line to check out, Rosy sees a rack of pastel headbands—in pink, blue, and yellow—with little unicorns on them. She desperately wants them. "But, Mama, can I have just one?"

"Sorry, Rosy, we do not need another headband," I respond.

A tantrum begins to brew. "But I want one! I want one!" she screams.

I launch into my usual routine: a combination of sternness, rational logic, and demands for her to stop whining. I meet Rosy's screaming with a high-energy list of requests. The tension between us starts to flicker like lightning. Bolts of anger creep into my voice and flash from my eyes. Rosy senses the anger and starts to send out her own lightning bolts, flailing her arms, and crying loudly. She is losing control of her emotions.

Thank goodness Elizabeth is there. She walks over to Rosy and does the exact opposite of what I'm doing: she brings the energy down. Way down. Instead of getting firm and stern, she becomes sweet, tender, and calm. So calm! Her facial expression is soft; her body is relaxed. Her movements are small and gentle. At first she's quiet. She waits a few seconds. Then she begins to speak to Rosy in the most quiet, loving voice I've ever heard her use. Her words are slow and deliberate. And she doesn't say much. She simply meets Rosy's storminess with tenderness, as if she is offering a soft blanket to a lightning bolt. Rosy is spellbound. The screaming stops—right away. Then she turns to Elizabeth and says in her own sweet voice, "*Iqutaq*" (the word for "bumblebee" in Inuktitut).

Tool #1: Parent with calmness

If you master only one concept from this book, I hope you'll try for this one. It's hard but, I promise, it's worth it.

In many cultures around the world, parents believe that one of their key responsibilities is to help children learn how to calm themselves down—to teach them to respond to everyday frustrations of life with aplomb and composure. And they take this responsibility as seriously as they do teaching a child other skills, such as how to read, do math, or eat healthy foods.

"I tell the new generation, 'Don't let the kids cry too much. Try to calm the kids down,'" Maria Kukkuvak tells me, sitting at her kitchen table. "Parents and grandparents need to calm kids down."

And the best way to do that—whether the issue is crying, screaming, or an endless stream of demands—is for the adult to interact with the child from a place of the utmost calm. Seriously, we are talking about a degree of calmness that we rarely see in Western culture. Think lying-facedown-on-a-massage-table calmness. Or the way you feel after taking a long, hot bath. Think Mister Rogers, stoned.

In Kugaaruk, the higher the energy a child brings to the situation, the lower in energy the parent goes. If the child starts screaming, thrashing, crying, or even hitting, the parent doesn't rush over issuing commands, nor do they tell the child to calm down. They don't make threats ("If you don't stop screaming . . .") or sweet offerings ("What's wrong? Do you want a drink? Do you want to go to . . .").

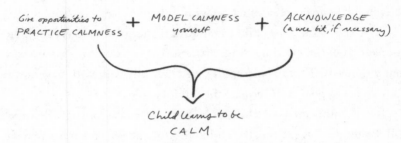

HOW
CALMNESS
TEACHES

Give opportunities to PRACTICE CALMNESS + MODEL CALMNESS yourself + ACKNOWLEDGE (a wee bit, if necessary)

Child learns to be CALM

Instead, the parents *show* the child how to be calm by being calm themselves.

Whenever children are upset—crying and screaming—the parents say very few words (words are stimulating). They make very few movements (movement is stimulating). And they show very little expression on their faces (again, emotion is stimulating). Parents aren't timid or fearful. They still have a confidence about them. But they approach the child the way you might approach a butterfly on your shoulder: Gently. Slowly. Softly.

Anthropologist Jean Briggs documented this style of parenting several times during her stay with Allaq and Inuttiaq's family in the 1960s. "There was consistency also in the calmly rational quality of the adults' responses to childish misbehavior. . . . When Saarak [a three-year-old girl] hit at her [mom's] face with a spoon, she turned her head away, saying calmly, 'She has no reason (*ihuma*).'"

Later on, the three-year-old had to deal with the arrival of a baby sibling. And when her mother no longer let the toddler breastfeed, all hell broke loose. She launched a "storm of wails and slaps." Her mother didn't admonish her, but instead responded in a "tender voice," almost unbelievable to Jean. "I had never imagined that the crisis [of being dethroned by a sibling], when it came, could be handled as gently as it was."

Why is this strategy so darn effective? It's pretty simple: children's emotions—and energy level—mirror those of their parents, says child psychotherapist Tina Payne Bryson, who has coauthored two *New York Times*–bestselling parenting books.

"Emotions are contagious," Tina says. The human brain contains neurons and circuitry with the sole purpose of mirroring other people's emotions. "We have a sort of social resonance circuitry in our brains that gets activated when you're interacting with someone else."

So if you want your child to have high energy, then have high energy yourself. Ask the child a string of questions. Give her instructions. Issue many requests. Talk to her rapidly, emphatically, and with urgency. Raise your voice. Repeat your request. Be intense.

But if you want your child to be calm, be calm yourself. Be quiet. Be still. Be tender. Over time, the child will come to see you as a safe haven in their emotional storms.

There's no question about it: parenting with calmness works. And here's the amazing part: the sheer act of the parent being calm has a massive influence on an upset child, not just in the moment, but over the long run. Over time, the child learns to calm herself down without the parent's aid, Tina says.

"What's really cool is if you get a lot of practice going from a kind of falling-apart, stressed state back into a controlled state with the help of your parent, your brain learns how to do that on its own," she says. "So it's very much about skill building."

Think back to that darn formula: practice + model + acknowledge = skill learned.

By contrast, when we come to a child in a state of high energy—talking loudly, issuing commands and questions—we will likely make the tantrum worse. And we can easily get stuck in the anger cycle—your anger makes the child's anger worse, which in turn fuels your anger more. At the same time, the child misses out on the opportunity to build executive function.

The calmness tool is our exit route out of this vicious cycle. It gives us a way to escape power struggles. When we react to a child's emotional outbursts with quiet, low energy, the child has an opportunity to find this response in themselves and to practice being calm.

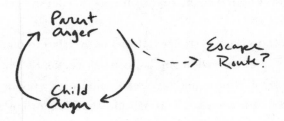

CYCLE OF ANGER

Parent anger

Escape Route?

Child Anger

As Tina puts it: "We need to *model* calmness. We have to be regulating our own internal states first before we expect our children to learn to regulate theirs."

Raising Rosy

So, Mama Doucleff, how on earth do you find your inner calmness when your child acts like a raging maniac? How do you become the calmest person you've ever been when your three-year-old slaps you across your face? It certainly hasn't been easy. And it has taken months of practice. But the more I miraculously hold myself together and stay calm when Rosy isn't, the easier and easier it becomes. And the more Rosy and I enjoy being together.

Personally, I use sensory imagery to hold on to my calm. I imagine that I'm in one of those fancy hotel spas getting a massage. I close my eyes and I can see the space. I'm in a dimly lit room with the walls painted mauve. Nepalese chimes play a tranquil song, and the scent of lavender wafts through the air. Aaaah.

If imagery doesn't work, I begin to hum "Edelweiss" and channel my inner Julie Andrews. Find what works for you, where you are your calmest, most imperturbable self. Where you can get milk spit in your face and simply chuckle a bit in response. Pull out that alter ego whenever your child gets worked up. My husband has his own trick: "I just pretend like I'm a little stoned."

Tina told me that she imagines that her child is a bit like a stereo. "Think about your kid's nervous system almost like a volume dial. My job is to help my kid's dial go down. And to do that, it first starts with me. If I yell at him or I join the chaos, I'm turning his volume dial up. So my job is to think about my own dial and make sure my dial doesn't get turned way too high or too low."

After I learn to use this strategy, Rosy's outbursts and tantrums begin to melt away. The emotional storms happen less frequently and, when they do arise, they resolve more quickly. Eventually, after a few months, they almost disappear completely. We're talking about an astonishing decline from several tantrums a day to one or two a month.

The difference is so striking that even my mother has admitted that yes, maybe this approach works better.

Tool #2: Parent with Touch or Toss (Physicality)

During our second night at Maria's house, one of her great-grandchildren puts her parenting to a major test. Eighteen-month-old Caleb is a spitfire. He's smart, curious, strong, and fearless. He marches into the living room and immediately begins to climb on chairs and tables. He pulls the Xbox

off the table. And then he goes over to the family's tiny Yorkshire terrier, Missy, and grabs her tail.

Sally picks Caleb up, and the little boy grabs on to Sally's cheeks so hard that he draws blood. Small red droplets appear on Sally's cheeks. I see she's in pain. Her teeth clench. Her eyes squint. I think for sure she's going to scream. But she remains calm and slowly peels his chubby, short fingers off her skin. She says with incredible kindness, "You don't realize this hurts, do you?"

Then she uses the physicality tool.

She slowly flips Caleb onto his stomach and gently pats his butt a few times, like you'd pat a rump roast before cooking it. "Ow, that hurts me," she says with the same sweet, calm voice. "We don't hurt people." Then she flies him in a circle, like an airplane. Caleb giggles. His urge to scratch has vanished. His anger evaporates. And Sally, through physicality, has calmed him—while also showing him who's strong and loving (aka, who's boss).

A few days later, a similar incident happens with me and Rosy. I'm trying to interview an elder while Elizabeth interprets. Rosy wants us to go back to Maria's house. But we need to finish the interview first. Rosy and I begin to argue. She hits me, and Elizabeth knows a tantrum is imminent. Elizabeth turns to me and says, with an unusual amount of urgency: "Pack her, Michaeleen! Just pack her." That is, put her on my back in the baby carrier—or the "pack." *Really?* I think. *That's going to stop the tantrum? She's 3.5 years old, she's not a baby.*

"Isn't Rosy too old for the baby carrier?" I say.

"Some moms pack their children until four or five if the child needs it—and if there isn't another baby," Elizabeth says, adding that I shouldn't feel ashamed of using it. If carrying the child helps them to calm down, then it's okay. "Every child is different. Some take longer to learn to calm down."

And so I strap on the baby carrier and invite Rosy over. Sure enough, the little demon hops in the "pack" without hesitation. Immediately, she stops screaming and crying. After a few minutes, I look over my shoulder: fast asleep, Rosy looks like an angel.

In both instances, physicality—touch, holding, spinning around—helped Caleb and Rosy to move past their anger and settle down. In Caleb's case, Sally used a high-energy type of physicality, which reduced the rising tension between the two of them, while also distracting the little boy from his destructive behavior. For Rosy, I used a low-energy type of physicality, which soothed her nervous system and brought her energy down.

In this way, physicality is a bit like a Swiss Army pocketknife. It offers several tools in one. You can gently touch a child's arm or rub her back to curtail a rising tantrum, or you can pick her up and bounce her on your knee when you see an outburst gathering. Physicality can also land somewhere between the two ends of the spectrum. You can give a child a bunch of Inuit kisses or *kuniks* (e.g., sniffs with your nose) on the cheek, a little tickle under the arm, or a raspberry on the belly. Either way, the physicality tool is a way of showing a child that they're safe and loved, and that there's a calmer—and stronger—person taking care of them.

"Physical touch breaks the tension between a child and parent," says psychologist Dr. Larry Cohen, who has written several parenting books, including *Playful Parenting*. "Children have a natural urge to cooperate. They love to please you. And when that's not happening, it's because they're overloaded with tension."

I saw a similar technique practiced on Rosy when we stayed in the Maya village. Whenever she became a bit out of control, the teenage girls would tickle her. They would pick her up and just start tickling her—under her arms and on her stomach. Sometimes she would end up on the floor laughing, and they would all gather round to give her hugs and kisses. She would run away, shrieking, and I wasn't sure if she liked it. But when I mentioned it to her, her opinion was crystal clear: "I love it, Mama. I love it."

From a scientific perspective, there are oodles of reasons to parent with physicality. Touch lights up a child's brain like fireworks. Roughhousing releases a chemical in the brain, called BDNF, which helps the brain mature and grow. Tender gentle strokes release the "cuddle" hormone oxytocin, which signals safety and love to a child.

Like eating well and getting enough sleep, "touch is good for your health," neuroscientist Lisa Feldman Barrett writes in her book *How Emotions Are Made: The Secret Life of the Brain*.

And for kids of all ages, physicality is more effective than lecturing, scolding, or long explanations. When children feel upset, they don't have access to the "left" or logical side of the brain, says child psychotherapist Tina Payne Bryson. During emotional outbursts, the "right side" of a child's brain calls the shots—and the right side is all about nonverbal communication, Tina and her colleague Dr. Dan Siegel write in *The Whole-*

Brain Child. "Our right brain cares about the big picture—the meaning and feel of an experience—and specializes in images, emotions, and personal memories." And so, when you calmly hug a screaming two-year-old or softly touch the shoulder of a crying eight-year-old, you speak directly to the most accessible part of their brain, and in doing so, you communicate more effectively with the child.

In many ways, kids are hardwired to learn emotional regulation through physicality—not through verbal instruction. "In our society, we're trained to work things out using our words and our logic. But when your four-year-old is absolutely furious because he can't walk on the ceiling like Spider-Man (as Tina's son once was), that's probably not the best time to give him an introductory lesson in the laws of physics," the pair write.

Raising Rosy

With Rosy, physicality is quite useful, not just for stopping tantrums, but also for preventing them. When I feel like I'm going to get angry at Rosy and I don't want to raise my voice, I pick her up in a fun way. I flip her over or swing her in my arms like a baby. "Are you my sweet baby?" I say. Or I start tickling her stomach. My anger breaks almost immediately. And her tantrum melts like butter in a hot pan. She'll go from crying to laughing, or screaming to giggling, in a flash. "More tickling, Mama! More tickling," she exclaims.

Just this morning, while trying to make it out the door to school, we start spiraling into a bad state. We can't find her shoes. We can't find her bike helmet. We can't find her special water bottle ("I really need it, Mom!"). Tensions rise. And Rosy can tell I'm getting annoyed. In response, she yells, "Now I'm getting angry!" I'm about to scream, but I know that screaming will only make things worse. So I close my eyes and imagine the mauve massage room. I sniff the lavender, hear the chimes. Then I think about Sally and what she would do with Caleb in a moment like this. I kneel down close to Rosy and say, as gently as possible, "I don't want us to be angry." And then I pretend to be the Cookie Monster, eating her arm: "Nom nom nom!" Poof! The tension breaks and she starts to giggle. We walk out the door, both laughing.

Tool #3: Parent with Awe

One evening, Elizabeth, Rosy, and I are walking back to Maria's house at about ten p.m. Over our heads, the sky is majestic: the sun hangs low over the bay, and streaks of clouds glow pink and purple.

We've been working all day, and Rosy is cranky with tiredness. She sits down in the road and begins to whine. I ignore her. So she starts to cry and scream. Elizabeth walks over to her, kneels down, and says with the brightest wonderment in her voice, "Look at the beautiful sunset. Do you see the pink? The purple?"

Rosy looks over at Elizabeth suspiciously. Her brow furrows. But she can't resist Elizabeth's sweetness—nor the sunset. Rosy turns to look at the sky. And her whole expression changes. Her eyes soften. The crying stops. And she stands up and starts walking.

It occurs to me that Elizabeth just did something I've seen many other Inuit moms do while I've been in Kugaaruk. The moms practice an incredibly sophisticated psychological tool with children from ages one to sixteen: they teach them to replace anger with awe.

About a year before our trip up north, I reported on a story for NPR about how adults can control their own anger. During an interview, neuroscientist Lisa Feldman Barrett gave me one of the best pieces of advice ever: "Well, you could try cultivating awe," she said.

Cultivate what?

"Awe."

"The next time you are outside walking, take a moment and find a crack in the sidewalk where there is a weed poking out and attempt to create the feeling of awe— awe at the power of nature," she explained. "Practice that feeling over and over again. Practice feeling awe at the

sight of a butterfly. Or the sight of a particular lovely flower. Or at the clouds in the sky."

She shared how she uses this technique in her daily life. "For example, when I am video chatting with somebody in China, I can feel irritated very easily when the connection isn't very good. Or I can feel awe at the fact that someone can be halfway around the world, and I can see their face and hear their voice, even if it is imperfect, and I can be grateful for that ability."

As Lisa views it, emotions act a bit like muscles. If you don't use them, you lose them. And the more you flex particular ones, the stronger they become. So the more you experience awe—the more you flex this neural muscle in your brain—the easier it becomes to access this emotion in the future. When you start to feel an unproductive emotion, such as anger, you can more easily swap that negative feeling for a positive one, such as awe. When you feel annoyance, you can swap it for gratitude.

Under the purple sunset, Elizabeth does exactly this with Rosy. And I see Sally's mom, Maria, do it with her great-grandson Caleb many times. During our stay with them, every time the little boy cries or whines, Maria takes him over to a window to show him the beautiful bay. In doing so, she reminds the child of something wonderful in his life, something to feel grateful for, something bigger than himself. And this redirection soothes him every time.

"It may sound hokey in the abstract, but I guarantee that if you practice awe, that practice is essentially helping to rewire the brain. So that you can make that emotion [awe or gratitude] much more easily in the future," Lisa said.

This practice is especially important for children because their brains are malleable. "Children's brains are waiting for wiring instructions from the world," she says.

Thus the awe tool not only helps to stop tantrums in the moment, but it also helps reduce them in the future.

Tool #4: Take the Child Outside

I hesitated to include this tool because it seems a bit thin. But ever since our return to San Francisco, this simple strategy has been so useful in helping

Rosy learn to calm herself down that I need to mention it. It's a great idea to keep in your back pocket for when you're out in public, too. It's easy, works more often than not, and moms from several cultures suggested it.

I first heard about it from Suzanne Gaskins. "When a child asks for more than their level of understanding should suggest, Maya parents send the kid outside," she told me. This action tells the child that their behavior or demand isn't acceptable given their age or level of maturity. "It's a nudge to the child that they need to up their social responsibility game," Suzanne said.

I heard a similar idea from Dolorosa Nartok in Kugaaruk. "When children are small and out of control, it is because they have been in the house or igloo too long," she says. "Let them be outside for a few minutes."

Dolorosa learned the technique from her mother-in-law. "Little children get cranky when they have been inside too long," she says. "So pack them [that is, put them in a baby carrier], go outside, and walk around a bit."

The tool is as straightforward as it sounds: When a child is having a tantrum, you calmly pick them up and put them outside. You can just set them down, walk back in the house, and watch them from a window, as a Maya parent might do. You can put the child in a baby carrier, like Dolorosa suggested, and walk around a bit. Or if you live in a city without much outdoor space, as we do, you can just hold the little one in your arms on your tiny porch and be silent. If you *have* to say something, try something like "You're safe. I love you." When the child starts to settle, you can say something like "We can go back inside when you calm down a bit."

As children get older, you can't pick them up and take them outside as easily. In my experience, Rosy no longer wants me to pick her up when she gets upset. So instead, I gently take her hand and lead her outside. If I say anything at all, I tell her something like "Let's get some fresh air. You'll feel better in a few minutes." But in general, you don't need any words. Your calm, gentle action is enough.

Tool #5: Ignore It

In many cultures around the world, parents ignore tantrums. Anthropological studies overflow with examples of a small child who lashes out at a parent, and the adults in the room respond by simply pretending that the child isn't there.

But many Inuit parents take a more nuanced approach. They sometimes wait a bit before reacting to a tantrum, to see if the emotion passes. In general, however, parents don't let toddlers and very young children cry for very long. An adult or sibling will comfort them with one tool or another. For older children, it's a different issue. Once the parent believes a child is capable of calming themselves down, parents can—and do—ignore their emotional outbursts.

For example, in Kugaaruk, while we are out with Elizabeth, we see a girl, maybe about age seven or eight, crying in the front seat of a pickup truck, near a fishing camp. Elizabeth tells me that the girl's grandparents have intentionally left her alone. "See, we ignore tantrums," Elizabeth says. Then the girl's grandmother explains what happened. "She [the little girl] wanted to stop at the airport on the way to the camp, and we didn't stop," the grandma says, her voice matter-of-fact. The grandmother knows the young girl can calm herself down, and so she simply leaves her granddaughter alone to do so.

At what age does a child acquire this coveted skill? It varies from child to child and situation to situation, but getting there probably takes more time than you might expect. As I've mentioned, Americans tend to overestimate children's emotional skills (and underestimate their physical skills). My pediatrician told me to ignore Rosy's tantrums when she was only eighteen months old. That strategy backfired horribly, making Rosy's tantrums—and our lives—much worse. Rosy didn't yet have the skills to calm herself down, and being left alone to cry only fueled the fire in her chest. She needed gentle, calm love. She needed physical connection.

As I have to keep reminding myself, there's no race to acquire emotional maturity (I'm still acquiring it at the ripe old age of forty-two). It never hurts a child to give them a hug when they're upset, to model awe or gratitude when they start screaming, or to offer them some fresh air and time outside when a tantrum erupts. You're not giving into their demands, but rather using the tantrum as a moment to help them flex other neurological circuitry. See tantrums as a chance for the child to *practice* calming themselves down, and for you to *model* calmness—not the time for you, as their parent, to prove a point.

As Inuit moms keep telling me through their words and actions: Go easy on the little ones when they lose control of their emotions. Throw out your own anger and frustration (think of that spa room) and replace it with empathy and love. Remind yourself that children don't have the emotional skills that we adults do. We need to show them how calmness works, over and over again, before we can expect them to master the concept.

II: Tools for Everyday Misbehavior

A big goal of Inuit education is to trigger thought. "Children need to think about what they're doing. They always need to think," says seventy-one-year-old Theresa Sikkuark. Indeed, the word for "education" in one dialect of Inuktitut is *isummaksaiyug*, "which means roughly, to seek thought, to seek mind . . . and other cognitive kinds of things," anthropologist Jean Briggs has noted. "This exercising of the thought processes goes on all during a child's life."

As we examine the next set of tools, we'll start to understand the importance—and power—of triggering thought. With these tools, you are *not* telling children what to do, but instead giving them the clues they need to figure out the proper behavior on their own. In other words, you use these tools for *encouraging* and guiding, versus demanding and forcing.

You can apply these tools for everyday, run-of-the-mill misbehaving from kids of all ages, from toddlers to teenagers. (I have also seen many of the tools work wonders on adults.) Maybe the kid won't leave the playground or help clean up a messy living room. Maybe they won't go do their homework or stop hitting their little sister. Or maybe, just maybe, they just won't go to bed! In all these cases, the child refuses to behave, but—unlike during a tantrum—they still have control of their emotions (or at least partially). Their rational, logical self is awake and open to input.

These tools accomplish a few key goals:

1. They work in real time. They change behavior right away, so they can help keep kids safe.
2. They build toward long-term goals, such as helping children learn key values (e.g., respect, gratitude, and helpfulness).
3. They teach children to think.
4. They sidestep power struggles, arguing, and back-and-forth negotiations. They avoid the anger cycle.

Everyday Tool #1: Learn the Look

Eeeeeek! This tool is so powerful I get excited just thinking about it.

Did you know that children can read their parents' faces really well? I mean, really, really well. Even teeny-weeny babies and toddlers can do it. So most of the time, parents don't have to say a single word to change a kid's behavior. We simply have to give them "a look."

Take everything you want to say, every bit of emotion you feel toward the child, and channel it through your eyes, your nose, your furrowed brow—or just any part of your face.

Across the world, parents use all types of facial expressions to direct children's behavior. One well-executed look can be magical. You can get a child to walk away from a rack of candy bars in the grocery store. You can get a child to stop hitting his brother or encourage him to share his granola bar with a friend on the playground.

"My mom could give us one look, and our blood would run cold," a friend tells me.

Inuit are ridiculously good at giving and reading facial expressions. A quick wrinkle of the nose says, "No," while a flash of the eyebrows upward says, "Yes." (Some of the teenage girls in Kugaaruk make such subtle expressions with their eyebrows and noses that, at first, I didn't catch them.)

Moms and dads can make "the look" in many ways—with eyes wide open, eyes squinty, or even a blink. "When my mother wanted me to stop a behavior, all she had to do was slowly but firmly blink at me and that was a stern 'No,'" says teacher Kristi McEwen, whose mom belongs to another indigenous group in the Arctic, called Yupik.*

"The look" has many advantages over words. It works at a distance— across the playground, the living room, or the dinner table. And since it's silent, children have a very hard time "arguing" with "the look." Kids can't negotiate with a nose or a pair of eyes like they can a verbal command.

In my experience, "the look" proves more effective than telling a child "No" or even "Don't do that." The look says everything you need to say in a quick, calm glance. It shows who is cool and in charge.

The look has saved me much grief, especially while shopping. One afternoon in the grocery store, Rosy grabs a giant Snickers bar from the shelf in the checkout line. As parents often do, my husband issues verbal commands: "Rosy, you can't have that. Put that back." Rosy, deciding to make it a fun game, takes off running up the aisle with my husband yelling after her. So I decide to put an end to this power struggle.

I turn toward Rosy, lock eyes, and fire off "the look." I scrunch up my nose as if I just smelled something stinky in the air, close my eyes a bit, and think to myself firmly, "No way, sister." Guess what Rosy does? She looks back at me with a little grin on her face, goes over to the shelf, and puts the candy bar back. She knows the right thing to do. The look just reminded her.

Everyday Tool #2: Parent with Consequence Puzzles

"Tell them the consequences of their behavior. Tell them the truth,"
says Theresa Sikkuark.

———————

Three days into our stay in Kugaaruk, I have a major parenting epiphany regarding the way I talk to Rosy. I realize my approach is not the most productive—and likely causes strife.

Rosy and I are spending the day with Elizabeth, who doesn't just interpret

———————

* Kristi also shared an interesting way her mom would stop bickering between cousins: "She would have us stand in front of her and raise our arms above our heads while she commanded, 'Don't laugh.' Of course, we were in fits of giggles before we knew it."

interviews but also teaches us about Inuit history and traditions. She takes us to visit a fishing camp, about an hour away from Kugaaruk. On the way, we come to a high bridge crossing the *kuuk*. The bridge terrifies me. It rises forty feet above the river and has no railing to prevent children from falling. Rosy runs over to the bridge, and I begin to yell, "Wait! Don't go near the edge!" But before I can get the words out, Elizabeth has already reached Rosy. She gently takes Rosy's hand and says calmly, "You could fall and hurt yourself."

And that's when it hits me: Elizabeth and I have a completely different way of talking to Rosy. My commands almost always begin with "Don't": "Don't climb on that chair," "Don't spill the milk," "Don't grab the toy from the baby," "Don't, don't, don't, don't . . ."

But Elizabeth never—or rarely—seems to use that word. Instead, she and many Inuit moms and dads I met take a more productive approach with their commands. Parents tell children what will happen if they continue misbehaving. Parents tell children the *consequences* of their actions.

Take for instance, juggling rocks. At the playground one afternoon, Rosy decides to juggle rocks. She picks up three rocks, about the size of lemons, and starts throwing them in the air. Before I can tell her to "Stop throwing rocks!" a ten-year-old girl named Maria takes care of it for me. She says calmly, "You're going to hit somebody with the rocks, Rosy." Then she walks away and climbs on the monkey bars. That's it. Maria simply states the consequence of Rosy's action, matter-of-factly, and allows Rosy to figure out the proper reaction. To my surprise, it works. Rosy pauses for a second, looks at the rocks, then puts them down.

As I watch this scene unfold, the words of Jean Briggs echo in my head: "The goal of Inuit education is to cause thought." The little girl Maria has done exactly that: she has prompted Rosy to think.

Come to think of it, telling a child "don't"—don't throw, don't grab, don't climb, don't scream—contains very little information. Rosy already knows she's throwing, grabbing, climbing, or screaming. But she doesn't know (or realize) the consequences of these actions. And she might not realize, in the moment, why she shouldn't do these things. When you tell a child "don't" and "stop," you assume they'll obey the command as an automaton would: without a thought of their own.

Inuit parents think more highly of children than that. They believe that even young children can think for themselves—or at least they can learn to. So they give a child useful information about their behavior. They give the child a reason to think twice about continuing to do it.

After that incident at the playground, I start to see this form of guidance and discipline everywhere in Kugaaruk, not just with Rosy, but with kids of all ages. A seven-year-old girl climbs on top of a shed, about fifteen feet off the ground, and an older girl says matter-of-factly, "You're going to fall, Donna, and hurt yourself." Donna pauses on the roof, waits a bit, and then gets down. At Maria's house, six-year-old Samantha climbs on the edge of the couch near a shelf of fragile porcelain figures. Samantha's mom, Jean, tosses off the warning, "You're going to knock something off the shelf." Later that day, Samantha's three-year-old sister, Tessa, squeezes a loud dog toy while her grandma sleeps nearby. Jean says calmly, "Too loud. You'll wake up Grandma."

After delivering that warning, I notice, Jean doesn't say anything else. She doesn't press Tessa to stop squeaking the toy. She doesn't nag or yell. She, as the adult, simply prompts the child to think about their behavior and its consequences, then the mom leaves the child to extrapolate the proper response to that information. This way of communicating with children respects their autonomy and their ability to learn.

Raising Rosy

I think this approach works especially well for "willful" kids, who like to experiment and figure out how the world works for themselves (or as we like to put it in Western culture, kids who like to "push boundaries"). Yes, I'm talking about Rosy. Now when she screeches like a pterodactyl in the

You're going to fall, Donna, and hurt yourself!

morning, I say calmly and gently, "Too loud. You will give me a headache." When she doesn't share a toy with a friend, I say, "Kian won't want to come over and visit if you don't share." And so on. (I always try to say it as calmly and emotionless as possible. Any sternness or condemnation will just start a fight.)

Quite often it works. Rosy doesn't always do what I'd like, but most of the time she does. And she listens with much less resistance.

When she continues to misbehave, I (try to) let it go and feel confident that she hears me and is on her way to learning. I often sense that Rosy is considering what I said. And it feels good to know that I have passed along information that will help her make the proper choice next time.*

If she puts herself or others in real danger—if, say, there's going to be copious amounts of blood, head injuries, or broken bones—I'll go over and physically help her. But I don't scream at her or respond with a sense of urgency. I explain the consequence of the behavior and help move her so that the consequence doesn't occur.

Everyday Tool #3: Parent with Questions

Here's another golden nugget of parenting that I learned in Kugaaruk (and I heard it again in Tanzania with the Hadzabe): turn commands, criticisms, and feedback into questions.

I first witness Sally use this strategy one afternoon after coming home from work. In addition to raising her fifteen-year-old son and helping with her three grandchildren, Sally works full-time at the health clinic. When she walks into the house, tired after her long workday, she finds a complete mess in the living room. Playing cards lay strewn across the floor. Candy wrappers litter the table. But Sally doesn't get upset. She simply looks at the culprits—Rosy and her friend Samantha—and says in a kind voice, "Who made this mess?"

Hmmm, I think. *Interesting.*

---

* I have more trouble "letting it go" around other parents because I feel a sense of shame if Rosy ignores me. But I stiffen my spine and say this to the other parents: "I find she learns better if I don't push so hard."

After that, I notice the tool cropping up everywhere. "Who's ignoring me?" Sally's sister-in-law Marie says when her four-year-old daughter ignores a request to leave the house. "What did you bring back for me?" Sally asks a grandchild returning from a trip to the grocery store. And when a child hands Sally a bunch of trash to throw away, she responds with a brilliant question: "What am I, a trash can?"

Over in Tanzania, questions abound as well. When a two-year-old hits a younger child, her mom asks, "What are you doing to your friend?" When a three-year-old wants another dad to carry him during a long hike, the dad asks, "What am I, your donkey?"

The parents often state these questions with a half-sarcastic, half-serious tone. The questions aren't accusatory or denigrating. They aren't meant to make a child defensive. Instead, the questions are more like a puzzle for the child to solve, a prompt for the child to consider their actions and the potential consequences.

The strategy is genius. And it's perfect for those moments when you feel like the child is "pushing your buttons" and you don't want to get angry, but you also don't know what to do or say. Or when the child acts out and you want to just ignore the behavior but you also just *have* to say something. The question allows you to get your point across without causing a power struggle.

Raising Rosy

I start using the question tool as soon as we get back to San Francisco. In particular, I want to reduce the screaming and demanding in our home. So I'll say, "Who's screaming at me?" When Rosy complains about food at dinner, I'll say in a matter-of-fact tone, "Who's being ungrateful?" After that, I just move on with life. I am not there for an answer or a debate—or even to make her change right away. I just need Rosy to think.

I find this method particularly useful when I try to teach Rosy broad concepts about behavior, such as acting respectfully. I have assumed that Rosy knows the meaning of "respect," but it turns out, at age 3.5, she has no clue (another example of me overestimating her emotional skills). No one has ever taught her about respect, so I start using the question method to teach her.

One day I pick her up at school and ask her politely, using the consequence tool, to put on some sunscreen. "It's sunny out," I say. "You'll get a sunburn if you don't use a little sunscreen." She screams, "No!" and throws the sunscreen onto the sidewalk. The old Michaeleen would have snapped and likely yelled.

But the new Michaeleen pulls out the question tool and stays calm. In a matter-of-fact way, I say, "Who's being disrespectful?" I look away from Rosy as I say it, because I'm not trying to accuse her—I'm trying to get her to think. And then I move on. I pick up the sunscreen without getting upset and put it back in my purse. I think the interaction ends there. But about a minute later, Rosy says, "Okay. Give me that sunscreen." And she puts on the sunscreen without a complaint.

By that point, I had been using the question "Who's being disrespectful?" for about a week. Every time Rosy said something nasty, or screamed that she wanted two cookies instead of one, or just acted bratty, I said in that same matter-of-fact way, "Who's being disrespectful?"

I couldn't tell how much she had absorbed. But ten days into this experiment, I finally receive a clue. While the two of us lie next to each other in bed, chatting about the day at school, she suddenly asks, "Mama, what does disrespectful mean?" Aha! She *is* listening—and she's thinking.

A friend in San Francisco tried this method with her three-year-old daughter and called me up a few hours later to rave about it. "It worked! It worked!" she exclaimed. Her three-year-old had been hitting her baby brother with a stuffed animal, and my friend responded by saying, "Who's being mean to Freddy?"

The little girl stopped hitting, and then five minutes later came over to her mom and said, "I'm sorry for being mean, Mama."

Everyday Tool #4: Parent with Responsibility

This tool I learn from the Maya supermom Maria de los Angeles Tun Burgos in the Yucatán. Before the trip, Rosy presented a new challenge

to me and Matt: she began leaving the house without us. At only two years old, she had figured out how to unlock two doors, including a bolt lock. And one morning, we woke up and couldn't find her. I looked out the kitchen window and there she was, running up the sidewalk, buck naked. *Well, at least she's not in the road*, I thought.

The problem got so bad that we considered adding another lock to the door. "Lock her in!" my mother-in-law exclaimed one night on the phone.

But when I tell Maria about Rosy's escapades, she has another idea. "Can Rosy go to the store and run an errand for you?" she asks. Her point: Rosy needs more freedom and more responsibilities.

Now, Maria lives in a small town with only about two thousand people or so. The town has very little traffic or crime, and everyone knows everyone. So a 2.5-year-old toddler would be perfectly safe walking a half block to the corner store, where the owner knows the child. But in San Francisco, unfortunately, we don't have that kind of setup. Our house sits on a busy street, where cars whiz by at thirty miles per hour around a steep curve. And even if the environment was safer, I don't think our neighbors would be ready for a toddler running errands. If two-year-old Rosy walked into the corner store, alone, and plunked a half gallon of milk and a five-dollar bill on the counter, Matt and I would surely have the police at our front door.

But Maria's suggestion has a broad meaning behind it, one that I can put to use in our San Francisco home: misbehavior is a child's way of asking for more responsibility, more ways to contribute to the family, and more freedom. When a child breaks rules, acts demanding, or seems "willful," their parents need to put them to work. The child is saying, "Hey, Mom, I'm underemployed over here and it doesn't feel good."

Think about it. If you feel bored at your job, or your manager doesn't take advantage of your full potential, you get cranky and squirrely, too. You might not sprint out of the office buck naked, but you might feel like crying out, "Hey, Manager, look at me over here! I'm capable of doing all the work that others are doing. Give me a chance."

In our house, this tool helps with two big parenting goals: teaching Rosy to whine less, and encouraging her to pitch in and help out the family. Now when she complains about what I prepare for her lunch, I view those whines and complaints in a new way: I see them as Rosy's way of asking for work. In other words, whining can be a small child's way of showing interest in learning a new skill. You can harness that interest and get the child to help and contribute. Instead of simply telling them to stop whining, give them a job.

Even the most basic tasks can pull a toddler or small child out of a diva moment. For instance, one morning Rosy wakes up cranky and starts the day by complaining about the music playing on the Google Home device (twenty-first-century toddler problem, I know). "But I want the other Moana song, not this one!" she says, crying. Before she can launch into a full spiral of whining, I give her a job to do: "Looks like Mango is hungry. You know, little girls can't make requests if they're not helpful. Go feed the dog, and then we'll fix the song."

My husband shoots me a stern look because he thinks this command will trigger a tantrum. But Rosy simply nods her head in agreement and walks over to the dog bowl. The job breaks her out of her whining. She has more important things to do. And the rest of the morning goes much smoother.

"That was interesting," Matt says. It feels great to share something I learned from mothers like Maria. "Kids need jobs," I say. "They don't like to be unemployed. Makes them nervous."

Everyday Tool #5: Parent Through Action, Not Words

When you watch parents interact with kids in the Arctic or the Yucatán, one of the most striking aspects is how quiet everyone is. You feel like you're watching a ballet without any music. Everyone's movements seem choreographed and well-rehearsed. Their interactions flow with ease. And everyone says very few words. I mean, very few words. All you can hear are the dancers' feet moving across the floor.

In the vast majority of cultures, parents don't constantly talk to kids or give them endless choices. Instead, parents take action.

In the vast majority of cultures, parents don't constantly talk to kids or give them endless choices. Instead, parents take action. That action comes in three flavors:

1. They do what they want the child to do. In the Arctic, Sally's sister-in-law Marie is ready to go fishing, so she puts on her boots and says to her daughter, "Okay, Victoria, let's go fishing." Then she walks out the door and hops on the ATV. Victoria eventually follows.

At lunchtime in the Yucatán, I see a mom put plates of food on the kitchen table and then wait for her two daughters, busy coloring outside, to come and eat. "They will come when they are ready," she tells me. And she's right. A few minutes later, both girls come inside and begin to eat, no cajoling needed.

2. They gently help the child do what is needed. In the Yucatán, Rosy climbs onto an adult bike that's way too tall for her. She's clearly going to fall off. No one screams at her or yells instructions. Instead, sixteen-year-old Laura comes over and gently takes Rosy's hand and helps her off the bike. All Rosy needs is a sturdy hand to help—and then a big hug.

3. They change the environment so the child does not need to change their behavior. One evening in the Yucatán, we are all sitting around the dinner table chatting and sharing a pineapple. Suddenly, Rosy grabs a giant butcher's knife off the table. Nobody gasps or tries to grab the knife from her. Instead, one of the moms, Juanita, walks over calmly, waits for Rosy to set the knife back down, and then moves it out of reach. There's no arguing. No whining. No break in the harmony of the moment.

In the vast majority of cultures—and throughout human history—parents don't discuss with children what activity they'll do next, or debate whether a child wants a peanut butter sandwich or pasta for lunch. Parents don't ask "Do you want" questions: "Do you want butter or tomato sauce on your pasta?" "Do you want to go to the store with me?" "Do you want to take a bath?" Instead, the parent just takes action. The mom makes black beans for lunch; the dad grabs his jacket and heads out the door to the store; the grandma goes to the bathroom and draws water for bath time.

I think this low-talk parenting style is a big reason kids in these cultures seem so calm. Fewer words create less resistance. Fewer words cause less stress.

Words and commands are energizing and stimulating, and they often incite arguments. Every time we ask a child to do something, we create an opportunity for fighting and negotiating. But when you keep the conversation to a minimum, you keep the energy low. The chance for debate and fighting plummets. Even the raging beast inside Rosy eventually caves in and relaxes.

Same goes for choices. Even for adults, choices are hard. They can cause stress and anxiety because we don't want to miss out on the option we don't choose. Why would the little ones feel any differently?*

After I observe how well this low-talk parenting works, over and over again, both in the Arctic and in the Yucatán, I begin to question my own verbose parenting style. Why do I constantly talk to Rosy? Narrate? Ask? Supply choices? Taking action seems way more powerful.

I know my parenting will never be as quiet and calm as the Maya and Inuit moms and dads. I'm a boisterous, energetic American. Words will always be my go-to parenting tool. But I can greatly reduce the

---

* The other day, Rosy actually said, "Mama, choices are hard. They are so hard." So even kids realize that choices cause stress. Plus, fewer choices helps kids accept and be grateful for what's in front of them.

stress in our family—and add a bit more flow—by reducing the verbiage involved in everyday tasks. I can say one time, "We're leaving in
five minutes," and then just go, without shouting reminders every thirty
seconds. I can say, "Come to lunch, Rosy and Matt," and then wait for
them to join me.

And I can get Rosy to take action by taking action myself. For example,
every morning when we arrive at her preschool, Rosy needs to wash her
hands and put on sunscreen. I used to ask a few times, then nag, and then
threaten. But the Inuit moms inspire me to try a different approach: Go
wash my hands myself. Or ask Rosy to do it together. "Let's go wash hands,
Rosy," I'll say as I walk over to the sink. I put sunscreen on myself and ask
Rosy to join me. Or I ask Rosy to put the sunscreen on me and then switch
up and put it on her.

These minor changes have produced phenomenal results. Not only
does our household have less frenetic energy and resistance, but Rosy is
more autonomous. After a few months of us washing hands together, she
does it without me having to ask. She simply puts the sunscreen on herself.
And leaving the house has become a breeze. She knows I'm not going to
debate or negotiate. When I start walking down those stairs at 8:15 a.m.,
she understands that the train is leaving the station soon and I'm not going
back in the house to ask her again. "Wait for me," she often screams now as
I get the bike out of the garage.

Finally, I can give Rosy less choices. I can completely cut out the question "Do you want . . . ?" Why on earth do I constantly ask a three-year-
old what she wants? How can a child learn flexibility and cooperation
if we always ask them, "Do you want . . . ?" Rosy has never shied away
from telling me what she wants; we don't need to encourage choice. Offering options frequently generates negotiations, unneeded decisions,
and eventually tears. And most of the time, her "wants" are irrelevant to
our lives. The family's priorities come first. For example, during meals
and snacks, I no longer act like a waitress, listing off the specials. When
she says she's hungry, we go prepare food together and we eat it. End. Of.
Story.

Everyday Tool #6: Mastering the Art of Ignoring

When I first witness Elizabeth execute this tool, it throws me off guard. It's so different than what I've been calling "ignoring." It's so much stronger. So much more effective.

Elizabeth and I are drinking coffee together at her sister's kitchen table one day, and Rosy starts demanding Elizabeth's attention. "Miss Elizabeth, look at me! Look what I'm doing. Miss Elizabeth, look," Rosy keeps saying. "Look at me."

Miss Elizabeth is definitely not looking at Rosy. In fact, Miss Elizabeth isn't changing her expression at all. She keeps a perfect poker face. Instead of looking at Rosy, she steadies her eyes and then slowly turns her head and looks out into the horizon above Rosy's head, as if Rosy is invisible.

My first thought is super negative. *Goodness, she is being rude to Rosy*, I think. But quickly I realize Rosy's behavior is inappropriate, and Elizabeth lets her know that in an incredibly gentle yet potent way. Elizabeth continues our conversation, and Rosy stops being demanding.

Elizabeth is a master at ignoring Rosy. Sometimes all she needs to do is ignore Rosy for ten seconds and, poof! Misbehavior ceases. Calmness ensues. Once Rosy realizes that her misbehavior doesn't deserve attention—that maybe, she doesn't need our attention—she falls in line and starts cooperating. And Elizabeth welcomes Rosy back into the social circle with a smile or nod.

Watching Elizabeth, I realize that when I thought I was "ignoring" Rosy, I was actually doing just the opposite. I was, in fact, giving Rosy's bad behavior a lot of attention. I was looking at her. I was making faces and comments. And most ridiculously, I was telling her that I was ignoring her. Rosy even enjoyed my "ignoring" game. What fun!

In many cultures, parents completely ignore misbehavior from children of all ages, says Batja Mesquita, a cross-cultural psychologist at the University of Leuven in Belgium. Parents don't look at the child, don't talk to them, and, perhaps most important, give no sign that they even care about the misbehavior (remember, many cultures expect children to misbehave).* And in doing so, the parents convey a huge amount of information to the children about that behavior, especially in terms of its usefulness and how much the culture values it.

What if a child starts hitting her mom with a microphone, for example? "Yes, there are lots of mothers in the world who would just completely ignore the hitting," Batja says. "And in doing so, the child's anger gets dampened. The anger eventually dies out. Or you can replace it with another emotion. Children's emotions become what they are by other people's response to them."

So parents can teach children which emotions aren't valued in the home by not responding to those emotions. By contrast, responding even negatively to the emotional behavior signals to children that those emotions are important and useful.

In Western culture, Batja says, parents often give children's anger and misbehavior a large amount of attention. We engage with a misbehaving child, ask them questions, and issue demands.

"If you say, 'Stop it,' that's attention," Batja says.

Remember the formula. The stronger we respond to a child's misbehavior—even in a negative way—the more we *acknowledge* that behavior and, in essence, the more we train the child to behave that way.

So even when I say "Stop" or "Don't" to Rosy, I reinforce an emotion or behavior with her—a behavior that keeps her from learning to control her emotions and actions. When, of course, I think I am doing the opposite.

But when I actually ignore Rosy—when I actually stop looking at her and stop caring about her misbehavior—something magical happens. Rosy stops misbehaving. "See," Elizabeth says one afternoon. "Once you really ignored her, she settled down."

---

* The ethnographic record is littered with examples of this parenting tool. Jean Briggs documents it throughout her books, both near Kugaaruk and in eastern Canada on Baffin Island. "Often, childish misbehavior was met by silence, not the heavy silence of gathering tension but an apparently relaxed and rational one that seemed to recognize that the child was not being reasonable but that sooner or later he would come to his senses and behave more maturely again," she writes in *Never in Anger*.

Try It 5: Discipline without Words

Dip Your Toe

- **When in doubt, turn away.** The next time your child misbehaves, just walk away. Don't react or change your expression; simply turn your body around and walk away. What happens? Try the same experiment if you feel a power struggle or an argument approaching. Simply turn around and walk away.

- **Practice being silent.** Challenge yourself to periods of silence. Tell your children, "We're going to be quiet now for five minutes." If they continue to talk, just stay silent yourself. The next day, try ten minutes, then twenty minutes. Work up to an hour or more, and you'll find yourself luxuriating in incredible peace in your home.

We do this when the energy in our home has gotten too high and frenetic—when Rosy can't seem to settle down and stop asking questions or demanding. After five or ten minutes of silence (at least on my part), she'll settle and the rest of the day or evening will go easier.

- **Turn crankiness into contributions.** The next time your toddler or small child acts cranky or demanding, use the responsibility tool and try putting them to work. Get them to help you make a meal. They can stir a pot, crack an egg, chop herbs, or wash vegetables. Or show them how to feed a pet, sweep the floor, or take the garbage out. Have them help fold clothes, rake leaves, or water plants.

"Look around the house and see what needs to be done," one mom told me in Kugaaruk. "There's always a way that children can help out in the house." (Refer to chapter 4 for more ideas.)

Then simply invite the child to help. One mom in Berkeley said this technique worked well with her five-year-old daughter. The little girl seemed cranky on a Sunday afternoon, whining and misbehaving. So the mom said, "Come help me with dinner. Come cut up the rosemary leaves."

"It was such a simple task," the mom later told me. "And yet she loved it! She was so proud of what she cut up. She kept showing me the leaves." The rest of the evening went more smoothly, too.

- **Use responsibilities as rewards.** Keep in mind that working together with an adult is a privilege for a child. If a child really wants to join an adult errand or activity, use their desire to teach adultlike behavior. For example, Rosy cherishes grocery shopping. She loves Trader Joe's. But joining me is a privilege for "big girls" (or at least, that's how I sell it). So I use her zest for shopping to help her practice mature behavior. If I hear a lot of whining and demanding on grocery day, I might ask, "Do whiny babies get to go to Trader Joe's?" And within seconds I'll hear "I stopped, Mama. I stopped."

Jump In

- **Stop issuing dos and don'ts (or issue them sparingly).** This is a tough one because these words are entrenched in our dialogue with children. But even cutting out half of your dos and don'ts will have a big impact on your relationship with your child. I guarantee you'll argue less, and at the very least, your child will have more opportunities to think and learn instead of simply doing (or not doing) what you tell them.

The next time you would like to change your child's behavior, pause for a moment. Wait before you talk. Think about why you are issuing this command. What is the consequence of their behavior? Why are you trying to change it? Or even, what do you fear will happen if the child continues that behavior?

Then tell the child the answer to one of these questions, and let them be. That's it! You don't need to say anything else. For example, Rosy starts to climb on top of the dog's back. Instead of saying, "Don't climb on the dog's back," I pause and think, *What will happen if Rosy climbs on the dog's back?* Then I say to Rosy, "If you climb on her back, you will hurt her," or even "Ow, Rosy, you are hurting the dog."

After a few days (or weeks) of practice with the consequence tool, try other tools to replace the dos and don'ts. You can turn your consequence statement into a question ("Rosy, are you hurting the dog?" or "Who's being mean to the dog?"). You can lock eyes with the child and give them a stern look to convey your displeasure with their behavior. Or you can simply walk away and ignore them.

• **If you really want to change how you communicate with your children, try this experiment.** During a regular morning or evening, take out your smartphone and use it to record your time with the kids. Set it on the kitchen counter while you make dinner or on the table while you eat. Then record for long enough that you and your kids forget about the phone. The next day, go and listen to the recording.

What impressions first come to mind? Do you tend to talk all the time? Are there any moments of silence and calm? Do you issue many commands? How many times do you offer your child options or ask what they want? How many times do you say "Don't" or "Do"? Are those commands really necessary? Do the kids listen? Do *you* listen?

As I mentioned earlier (see chapter 6), I ran this experiment unintentionally once. And when I went back and listened to the tape, I started to cry. I realized that I was talking all the time and wasn't listening to Rosy. I thought I was listening. But I actually was not considering her words and thoughts. And she was incredibly frustrated by it (as I would have been).

• **Learn the art of ignoring.** Is there some misbehavior or bad habits that you'd like to eliminate? Maybe it's whining, or excessive demanding. Or maybe it's mistreating the dog, or throwing silverware at dinner. Try this approach for one to two weeks, and I'm confident the behavior will decrease, if not cease altogether. Each time the child displays the unwanted behavior, do the following:

• **Keep your expression flat.** Don't flinch or react in the slightest. Pretend like you can't even hear or see them. With this flat expression, look into the horizon above the child's head or to their side.

• **Then walk away.** Just turn around and walk away until the child is out of sight.

Now, you don't have to be mean to the child or hurt their feelings. You're still responding to their needs and you're not acting angrily toward them. You simply aren't responding *emotionally* to their misbehavior. You are staying neutral and showing them that you have zero interest in that behavior.

For example, one Wednesday afternoon when I arrive to pick up Rosy from preschool, she says, "I'm hungry, Mama" in a whiny, baby voice. I respond by saying kindly, "I'm hungry, too. I have no food with me. So let's stop at a store and get a snack on the way home."

What a nice proposal, right?

Unimpressed, Rosy launches into more whining and demanding. "But I'm hungry. Mama, I'm hungry," she repeats until she's crying.

A few months before, I would have unleashed a series of explanations ("I hear you. You are hungry. But I don't have food now"), which would eventually turn into tension and anger ("What did I just say? We can stop at a store when we get home. I don't have any food!" and so on). But now I pull out the ignore tool. I can't do anything at this point to provide her with food. She has no choice but to sit with her hunger and wait. So I keep my expression completely neutral, look over her in the distance (just like Elizabeth did), and proceed as if Rosy doesn't exist. I hop on the bike and ride away from her school while Rosy continues crying. And guess what? Within fifteen seconds or so, she stops. Completely. She accepted her discomfort. She learned to control her emotions, and she did it all by herself.

At the same time, I avoided a heated discussion and negotiations, which could have easily escalated into an argument and a tantrum. I turned a potential battle into an opportunity for Rosy to calm herself down. Instead of raising the energy of the situation, I lowered it. And along the way, Rosy built up her executive function.

Summary for Chapter 10:
Tools for Changing Behavior

Ideas to Remember

➤ American parents tend to rely on verbal instruction and explanations to change children's behavior. But words are often the least effective way to communicate with children, especially young children.
➤ Children's emotions mirror our emotions.
  • If you want your child to be calm, be quiet and gentle. Use few or no words (which are stimulating).
  • If you want your child to be loud and have high energy, have high energy yourself. Use many words.
➤ Commands and lectures often cause power struggles, negotiations, and cycles of anger.
➤ We can break out of the anger cycle and power struggles by using nonverbal tools or by helping the child to think instead of telling them what to do.

Tips and Tools

➤ **Taming tantrums.** Tantrums go away if we respond to a child with calmness. Next time a child has an emotional outburst, stay quiet and try one of these tools:
  • **Energy.** In the calmest, lowest-energy state possible, simply stand near the child, silently, and show them that you are close by, supporting them.
  • **Physicality.** Reach out and gently touch the child on the shoulder or offer a hand. Sometimes a soft, calm touch is all a child needs to calm down.
  • **Awe.** Help the child replace their anger with the emotion of awe. Look around and find something beautiful. Tell the child,

in the calmest, most gentle voice, "Oh wow, the moon is so beautiful tonight. Do you see it?"

- **Outside.** If the child still won't calm down, take them outside for some fresh air. Gently lead them outside or pick them up.

➤ **Changing behavior and transmitting values.** Instead of telling the child "Don't," prompt the child to think and figure out the proper behavior themselves with:

- **The look.** Take whatever you want to say to a misbehaving child and channel it into your facial expression. Open your eyes wide, scrunch up your nose, or shake your head. Then shoot the look over to the child.
- **Consequence puzzle.** Calmly state the consequences of the child's actions, then walk away (e.g., "You're going to fall off and hurt yourself").
- **Question.** Instead of issuing a command or instruction, ask the child a question (e.g., "Who's being mean to Freddie?" when a child hits a sibling, or "Who's being disrespectful?" when a child ignores a request).
- **Responsibility.** Give a misbehaving child a task to do (e.g., say to a whining child in the morning: "Come over and help me make your lunch").
- **Action.** Instead of asking a child to do a task (e.g., leave the house), just do the task yourself. The kid will follow.

CHAPTER 11

Tools for Sculpting Behavior: Stories

While in the Arctic, I noticed that a big chunk of Inuit parenting happens well after a child misbehaves. Not in the moment and not immediately after, but later on, when everyone has calmed down. In these peaceful moments, children are more open to learning, observes eighty-nine-year-old Eenoapik Sageatook, from Iqaluit, Canada. When a child is upset or defying the parent, the child is too emotionally charged to listen. So there's no reason to try to teach the child a "big lesson" in those moments. "You have to remain calm and wait for the child to calm down. Then you can teach the child," she says.

Now we'll look at two tools that change a child's behavior over the long term. These are your big power tools that shape children's values and ways of thinking. But the key is to use them at the right time.

This wait-to-fix strategy has a couple of big advantages. First, it averts power struggles. Instead of jumping in as soon as a misbehavior occurs to scold a child, you keep your focus on the long game, knowing there will be an opportunity later on to teach your child the proper behavior. So in these hot-button moments, you don't need to "prove a point." You can easily let issues go. You can ignore a disrespectful comment in the car, a refusal to help set the dinner table, or even a full-out food-throwing fest at dinner because, later in the evening, you will execute one of the following tools. And you know that these tools will work more effectively than yelling, scolding, or debating about the problem.

> You have to remain calm and wait
> for the child to calm down.
> Then you can teach the child.
> —EENOAPIK SAGEATOOK

Second, these tools open up communication between children and parents instead of cutting it off as punishments and anger do. These tools build connections and ease tensions. They do what almost seems impossible to me: they turn misbehavior into play and replace power struggles with stories.

———————

Life in the Arctic is remarkably similar to life in San Francisco in one major way: the prevalence of danger.

As I've mentioned, in San Francisco we live on a busy street. Buses the size of whales zoom downhill at thirty miles per hour and cars zip around the corner without stopping at the crosswalk. In the Arctic, danger comes in the form of deadly bears and icy water. Polar bears often lurk at the edge of town. A family's home might sit mere steps away from the icy Arctic Ocean. In the spring, a toddler could fall through thinning ice; in summer, swift currents could sweep a child out to sea.

So when a three-year-old runs out toward the icy waters, parents must have to yell to keep them safe, right?

Nope, says Goota Jaw, a college instructor, who teaches a class on traditional Inuit parenting at Nunavut Arctic College. "Instead, we use storytelling for disciplining."

Oral storytelling is a human universal. Every culture today—and throughout human history—tells stories. Storytelling was likely essen-

tial for the evolution of *Homo sapiens*. Without stories, our species probably wouldn't have developed certain skills critical to our success, such as
designing tools, hunting cooperatively, and harnessing the power of fire.
Why? Because such skills require a person to remember a series of steps,
past events, and actions, similar to a story line or plot.

Storytelling is one of the unique characteristics that makes us human. It
connects us to our environment, to our families, to our homes. It makes us
cooperative and powerful. And it serves as a key tool for training children.

In addition to transmitting important skills, stories also transmit cultural values to children. For tens of thousands of years, perhaps longer,
parents have used oral stories to teach a child how to behave like a good
member of their community. Today, modern hunter-gatherer groups use
stories to teach sharing, respect for different genders, anger control, and
how to stay safe around their homes.

But the storytelling tool does not belong exclusively to hunter-gatherers.
Not in the slightest. In fact, I challenge the reader to find a culture in which
this tool *doesn't* exist.

Not that long ago, the tool formed a huge part of Western parenting,
says Celticist researcher Sharon P. MacLeod. "Celtic cultures are steeped
in supernatural beings," she says. Fairies filled the woods, ghosts roamed
the roads, and monsters lurked in lakes and bogs. Some of the creatures
were helpful; some were dangerous. And a big function of these mythi-
cal creatures was to help keep children safe. "Bogs and wetlands could be
treacherous," she says. "Sometimes a bog looks like land, but it's actually
water. Before kids have skills in this arena, stories kept them away from
the wetlands."

For example, one Celtic story centers around a horse that lives in the
water and likes to steal kids. "If children came too close to the water, the
horse would put them on its back and take the kids down under the water,"
Sharon explains. "No matter how many kids hopped on, the horse's back
would get longer and longer." And so parents didn't have to hover over
young children—or yell at them—when they played by the beach or a river,
because the parents had taken a preemptive approach. They had already
told their children tales about the water horse. Steeped in these stories,

even small toddlers understand that to stay safe, they should stay clear of the water.

Remarkably, Inuit parents have a similar story with an identical purpose, says Goota Jaw. "It's Qalupalik, the sea monster," she says. "If a child walks too close to the water, the Qalupalik will put you in his *amauti* [parka], drag you down into the ocean, and adopt you out to another family."

Stories like these abound in Inuit parenting. To ensure children keep their hats on in the winter—and avoid frostbite—parents use the northern lights, says Myna Ishulutak, a film producer and language teacher in Iqaluit. "Our parents told us that if we went out without a hat, the northern lights are going to take your head off and use it as a soccer ball. We used to be so scared!" she exclaims, erupting in laughter.

Inuit parents also use stories to transmit important values to children, such as respect. For example, Myna's parents told her a story about earwax, which taught her to listen to her parents. "My parents would check inside our ears, and if there was too much wax in there, it meant we were not listening," she says. Another example: to teach kids to ask before taking food, Myna's mom and dad told her that long fingers could reach out from the container and grab her.

A big part of childhood, in both traditional Celtic and traditional Inuit cultures, involves learning how to treat these mysterious creatures—how to avoid them, respect them, or keep them happy. Parents and grandparents pass down knowledge through these captivating, sometimes scary stories. In the process, children learn to respect their parents and stay safe.

"The stories help children understand how serious parents are about needing to behave and listen," Myna says.

At first, these stories strike me as a bit too scary for little children, especially toddlers like Rosy. And my knee-jerk reaction is to dismiss them. *I don't think this approach is going to help me*, I think.

But when I return to San Francisco, I try out a story on Rosy. And her reaction takes me by surprise.

About a month after the trip to the Arctic, Rosy and I are in the kitchen, preparing dinner. She wants an item from the refrigerator. So she grabs her step stool, walks over to the refrigerator, and climbs up. Then she proceeds to stand there, with the refrigerator door wide open, for five minutes. I tell her to close the door, and she ignores me. I explain several times how she's wasting energy. It's like I'm talking to a wall. So I try pleading in a sweet, nice voice. Still, she ignores me. I can feel my anger rising up in my belly. A power struggle is imminent.

But I don't want to argue—again. I'm so tired of arguing. I'm just about ready to issue some kind of threat, when Goota Jaw and the sea monster pop into my head. *One monster in the house couldn't hurt*, I think. *Why the hell not, Michaeleen?*

So with a half-serious, half-playful tone, I say, "You know? There's a monster inside the refrigerator, and if he warms up, he's going to get bigger and bigger and come get you."

Then I point into the refrigerator, make my eyes wide, and exclaim, "Oh my goodness. There he is!"

Holy moly! You should have seen the look on Rosy's face. She closes the refrigerator door faster than a jackrabbit. Then she turns around with a big smile on her face and says, "Mama, tell me more about the monster in there."

Since that day, we have brought all sorts of monsters into our house. Rosy can't get enough of them. Storytelling has become our family's go-to parenting tool. She calls the stories "take-aways" because the protagonist—a little girl who's about three years old—often gets taken away (just as Celtic and Inuit kids do at the hands of water horses and sea monsters).

"Mama, tell me a take-away," she says every night before she falls asleep. Sometimes she even asks me to make them scarier, I kid you not.

Storytelling has become so infused in our lives that I can't imagine going back to life without these supernatural creatures flying around our house, coming through the walls, and hanging out in the tree of the park nearby. These creatures are the sole reason we get out of the house each morning for school. And the only reason why bedtime is not a complete hot mess, night after night.

With storytelling, I feel like I can finally speak Rosy's language. We can finally communicate smoothly.

Take, for instance, the pink dress challenge. For Rosy's birthday, Matt and I give her a pink dress with fabric roses knitted all over the bodice. The dress is sleeveless and a bit short for her (it falls right above her knees). So it's really not appropriate for the rainy, chilly winter in San Francisco. Nevertheless, once Rosy puts that darn dress on, she doesn't take it off for days. She wears it—day and night—for about a week. By that time, it's no longer pink but rather gray and brown. And it smells like mildew mixed with stale urine (yes, I think there was an incident in the bathroom).

For the life of me, I cannot get Rosy to take off that dress. I try my usual tactics, including long explanations and adult logic. "Rosy, if we wash it tonight, it won't have stains on it for school tomorrow." She looks at me as if I spoke in French.

Finally, one night, I kneel down to her height, move close to her ear, and whisper dramatically, "If the dress gets too dirty, spiders will start to grow in it."

Rosy doesn't say a word. Her face freezes. She steps away from me, slowly, and slips the dress off. I snatch it from her hands and throw it into the washing machine. Victory!

Later that night, when I take the dress out of the dryer, I hold it up and exclaim, "See, Rosy? So nice and clean!"

She doesn't miss a beat. "And no spiders," she says.

Try It 6: Discipline with Stories

Some American parents have expressed concern with the idea of "scaring" a child into complying or being cooperative. I had the same worry, but the point isn't to terrify the child and give them nightmares. The point is to get the child to think, to encourage a certain behavior, and to open up a discussion about a cultural value.

If you find yourself balking at the "scare factor" of this tool, as I did, you might consider that in Western culture, we also "scare" children into behaving. Children can become afraid of their parents' anger or punishments. This is what happened during my childhood; I behaved because I feared my father's anger. To be honest, I would rather Rosy be afraid of a "refrigerator monster" or the "spiders in a dress" than fear me or her father.

And just because parents don't tell children stories doesn't mean that kids don't learn through stories, points out historian Emily Katz Anhalt. Many families, including our family, outsource oral storytelling to Disney, Netflix, and YouTube. "People learn from all the stories they're told. That's how we transmit our culture," she says. "And I worry we've lost sight of our culture's creations. The motive to generate a profit from stories means they are often filled with violence"—and they might not teach children the best set of values.

In contrast, when *you* tell your child a story, you can personalize it just for them. You can see their response in real time and tailor the story accordingly. When a child becomes afraid, you can back off a bit. And when you find a tale that really tickles a sweet spot and connects with them, you can go deeper. Whenever I infuse the stories with Rosy's own experiences, I always know we'll have a winner.

At the end of the day, the proof is in the pudding. With stories to guide her behavior, Rosy is more cooperative, flexible, and easygoing. We communicate better with each other—with humor, instead of lecturing and scolding. And I can see how the stories really prompt Rosy to think and consider how her behavior affects others.

One day I ask: "Rosy, what do you like better, me yelling at you or me telling you stories?" She doesn't hesitate. "Stories."

Dip Your Toe

If you still feel a bit skeptical about the storytelling idea, start off with non-fiction. The story doesn't need to scare the child to open a communication channel—or to help the child comply with a request. You can also tell fun and truthful stories.

Here are two approaches to try:

• **Tell family history stories.** Try telling stories about your own child-hood or your family's origin stories. "Inuit *highly* value knowledge of our family trees and connecting to our relatives' lives," says Corina Kramer, of Kotzebue, Alaska. "In fact, when we traditionally introduce ourselves, we start by saying our name, who our grandparents and parents are, and which village our family is from." Children of all ages love to hear about what their parents and grandparents did when they were younger. They're drawn like magnets to these stories.

Family origin stories can pass along lessons from one generation to the next, and they can build intergenerational connections that have positive repercussions on children's behavior even as they grow into adolescence. Several studies have found that learning about their family's history buffers preteens and teenagers from mental health problems. In the studies, children ages nine to sixteen showed lower levels of anxiety, depression, anger, and behavior problems when they knew more about their family's past, such as when their parents met, where their parents and grandparents grew up, and what lessons their parents learned from the mistakes they made and the jobs they had as young adults. This knowledge also correlates with the overall functioning of a family, including how well family members communicate with each other. The scientists point out that what's important here is that parents share stories about their history, not that children learn specific facts.

You can start off with something as simple as "Let me tell you a story about when I was your age . . ." Then recount an incident or activity in your childhood that stands out in your memory. For little children, you can tell incredibly simple stories—where you loved to play outside, how you helped your mother in the garden, helped your dad with the laundry, or what you liked to do with your siblings. Sprinkle in details your child can use to visualize the story in their minds, such as colors, smells, and familiar objects.

Tell your children stories about where you were born, where you grew up, or where you and your spouse got married. Recount lessons you learned from making mistakes or from jobs you had as a teenager and young adult. Build up your family's stories by adding "characters," such as grandparents, uncles, aunts, cousins, family friends, and pets.

For a city kid like Rosy, she devours stories about my childhood in rural Virginia. She loves hearing about the huge garden in our backyard, where we grew corn, cucumbers, and watermelon, and how each summer we would pick green beans and shell them on the porch for dinner.

To help teach Rosy proper behavior and core family values, I often tell her stories about how my sister and I would get in trouble if we didn't share food or help clean up the dinner table. She also loves the story of how little Michaeleen got punished for disrespecting her mom by yelling at her, and then didn't get to visit her friend's house after school.

Over the course of writing this book, I have noticed a remarkable trend with Rosy: she is more likely to comply with a request if I first tell her that my mom made me do the same dreaded task during my childhood. For example, when Rosy refuses to eat asparagus at dinner, I say something like "When I was four years old, Granana made me eat asparagus, too. Man, I didn't like that, but I ate them because she's the boss." Then, voilà! Rosy starts popping the asparagus in her mouth.

• **Make science come to life.** Many ideas in biology, chemistry, and physics sound stranger than fiction—and just as interesting to young children. So why not use science knowledge as a way to create nonfiction stories? Just remember to use simple, relatable words, especially ones that paint a picture or will tickle the child's imagination.

For example, we help Rosy brush her teeth by telling her stories of the "critters" inside her mouth. They are so tiny you can't see them (yes, they are bacteria). But they live on your teeth, and you have to brush them off or they'll punch holes in your teeth at night and turn them black. In essence, we take real science and jazz it up with imagery, anthropomorphism, and hyperbole.

To help Rosy learn healthy eating habits, we tell her about the creatures in her stomach. Millions upon millions of friendly critters not only work to keep her insides feeling good, but they also help her brain function and her body fight off bad critters. The microbiome! These critters get sick when Rosy eats too much sugar. But they love fruits, veggies, beans, and nuts. "The creatures are screaming for chickpeas, Rosy," I find myself saying at lunch. "They are saying, 'Please, please, Rosy. Give us more chickpeas. More chickpeas.'"

Wade In

• **Embrace anthropomorphism.** The next time you find yourself struggling with a child or having difficulties "encouraging" a certain behavior, try this simple trick. Look around you, find the nearest inanimate object (even a shoe will do), and bring that object to life. Pretend it can talk. Have the object tell your child what you need her to do. With toddlers, I bet this trick will work nine out of ten times.

What types of objects work best? For Rosy, it's all about stuffed animals. But I have also used my body parts (including my belly button) and her invisible friends (including Maria from *The Sound of Music*).

At NPR, I've heard from several readers who've had wild success with this approach.

Listener Kathryn Burnham brings "Woofie" out:

"If we are running late and my three-year-old daughter needs to put on her shoes, I know that yelling, 'Put on the shoe' makes things worse. So I make my hand into the dog, Woofie, by bringing [two of] my middle fingers down to my thumb for a mouth. Then I say something like 'Can

Woofie have a turn trying to put on your shoes?' And I make silly whining, panting, and barking dog sounds while Woofie helps her put on her shoes. The more animated I make Woofie, the more she giggles and loosens up. The tense situation turns into a fun bonding moment."

For listener Penny Kronz, a stuffed animal leads the way:

"When my son doesn't want to join a meal or go to bed, I just tell him it's time for his favorite stuffed animal to go to bed or come eat. Then I proceed to do the activity with the stuffed animal, and he will quickly come join in."

And Adele Karoly lets her son's clothes do the talking:

"When my son doesn't want to put on his pajamas, I will start having the pajamas talk to me. They will say something like 'Elliot wants to wear us?' And I will answer, 'I don't think he does, let me ask him.' And if he says no, I will tell the pajamas and continue to have a conversation with them. Eventually, he will get drawn in and accept the pajamas, and they will be so excited and give him a big hug."

Jump In

- **Let monsters move in.** To harness the full power of storytelling, bring monsters into your home. You can make them fun with a dash of danger, or pretty scary with a dash of fun. "Scary" is a wide spectrum. The right level of "scary" in your household will depend on your child, their age, their disposition, and their experiences. Pay attention to your child's reaction and adjust accordingly. But, as Celtic researcher Sharon P. MacLeod says, "Children love to be scared!"

In general, fictitious stories for changing behavior likely work best with toddlers and young children about age six and younger, says psychologist Deena Weisberg at Villanova University, who studies how small children interpret fiction. Toddlers, age two and under, can't really tell the difference between fiction and nonfiction. A year or two later, this ability begins to grow. "I'm hesitant to put an age on it because all kids are so different. But around age three or four, a child may not one hundred percent believe the story." Nevertheless, they may still find the story interesting, scary, and thought-provoking, she says. "For example, I doubt your three-year-old

believes one hundred percent that spiders are going to grow in her dress."
But she took it off, nonetheless.

Around age seven, essentially all kids will know the difference between
fiction and nonfiction, Deena says. But they still like to play along with fan-
tasy for the fun of it. "They may think: 'I know there's not a monster there.
But I get what you're telling me,'" she says. And even if they don't take the
bait, the story may open up a new way to discuss problematic behavior. I
have found that many older kids, around age seven or eight, don't believe
the monster stories, but they have a strong desire to talk about the stories
and want me to "confirm" that they are indeed "not real."

Personally, Rosy loves getting scared—a bit. But I always keep a wink
in my eye when I tell her stories, and I keep a close watch to make sure I
don't scare her too much.

Here are a few popular stories in our house:

1. Sharing Monster. The Sharing Monster lives in a tree outside the
kitchen window. When little kids don't share, he grows bigger and bigger.
Eventually, he could come out, snatch you, and take you up in the tree for
seven whole nights. And do you know what he feeds little kids? Nothing
but cauliflower and brussels sprouts.

2. Yelling Monster. He lives in the ceiling and listens through the light
fixtures. If little kids yell too much or make too many demands, he comes
down through the lights and snatches you away. And just to be clear, the
yelling monster means serious business early in the morning.

3. Shoe Monster. She lives in the heating duct and makes sure that kids
get their shoes on in the morning—quickly—or else she'll take you down
into the vent. To make the Shoe Monster really come to life, sometimes my
husband turns on the heat just when it's time to leave the house. The sound
in the duct gets Rosy to put those shoes on lightning fast.

4. Jimmy-Jammy Monster. Matt came up with this one, and it has been
super helpful for reducing conflict around bedtime.

The other night, around 9:30 p.m., Rosy wasn't even close to settling
down for bed. She was doing a whole bunch of jimmy-jammin'—that is,

jumping on the bed, waving her arms and legs, and making a whole lot of noise. "Come on now, we need to calm down," I repeated over and over. But she just laughed at me!

Then Matt swooped in to save the day. He jumped up from the chair, pointed out the window, and said, with his eyes wide, "There's the Jimmy-Jammy Monster. I see him at the window."

Rosy ran over to Matt, grabbed on to his legs, and said, "Where? Where is he?" Then I whispered, very calmly: "He's out the window, and if we move too quickly or talk too loudly, he will come and take us away. I don't want that." Then I took her hand and led her into the bed. We lay there together and had a very quiet discussion about the Jimmy-Jammy Monster—what he looks like, where he lives, and where he takes kids who jimmy-jammy at night.

She fell right to sleep.

Now every night when we go to bed, I remind Rosy of the Jimmy-Jammy Monster. I talk very quietly, move slowly, and tell her that I really don't want him to come. And remarkably, months after the Jimmy-Jammy Monster first appeared near our home, he still proves quite effective at settling her down.

Tools for Sculpting Behavior: Dramas

Our last tool will help us to lighten our approach to discipline, while also giving us some surprising insights into why kids often do exactly the opposite of what we expect or ask them to do.

Are you a baby?

To learn about this tool, we'll fly out of Kugaaruk and go east about six hundred miles to a giant island called Baffin, right across from Greenland. About the size of California, Baffin Island is drenched in natural beauty. Glacier-carved valleys and rivers slice through six-thousand-foot snow-capped mountains. Massive ice walls, taller than the Empire State Building, overlook sapphire-blue seas, teaming with beluga, narwhals, walruses, and seals (along with the polar bears hunting them).

Baffin Island is the base for a growing movement in the Arctic to preserve and nourish the practice of traditional Inuit parenting. Over the past century, intense colonization has damaged this knowledge, elders told me.

So the community works hard to train new parents and caretakers in these ancient skills.

In early December, I travel to the largest town on Baffin Island, called Iqaluit, to meet Myna Ishulutak, one of the women at the forefront of this movement. She agrees to meet me for dinner at a restaurant that's across town from my Airbnb. I arrive early and wait for her at the bar. Outside, the temperature is a bone-chilling minus twenty-seven degrees Fahrenheit. The sun has been down since about two p.m. Tiny flecks of snow swirl in the air, coating the street with pink and blue glitter. Inside, the restaurant is warm and cozy, and the scent of fresh fish frying back in the kitchen carries to me where I sit.

Myna is late. Fifteen minutes go by with no sign of her, here or on my phone. I worry that she might have changed her mind about talking to me. I can understand her hesitation. Western culture, my culture, has mistreated Inuit, her culture, over the past centuries, continuing into recent decades. In the 1960s, the Canadian government forced or coerced many Inuit families to give up their traditional nomadic lifestyle and settle in permanent towns. Here on Baffin Island, some Canadian officials even shot sled dogs so that families couldn't hunt or track animals. Families starved. Many died of diseases. All this to say, if I were Myna, I probably wouldn't want to talk to me.

Nevertheless, Myna keeps her word. About five minutes later, she walks through the doors of the restaurant. In an instant, the whole energy in the room shifts, like somebody turned on the lights—and turned up the music. Wearing a bright blue parka and white fur boots, Myna looks regal. "They're caribou," she says, showing me her boots. Myna has a heart-shaped face with a broad, full smile. And when she laughs, it sounds like a power chord in a rock anthem. It makes you think anything is possible.

We sit down in a booth and start talking about her work. Myna is incredibly busy as a movie producer, an Inuktitut language teacher, a mother of two grown sons—and about a decade ago, she helped to develop a parenting class at the Nunavut Arctic College, which continues to be taught to this day. The class trains day care and preschool teachers on traditional Inuit parenting techniques—the same techniques Myna's parents used with her when she was a little girl, growing up "out on the land," as she says.

Myna was born and raised in a hunting camp, in a community of about sixty other people. They lived along the coast of Baffin Island. "We lived in a sod house. And when we woke up in the morning, everything would be frozen until my mother lit the oil lamp," she says. She remembers her grandfather telling her stories at night to help her go to sleep. "We didn't have books. So adults would tell us legends at night, especially my grandfather. He was a leader in our camp. I didn't want to fall asleep because I used to really enjoy his stories."

Myna's family ate only what the animals provided—"seals, caribou, fish, and sometimes polar bear meat," she says. "And we picked berries in the fall.

"I remember the first time I tried chocolate. Oh, it was so sweet! So sweet," she says, shaking her head. "We didn't have foods with so much sugar in them.

"I miss living on the land so much," she tells me, and then lets out a big "Hmm." The memories fill her face with melancholy.

When Myna was about twelve or thirteen, her family moved out of the hunting camp and settled in a town so her grandfather could access medical care. "It was very shocking to me to live in a town," she says quietly. "It was very hard for me to adjust."

Today Myna lives in the bustling city of Iqaluit, which has a population of nearly eight thousand people.

Given her childhood and current work, I'm curious what she thinks about the late anthropologist Jean Briggs and the parenting she describes in her book *Never in Anger*.

Myna pauses and then chuckles nervously. I worry that I've offended her. Then she reaches into her purse and brings out a book. I instantly recognize the cover: a black-and-white photo of a grandma snuggling her nose next to a little girl's face. It's the book Jean wrote, titled *Inuit Morality Play*. And it describes the anthropologist's second major trip to the Arctic, when she studies the life of a three-year-old girl, dubbed Chubby Maata.

Myna pats the cover and says, to my utmost surprise, "This book is about me and my family. I am Chubby Maata."

———————————

In the early 1970s, when Myna was just turning three, her family welcomed Jean into their home for six months. Her parents allowed Jean to study the intimate details of Myna's day-to-day life. What happens when Myna hits her mom? What happens when a new baby sister arrives? When Myna has a tantrum, bosses her mother around, or acts ungrateful? How did Myna's family transform her from a demanding, bossy toddler who strikes out at her baby sister into a kind, gracious—and calm—six-year-old?

Over and over again, Myna's mom, dad, and grandparents executed one key parenting tool, which aimed to increase the child's executive function. Jean called the tool "dramas." Here's how they work. When a child acts in anger—say, she hits someone or attacks a sibling—the parent may say something like "Ow! That hurts," or "Ow, you're hurting your brother," to show the consequences of the child's action. But there's no yelling, no punishments.

OW!
That hurts!

Instead, the parent waits. Then in a peaceful, calm moment, the parent stages a reenactment of what happened when the child misbehaved. Typically the performance starts with a question, tempting the child to do something she knows she shouldn't. For example, if the child hits others, the mom may start a drama by asking, "Why don't you hit me?"

Then the child has to think: "What should I do?" If the child takes the bait and hits the mom, the mom doesn't scold or yell, but she performs a reenactment of what happened, using a slightly playful, fun tone. She acts out the consequences. "Ow! That hurts!" she might exclaim.

The mom continues to emphasize the consequences by asking follow-up questions to the child. For example: "Don't you like me?" or "Are you a baby?" These questions continue to trigger thought. They also link the desired behavior with maturity and the undesirable behavior with infancy. The questions convey the idea that hitting hurts people's feelings, and "big kids" wouldn't hit. And the mom asks all the questions with a hint of playfulness.

A parent will stage these dramas for whatever problematic behavior or transition a young child might be going through, Jean Briggs writes. For example, if a toddler has problems sharing with a sibling, a dad may stage a "sharing drama" by tempting the child to be greedy. "Don't share your food with your brother," the dad might say one afternoon to the child while they're eating. Then if the child goes ahead and doesn't share, the dad acts out the consequences. "You don't like your brother? Poor thing, he's hungry."

The parent repeats the drama, from time to time, until the child stops falling for the traps. When the child acts properly, the parent may praise the behavior with a simple "Look how generous Chubby Maata is," Jean documents.

And so that snowy night on Baffin Island, sitting in a booth across from Myna (aka Chubby Maata), I feel like I have a remarkable opportunity. I have the opportunity to understand Jean's work—and this incredible parenting technique—at a deeper level. So I ask Myna about her relationship with the late anthropologist.

"She felt like family to us," Myna says. "We loved her."

Throughout the decades, Myna and Jean stayed close, all the way up until Jean's death in 2016. Jean regularly visited Myna on Baffin Island and Myna visited Jean in Newfoundland. "She will always be special to me," Myna says solemnly.

On occasion, Jean would read her book out loud in Inuktitut to Myna's family, recounting the dramas and the time she spent with them "out on the land." Myna says she doesn't remember much that Jean documents in the book. "I was just too young," she says.

But Myna does believe dramas are a powerful tool for helping children regulate their emotions. They teach a child to keep their cool and not to be provoked so easily, she says. "They teach you to be strong emotionally, to not take everything so seriously or to be scared of teasing."

The dramas do that in two ways:

1. Practice proper behavior.

Dramas give kids a chance to do something that, in Western culture, they don't often get the opportunity to do: practice fixing their mistakes. While taking part in a drama, kids can practice controlling their anger. Practice being kind to a sibling. Practice sharing with a friend. Practice not hitting Mama. Practice. Practice. (Remember, the first ingredient to teaching a skill or value? Practice.)

If you practice feeling awe or gratitude when you're not angry, you'll have a better chance of managing your anger in those hot-button moments.

In these dramas, children get to try out different responses to charged situations. Since their parent is relaxed and slightly playful, the child doesn't need to fear making a mistake. The child can act out the consequences of poor behavior in a moment when they feel calm, not upset. So they're more receptive to learning and thinking.

Practice is especially important when kids are learning how to control anger, says neuroscientist Lisa Feldman Barrett. Because once anger has already erupted, squelching it is not easy for anyone, children or adults.

"There's a big misconception that you can easily stop yourself when you're already mad," Lisa says. "But when you try to control your emotions in the moment and you want to change the feeling, that's a really hard thing to do."

But if you practice feeling awe or gratitude when you're not angry, you'll have a better chance of accessing those emotions when you start to feel angry managing your anger in those hot-button moments. "That practice is essentially helping to rewire your brain to be able to make a different emotion [besides anger] much more easily," she says.

For children, the dramas give them the chance to flex and strengthen self-control circuitry in their brains. Instead of getting angry, children learn to think. Instead of reacting, children learn to maintain their equilibrium.

2. Turn discipline into play.

Play makes a powerful parenting tool for changing behavior, one that many parents overlook, says psychologist Laura Markham. "Play is how children learn about the world. Play is their work."

Children use play to recover from hard experiences throughout the day and "emotional upheavals," says psychologist Larry Cohen. After an argument with a parent, play helps to release tension and move on. The air clears, the atmosphere lightens, and the parent and child are released from their locked-in cycle of anger and misbehavior.

"A big source of problems is this tension between a child and parent," Larry says. And the usual responses to misbehavior, such as lecturing, reasoning, or yelling—even in their mildest forms—build up tension. "Play reduces the tension. That's why I love it."

When a child has a tough time with a particular task, such as getting out of bed in the morning, doing their homework, or sharing with a sibling, Larry recommends a technique that's remarkably similar to the dramas. "I tell parents to bring the problem into the play zone," Larry says. The play zone makes a great tool for children of all ages, from toddlers to teens. (We'll see how it works in the "Try It" section.) Once the tension is released through play, the problematic behavior often fades away on its own, Larry notes.

Raising Rosy

After meeting Myna, I start to see Rosy's misbehavior in a different light. I realize that many times when I think she is "pushing boundaries" (or my buttons), she is actually trying to practice the proper behavior. She keeps repeating the wrong behavior over and over again, until she finally makes the right decision.

This realization really crystalizes one evening while we walk the dog through our neighborhood. Rosy rides her red tricycle on the sidewalk, no easy feat on the San Francisco hills. As I've mentioned, our neighborhood has a few terrifying intersections, including Market Street, with four lanes of cars going about thirty miles per hour. This evening, Rosy rides like a daredevil, and when we're about a block from Market Street, she zooms off, way ahead of me, straight for the busy road. My heart literally skips a beat! I want to scream, "Wait, Rosy! Wait for us." But before I can say anything, Rosy runs the tricycle right off the curb into the road.

Thank goodness she stops quickly and ends up only a few inches into the road. Cars whiz by her only a few feet away. *Phew*, I think, *she's safe*. But still, what on earth was she doing?

I really want to scold her. I want to pull her off the tricycle and carry her back home. That's my parental duty, right? But I don't. Instead, I think about Chubby Maata and what Myna's mom might do in this situation. I think how children want—and even *need*—to practice the proper behavior. *Maybe she is practicing how to stop at this dangerous intersection*, I think. So I stay calm and tell her the consequences, nonchalantly (Everyday Tool #2): "You're going to get hit by a car if you ride in the road." Then I parent with action instead of words (Everyday Tool #5). I go and stand between her and the traffic so I can stop her if she tries to go farther.

Then Rosy does something really interesting. She takes the tricycle and repeats the transgression. She walks up the hill a bit, hops on the tricycle, and rides it straight off the curb. Again, she stops only a few inches into the road. She repeats this maneuver about three more times. Then, finally, on the fourth try, success! She stops the bike *before* the curb. She has learned the proper behavior.

"Okay, Mama, let's go home," she says as she heads back up the hill to our house. *Hmm*, I think. *Toddlers are insane.*

Try It 7: Discipline Through Dramas

This chapter is really about converting problems into play and discipline into practice. And there are a cornucopia of ways to do that. No matter the route you go, keep two rules in mind:

1. Make sure neither you nor the child feels upset, angry, or emotionally charged when you work with these tools. Play happens when everyone is relaxed and peaceful.
2. Keep the tone fun and light. Try to keep a smile on your face or a wink in your eye. This is not the time for lessons or lectures. This is the time for kids to feel safe to misbehave and try out new skills, without any worry of upsetting parents.

Dip Your Toe

• **Put on a puppet show.** The next time your child struggles with a task or some facet of emotional control, try reenacting the problem with a puppet show. Take two stuffed animals—or even a pair of socks—and make them into characters who aren't related to you and your child. For example, with Rosy I often use Mango (our dog) as one character and Louis (the neighbor's dog) as the second character. This approach will help ensure the child feels relaxed and not like they're being disciplined or lectured. Then set the scene, act out the problematic activity, and then act out the consequences of that behavior.

Sometimes Rosy and I will even reenact scenes with Legos or Halloween candy playing characters. The idea is to help the child revisit a past problem in a stress-free, or even fun, way. Then she can think about the experience in a new, rational way while strengthening her self-control.

You can get the child involved in the show by asking them questions

("Is Mango a baby when she hits Louis?" "Did that hurt Louis's feelings?"), having them play one of the characters, or having them do the whole show. See what the child naturally does and build off it. If the child has older siblings, you might ask them to play a character, too.

• **Bring the problem to the play zone.** Earlier I mentioned psychologist Larry Cohen's concept of a play zone, a technique which he advises using with children of all ages, even teenagers. To see how it works, let's look at a common problem: getting a child to calm down at bedtime. To break the cycle of tension around bedtime, Larry says, wait for a calm, peaceful moment during the day (*not* at bedtime) and say something like this to the child: "Hey, Rosy, I've noticed there's been a lot of arguing around bedtime. Let's play a game about that."

Then you can just wait and see if the child already has a game in mind and let her explain it. If she doesn't, you can simply ask, "Who do you want to be in the play? Do you want to be the mom and I'll be Rosy?"

Then you and the child act out, in a lighthearted way, what happens when she won't go to bed and you get angry or upset. "Don't be afraid to be outrageous and really exaggerate the bad behavior and its repercussions," Larry says. "The goal is to laugh, have fun, and release tension that's built up around the problem. So the more outrageous the better."

Some parents may worry about modeling the wrong behavior. But children can tell the difference between play and real life, Larry says. "During this type of play, the child isn't going to remember the 'modeling.' But instead, she will remember the human connection, the creativity, and tension release."

Jump In

• **Stage a drama.** To see how dramas can work, let's look at a chronic problem in our house: hitting. When Rosy hits me now, no matter how hard she slaps, I don't get angry anymore. I try with all my heart to ignore it. Just completely ignore it. And if I can't, I say only "Ow, that hurt me" in the calmest way possible (just like Sally did when Caleb scratched her face).

Then later, when we are both calm and relaxed, I put on little hitting dramas. I go to Rosy and ask her to hit me. If she takes the bait, I act out the consequences again. I say in a dramatic way, "Ooh, that hurts! Goodness that hurts!" to show her that hitting causes pain, physically and emotionally.

Don't you
like me?

I can see the little gears in her brain churning. "Wait! Am I hurting Mom's feelings?" she seems to think. (And I can see that Rosy doesn't mean to push my buttons. She cares about my feelings. She just didn't realize how much the hitting hurt!)

Then I ask her this one question, with an exaggerated sense of pain and suffering: "Don't you like me?" Often she will respond with something supersweet and wonderful like "No, I love you, Mama."

To help her further understand the consequences of hitting, I connect the misbehavior to immaturity. The conversation typically goes something like this:

Me: "Are you a baby?"
Rosy: "No, Mama, I'm a big girl."
Me: "Do big girls hit?"
Rosy: "No, Mama."*

Oftentimes, Rosy wants to reverse roles and play the mama next. She'll say something like "Hit me, Mama!" I will gently tap her on the butt or push her shoulder a bit. Then she'll act out the consequence of the hit, very dramatically. She'll scream, run away, or say with a maudlin tone, "Don't you like me?" By the end of the second drama, we are both laughing.

After a month or so of staging the dramas, Rosy's hitting noticeably

---

* Associating unwanted behaviors with being a baby works incredibly powerfully on young children, who desperately want to be big girls or big boys. When our dentist told us to throw out Rosy's pacifier, the idea scared me; she had used it for three years. So I encouraged Rosy to stop using the pacifier by connecting it to infancy. Every time she wanted the pacifier, I just said, "Oh, because you're a baby." After three days, she walked over to me, handed me the pacifier, and said, "I don't need this. I'm a big girl."

declined, in both intensity and frequency. Sometimes she would even stop mid-swing, or intentionally miss my arms or legs.

But I have to say, the hitting didn't stop completely until I stopped caring so much about it. Once I learned to brush off a pinch on the arm—or even a slap on the face—as nothing more than a "little baby" losing control of her emotions, Rosy didn't see a need to "practice" this misbehavior anymore. And what do you know? I didn't need to practice controlling my own anger (as much), either.

Summary for Chapters 11 and 12:
Sculpt Behavior with Stories and Dramas

Ideas to Remember

➤ When a child feels upset, they will have a hard time listening and learning.

➤ When a child feels relaxed and safe from punishment, they are open to learning new rules and fixing mistakes.

➤ If the child isn't cooperating over an issue (e.g., doing their homework), there's likely tension between the parent and child over the issue. Once this tension resolves, through play or a story, a child will cooperate and behave better.

➤ Children love to learn through oral stories, especially when these stories include characters, experiences, and objects from their real lives. They have a natural inclination to learn this way. For example, children love to:

- Hear about their family's history and their parents' childhoods.
- Imagine objects coming to life and making mistakes.
- Imagine ghosts, monsters, fairies, and other supernatural creatures living around them and helping them learn proper behavior.

➤ Children love to learn through play. It's how they release tension and practice proper behavior. Children love to reenact problematic behavior or mistakes and watch the consequences unfold in a fun, low-stress environment (without fear of punishment).

Tips and Tools

Instead of using lectures and adult logic to change a child's behavior or teach them a value, wait for a calm, relaxed moment and try one of these tools:

- ➤ **Tell a story from your childhood.** Explain how you and your parents handled a mistake, problem, or misbehavior. Were you punished? How did you react?
- ➤ **Put on a puppet show.** Get a stuffed animal or a pair of socks to act out the consequences of the child's behavior and how you would like them to behave. Have them play one of the characters in the show.
- ➤ **Bring the problem into the play zone.** Tell the child, "I noticed we've been arguing a lot about homework [or whatever problem you have]. Let's play a game about it. Who do you want to play? Me or you?" Then reenact in a fun way what happens during the argument. Don't be afraid to exaggerate and act outrageous. The goal is to laugh and release tension built up over the issue.
- ➤ **Use a monster story.** Create a monster that hides out near your house. Tell the child the monster is watching and if the child misbehaves in a particular way, the monster will come and take them away (for only a few days).
- ➤ **Bring an inanimate object to life.** Have a stuffed animal, piece of clothing, or other inanimate object help you coax a child to complete a task. Have the object do the task itself (e.g., brush a stuffed animal's teeth) or have the object ask the child to do a task (e.g., have a toothbrush ask the child to brush their teeth).

Hadzabe Health

T
E
Autonomy
M

CHAPTER 13

How Did Our Ancient Ancestors Parent?

The hunt begins with a whistle. Wearing gray pin-striped shorts and a baboon skin across his chest, Thaa hops up from the fire, grabs his bow and arrow, and begins to whistle. Long, high-pitched whistles. *Fwheeeoo. Fwheeeoo.*

A dozen dogs run toward us, coming from every direction. Tan dogs, black dogs, white dogs. Even one with fur that reminds me of herringbone. The size of foxes, the dogs are all skinny, their ribs bulging from their flanks. And they seem eager to help.

Thaa whistles one more time. *Fwheeeoo.* A few more dogs rush up the trail from below us. Two of Thaa's friends rise from the fire and join him. Each man has a bow and a few arrows in their hands. All three are tall, slender, and fit as marathoners. Before I even realize what's going on, they've nearly disappeared into the bush. The dogs follow right behind, with their noses pointing at the earth and their tails pointing to the sky.

"Let's go!" I shout to Rosy. I kneel down to the ground and wait for Rosy to wrap her feet around my waist. A piggyback ride is the only way we'll keep up.

This dawn has found us on the side of a mountain, a few thousand feet up. The sun has yet to emerge, laying tucked behind another mountain to our east, but a warm yellow glow has begun to spill across the savanna below us.

We are just south of the equator, about a hundred miles from the plains of the Serengeti, and it's wintertime in Tanzania. The earth is dry and dusty. Pink and white boulders dot the hillside. Tree branches, bare and gray, twist up to the sky like long, skinny witches' fingers. Only the acacia trees have managed to hold on to some leaves, all clustered at their top branches. It makes them look like Frenchmen, wearing green berets.

Rosy and I catch up with Thaa and his friends. Our interpreter, David Mark Makia, has also come along with them, and all four men have stopped to study something on the ground. Footprints in the sand. This morning, the men hope to track down baboons. But they will go after anything they spot—a bushpig, dik-dik, civet cat, you name it. Hunting is the primary way Thaa provides for his family.

In his forties, Thaa is a father of seven kids. His age shows in the three deep crevices of his forehead, which deepen as he looks across the savanna. On his head, he wears a visor with a puff of baboon fur in the front. Thaa is a man of few words. When he talks, I can barely hear him. He chooses to *show* his feelings through actions. When Rosy and I first arrived at the

Hadzabe camp, Thaa helped us find a place to set up a tent, on the hillside about fifty feet from his family's hut. As I wrestled with the green canvas tent, Thaa bent over and carefully removed all the rocks and pebbles from the ground, ensuring we'd have a smooth surface to sleep on.

Thaa and his friends are some of the best hunters in the world. The men hunt almost exclusively with bows and arrows, which they make by hand from the branches of a common tree. To call them "sharpshooters" would be an understatement. All three men could pluck a small bird from a tree, thirty feet up in the air. They have hyper-encyclopedic knowledge of animals in the savanna: what they eat, how they move, where they like to hide, what prints they leave in the sand.

Today, the men decide the tracks aren't worth following. They start moving again, deeper into the bush. Technically, they are "walking," not running. But the word that comes to mind, as I watch them, is "gliding"; their movement is so effortless and smooth. And their pace is fast. I have to jog—with Rosy on my back—just to keep up.

It isn't long before my heart is pounding. My lungs strain for air. We hop over the roots of baobab trees as thick as telephone poles. We scramble over boulders. We duck under tree limbs, coated in thorns the length of my index finger. Every now and then, one of these giant thorns catches my sweater, and I have to stop and wrestle myself free.

"Rosy, I don't think we're going to be able to keep up," I say over my shoulder. The four men have pulled so far ahead of us, I can no longer see them.

Then they come into view, waiting in the distance, and we run to meet them. Everyone is silent. Even the dogs stop moving.

Thaa has his bow in his hands. He takes an arrow and places it between two fingers, aiming at the top of a tree. The wind rustles the leaves. He draws the bow and releases it. The arrow moves so quickly into the tree that I can't trace its flight. We hold our breath. Did he hit it? Then a dove flies from the tree above our heads. He missed.

Immediately the men take off again.

When Thaa was about two years old, his father gave him a small bow and arrow. He carried that bow everywhere he went. By the time he was

Rosy's age, he had already begun shooting mice, birds, and small reptiles near his home. For more than a decade he practiced every day, target shooting with friends. Then as a young teenager, he started joining older men on short hunts. By his twenties, he could track down a kudu or a giraffe.

Looking across the savanna, I find it hard to believe that Thaa and his family live almost entirely off this land. To my eyes, it looks dry, crackly, barren. But he and his wife manage to obtain all their family's needs— food, water, tools, clothes, and medicines—solely from the plants and animals found here. And they do it quite easily. Their way of life doesn't require large stores of water to feed livestock or expensive fertilizer to coax crops to grow. When an arrow breaks or gets lost in the bush, Thaa and his friends can simply make another one from the branches of a common tree.

Thaa is Hadzabe, a group of hunter-gatherers in Tanzania. No one knows exactly how old the Hadzabe culture is, but ancient stone tools and rock paintings suggest that Thaa's ancestors have hunted on this savanna for thousands of years, perhaps tens of thousands. And many scientists believe that the Hadzabe may be one of the oldest cultures on earth.

All humans are descended from hunter-gatherers in Africa. From Thaa here in Tanzania to Maria in the Yucatán, from my grandfather in Virginia to my husband's ancestors in Macedonia, all humans share that history. We all evolved, over a few million years, from a troop of peculiar humanlike apes in Africa, who survived by picking berries, digging for wild tubers, scavenging meat leftover from bigger predators, and—eventually— hunting and fishing.

No one knows for sure how our ancestors raised their children. We have no records of how a Paleolithic mom got kids to clean up after a meal, or how a Stone Age dad coaxed his toddler to sleep at night. We haven't uncovered cave paintings of bedtime routines or petroglyphs offering tips for toddler tantrums.

But we can make educated guesses about some aspects of prehistoric parenting—about how our little humans adapted to be disciplined, motivated, and loved. And we can make those guesses by learning about the extraordinarily diverse cultures that exist on every habitable continent on earth. We can identify which parenting practices persist across the vast majority of these cultures—practices that have stood the test of time or cropped up over and over again throughout human history. And we can pay particular attention to cultures that still hunt and forage for part of their livings, since they hold a unique position in human history.

Our species, *Homo sapiens*, has been on earth for (very) roughly two hundred thousand years. And we spent the vast majority of that time, about 95 percent or so, as hunter-gatherers. First, we foraged in Africa (including the region where Rosy and I are scrambling to keep up with Thaa as he hunts); and eventually, we spread to every habitable continent on earth. About twelve thousand years ago, some of us began to cultivate crops and raise livestock for our livelihoods. Then, less than two centuries ago, some of us ratcheted up the farming and ranching to such extraordinary levels that we now require gas-powered tractors, power saws, and robots to produce our daily calories.

So if we want to understand our species' past, we essentially have two tools at hand: bones left in the ground by ancient people and the study of modern-day hunter-gatherer communities. The latter, as I have mentioned, are not "living fossils" or "relics from the past." They do not show us how humans lived thousands of years ago. Instead, they offer a look at how humans can thrive as hunter-gatherers. On top of that, they're living in a way that's much closer to our species' past than, say, my life in San Francisco, and they've held on to many ancient parenting traditions and techniques that Western culture has lost. Put simply, many hunter-gatherer communities have an enormous amount to teach Western moms and dads.

———

When journalists write about hunter-gatherers, like the Hadzabe, they often use words such as "rare" and "last." But those adjectives give the wrong impression. First off, there are likely millions of hunter-gatherers currently living around the world. In 2000, anthropologists estimated that the population numbered around 5 million. These communities live across a huge swath of the Earth. They hunt monitor lizards across Western Australia. They track caribou across the Arctic tundra. And in India, where nearly a million hunter-gatherers live, they collect highly valued medicinal plants and wild honey.

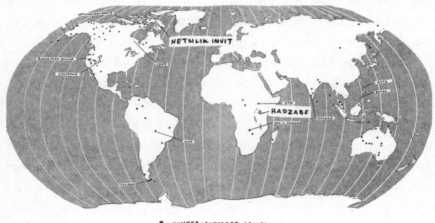

In 1995, archaeologist Robert Kelly compiled a summary of Western knowledge of foraging societies worldwide. The resulting book, called *The Lifeways of Hunter-Gatherers*, describes scores of cultures worldwide, including more than a dozen in what we now call the United States. Not that long ago, hunter-gatherers managed large areas of North America, from the Shoshone and Kiowa people in the Rocky Mountains to the Cree in the Midwest.

In fact, right now, as I write these words, I sit on a peninsula that, some two hundred years ago, belonged to a group of highly skilled hunter-gatherers called the Ramaytush Ohlone. They fished in the bay, foraged for acorns in oak forests, and collected mussels along the coast. These were the original people in San Francisco. Then Spanish missionaries arrived in the late 1700s, and almost every family died from disease or hunger.

Robert's book aptly illustrates not only how "common" hunter-gatherer cultures are, but also how remarkably diverse they are now, were in the past, and will be in the future. Some hunter-gatherer groups rely largely on hunting or fishing; some on foraging. Some live in large, settled groups; others in small, nomadic camps. Many have moral systems based on equality for all people; others, not so much. Some cultures tend to have lots of babies with big families; some tend to be more like me and Matt—one or two and done. And essentially all hunter-gatherer cultures do *more* than hunt, gather, and fish for a living. "The reader should know that many of these 'hunter-gatherers' grow some of their own food, trade with agriculturalists for produce or participate in cash economies," Robert writes. "Would the real hunter-gatherer please stand up!"

On top of that, none of these cultures are "undisturbed," "pristine," or "cut off" from the rest of the world. Every culture communicates and trades with other cultures, nearby and even far away. Every culture teaches and learns from other cultures. Every culture is interconnected and linked to others.

The Hadzabe in northern Tanzania are no different. For thousands of years, the Hadzabe have lived in a vast savanna woodland, about the size of Rhode Island, surrounding a massive saltwater lake. Throughout that entire time, they have hunted wild animals, including large ones (giraffes, hippopotamuses, eland) and small ones (rabbits, wild cats, small antelope, squirrels, mice). They have snatched fresh meat away from feasting lions ("easy food"), collected honey from trees (the "gold in life"), dug for yam-shaped tubers, and snacked on the tart, crunchy fruit of baobab trees. They have lived in dome-shaped huts made of branches and grasses, which women can easily build in about two hours.

In other words, the Hadzabe have lived similar to the way their ancestors have lived for thousands of years, not because the people have been isolated or not exposed to other ways of living, but because the people believe their way of living is optimal for the harsh environment in which they live. And it's true: Hadzabe have been quite successful for a long, long time. Why fix what's not broken?

The Hadzabe have been so successful, in large part, because of their long-standing relationship with the land. Westerners would call it "sustainable." Families work together with the plants and animals around them so that they all can coexist and thrive across millennia. It's a relationship based on minimal interference and respect, instead of control and transformation, as Westerners tend to practice.* The plant ecologist Robin Wall Kimmerer calls this approach to life the "gift economy." The land gives the Hadzabe families dik-diks, baboons, and tubers and in return for these gifts, the Hadzabe have a responsibility to the land—to take care of it and preserve it. The relationship is one of reciprocity. It's bidirectional.

In her brilliant book *Braiding Sweetgrass*, Robin writes:

> *In the gift economy, gifts are not free. The essence of the gift is that it creates a set of relationships. The currency of a gift economy is, at its root, reciprocity. . . . In a gift economy property has a "bundle of responsibilities" attached.*

Put another way, the giving flows in both directions, from land to people and back to the land. And so do the responsibilities. For every gift the land gives the people, the people are expected to give some of the gift back to the land.

During the short time I spend with the Hadzabe families, I can see the gift economy everywhere—in how they treat the animals they hunted, how they share every single plant they foraged, how they waste basically no food, and how they generate essentially no trash. I also see the gift economy in their relationship with their children. The parents don't aim to transform the children into some ideal, as fast as possible, through control and domination. Rather, they focus on giving to each other. The parent continually gives the child gifts of love, companionship, and food, and in return, the parent expects a "bundle of responsibilities." We coexist together, with minimal interference and mutual respect; and through reciprocity, we love and connect. In my clumsy Western way, I created a motto for this relationship style: You go about your business and I'll go about mine, and we'll always look for ways to help each other as much as possible.

This way of treating—and thinking about—children isn't unique

---

* The Western relationship with land is one of domination. People transform the land and use up its resources at near breakneck speed, leaving little for future generations. Gifts flow in one direction: the people take, control, and change the land and animals.

to the Hadzabe. You can find a similar style across many, many hunter-gatherer communities and other indigenous cultures. And that commonality makes this parenting approach so extraordinary and so important: despite the vast diversity that exists among hunter-gatherer cultures, you can still trace a common way of raising and interacting with children—a way that has likely survived thousands, perhaps tens of thousands of years (or even more). This way, as we'll learn, fits children's needs—mentally and physically—like a hand fits a perfectly tailored glove. Or even better, like a Nejire kumi tsugi Japanese wood joint. It's beautiful.

Back at the hunt in Tanzania, I have my first lesson in this beautiful way of parenting. Rosy and I are trailing a quarter of a mile behind Thaa and his friends, and I don't see how we can possibly catch up, especially with Rosy still riding on my back. I begin to worry that we might get lost in the bush. Rosy is almost in tears. "Mama, I'm not comfortable. Ow! Ow! I want to walk," she cries.

Just let her go. She can go in front and you can follow behind her. She'll be okay.

—DAVID MARK MAKIA

"Okay. Hop off," I say as I kneel down. "Take my hand."

I grab Rosy's wrist, and we rush to catch up with the guys. I hold her tight and help her scramble over the rocks. I push her head down, under spiky branches. "Watch the thorns!" I yell several times. I keep pulling on her arm to get her to go faster. At one point, I feel like I'm literally dragging her across the bush, like a reluctant dog on a leash.

She begins to cry, and I think we should just give up and go back to camp. I call up to the interpreter David to come back and help us. He has two daughters of his own, including a four-year-old girl. Right away, David spots my parenting problem. And without hesitation, he gives me a piece of parenting advice that encapsulates so much of what the dads and moms teach me on our trip here, so much of what the gifting style of parenting is all about.

"Let go of her hand. Just let her go," David says with a hint of exasperation in his voice. "She can go in front and you can follow behind her. She'll be okay."

"Really? You think so?" I ask doubtfully.

"Yes, she'll be fine," he says.

"Okay . . . But, I don't think . . ." Before I can finish my sentence, Rosy runs off, scrambling over the boulders like a baby baboon.

Turns out, David is spot-on about Rosy. Once I "let her go," she actually does a great job on the hunt, walking on and off for three hours.

In that moment, I see firsthand what a little autonomy can do for a small child—and their relationship with their mother.

CHAPTER 14

The Most Confident Kids in the World

On the third day in Tanzania, I meet a little girl who shows me just how self-sufficient and kind children can be, even when they're still quite young. She also makes me wonder if I interfere way too much with Rosy—and in the process, make her more anxious and bossy.

By this point, Rosy and I have been camping near the Hadzabe families for a few days. And we already have a sense of the daily rhythm of life here, a gentle tempo, one set largely by two elements: fire and friendship.

Every day begins the same. Right before dawn, when the sky is a milky gray filled with lingering stars, Thaa walks by our tent, climbs a nearby tree, and chops down a log about the size of my body. He brings the wood over to a circle of stones and starts the morning fire.

The dawn air is downright cold. You can almost see your breath. And Rosy and I are tempted to stay snuggly warm under our sleeping bags. But a few minutes later, several other men join Thaa around the fire. Their soft chatter lures me and Rosy out of our tent. "Come on, Rosy," I say, pushing the sleeping bag off of us. "Let's go see what they're talking about." I help

Rosy put on a sweater, and we head out to the fire circle, under one of the most majestic trees I've ever seen.

Every morning, for about an hour, the fathers sit under a massive, thousand-year-old baobab tree. About the size of a two-story townhouse, the ancient tree is a marvel of nature. It looks like a giant pillar candle stuck on the hillside. Its smooth maroon bark seems to drip down, like hot melting wax. At its top, green velvety pods dangle from outstretched arms, offering a gracious gift to the Hadzabe. Packed with vitamins and fat, baobab fruit and seeds give families a big portion of their needed calories, year-round—more than any other single plant or animal.

I love this tree. Sitting under it, with the fire's warmth on my face and fingers, I feel like the tree is almost hugging me. Rosy sits next to me, bundled under a red plaid blanket and munching on a yellow muffin that I stashed away from our flight here. One of the young men in the group, Ima, walks over to the fire with a small furry creature strapped across his back, the bounty of an early-morning hunt. The critter looks like a cross between a raccoon and a house cat. The men work together to skin the animal, butcher it, and then BBQ the chunks over the fire. They all share the meat and throw the scraps to a few eager dogs, also idling near the fire.

From our perch on this mountainside, we have a spectacular view of the valley below, which includes fields of green-onion farms and a sparkling saltwater lake. *What an incredible place to raise a family*, I think. Just being in this environment every morning has to be good for one's mental health. The pace of life also feels great. Throughout the day, moms and dads will stop what they're doing and simply sit together for an hour or sit alone quietly. *Why do I feel the need to talk or do something at every moment?* I wonder.

Then down the hillside, I spot a small figure walking on the trail below us: a little girl. Her head bobs up and down as she climbs over a few boulders in the path. When she comes closer, I can see she's hunched over and carrying something on her back.

With short black hair and delicate facial features, the little girl looks to be about five or six years old. She wears a red fleece jacket, gray flip-flops, and a black-and-white-striped skirt, which perfectly matches the print on Thaa's shorts. A sling, painted with brown and orange flowers, wraps around her shoulders. Inside the sling, a baby about six months old snuggles against her back.

"She's my daughter," Thaa says through David's interpretation. I ask Thaa her name.

"That's Belie. The baby is mine, too," Thaa says, gesturing toward Belie's back. *Ah, she's carrying her baby brother*, I think.

Belie sits down around the fire, between me and her dad. Close up, I realize that I've seen her at other times during the trip. She's been hanging around me and Rosy for the past few days, watching us. She never ventured within five feet of us, but I could tell she was very curious. She couldn't keep her eyes off Rosy.

Today she seems braver, like she wants to talk and learn more about us. I offer her one of the airplane muffins. "Would you like one?" I ask. Belie slowly takes the muffin, looks at it, and then without missing a beat, tears off a piece and gently puts the mushy cake in her little brother's mouth. The baby looks over and smiles at me.

Wow, so generous, I think. Then, over the next five minutes or so, Belie feeds the *entire* muffin to her baby brother, without saving one bite for herself. No one asks her to share. She does it entirely on her own. And this voluntary act of kindness, from such a small human, is so beautiful to me, I almost start crying. Would Rosy have done the same? Would I have done the same at that age—or even now, as an adult?

Little do I know that I'm just at the beginning of what I will learn about kindness and respect while with the Hadzabe.

Just as the Hadzabe's days begin with a fire, they end with one, as well. Every night, right after sundown, Thaa and the other men gather under the baobab tree for more chatter, stories, and songs. Tonight the sky is so black and clear that we can even see the Milky Way, streaking a white, fuzzy brushstroke across the southeast horizon.

One of the young men, in his early twenties, brings over a handmade string instrument made from a gourd (a *zeze*), and begins to teach us a song in the Hadzabe language. The song tells the story of a baboon visiting women in a camp, while the men are away hunting. Hadza is one of the last few languages on earth that uses so-called click sounds, which you can make by banging your tongue on the roof of your mouth in various ways. Hadza contains three distinct clicks, depending on the shape of your mouth and the motion of your tongue. Hadza speakers then modify those three clicks in three other ways, creating nine different sounds, which all sound basically the same to me (like the sound of a horse walking on a road). I can barely say one or two lines of the song, but Rosy seems to have no problem with any of it and sings her little heart out, under the baobab tree.

Then one of the young dads, named Pu//iupu//iu (those "//" are clicks), decides to give me and Rosy Hadza names. Pu//iupu//iu is only in his early twenties, but he's already such an amazing parent. He spends almost every afternoon and many evenings holding and snuggling with his first son, who's only about one. Pu//iupu//iu speaks to the baby softly, nuzzles him, and sings to him for hours around the fire. And the boy loves it! They never seem to get bored of simply sitting and spending time together—no iPad needed.

Pu//iupu//iu points to Rosy and says, "She's Tok'oko" as he bounces his baby boy on his leg.

" 'Tok'oko' is a small, wild cat," he says. "Because she's always running around camp, like a small cat." *And screeching like one, too*, I think. *That's appropriate.*

Then Pu//iupu//iu turns to me and smiles. "You're Hon!o!oko."

"What?" I exclaim, laughing.

"Hon!o!oko," he repeats, over and over again. "Hon!o!oko, Hon!o!oko, Hon!o!oko."

Those two "!"s are two loud popping noises. And then you add a hard, loud "oko" at the end. But in practice, I have no clue how to make those sounds with my mouth and tongue. Every time I try, all the men find it hilarious. Everyone erupts with laughter.

Then a few men start singing again, and soon we're all singing the baboon song over and over again, smiling and nodding heads together. It all feels extraordinarily joyous. I start to see how all you need for an amazing evening is a fire, a few favorite songs, and friends you know like the back of your hands.

Finally, the singing and laughing peters out, and I ask Pu//iupu//iu about the meaning of the name Hon!o!oko.

"It means 'Wait-a-bit,' " Pu//iupu//iu says, smiling and showing me these gleaming white teeth, perfectly straight and aligned.

"Wait-a-bit? Why that?" I ask.

At this point, Pu//iupu//iu and the interpreter, David, start having a long, boisterous conversation about my name, involving a lot of big hand gestures and big facial expressions. Then they all erupt in laughter. A few men even start singing. I get the feeling that I'm the joke.

"Wait-a-bit is the name of acacia trees," David says, smiling. "You know, the trees with big thorns on the branches. They call those trees 'wait-a-bit' because if you get stuck on a thorn, all you need to do is wait-a-bit and you'll get unstuck."

"So I'm named after acacia trees?" I say, feeling pretty good about that. Who doesn't want to be named after one of those beautiful trees?

"Yes," David says, laughing. "Because during the hunt, your sweater kept getting stuck in acacia thorns. So your name is Wait-a-bit. You need to wait-a-bit."

Hmm, I think, *Rosy and I were so far behind during the hunt. How did they know I kept getting stuck? Was somebody watching me and I didn't realize it?*

I almost get the impression the men are trying to teach me something with this name, something more than simply pausing on the hunt.

I smile and laugh, but now I have a new challenge: Why did they name me Wait-a-bit?

––––––––––––

The next morning, Rosy and I wake up a bit late. The sun, already perched above the mountains to our east, quickly warms the cool air. The scent of smoke and campfire surrounds us.

Rosy and I walk down the hill to the family's huts and find a few of the moms getting ready to go foraging for tubers. All of them wear beautiful sarong dresses strapped across their shoulders in an array of primary colors: blue with yellow flowers, red with gold leaves, and a blue-red plaid.

First we sit around a fire, chatting a bit—who needs to rush? The tubers aren't going anywhere. As I soon see, the women can gather all the roots they need in about one to two hours.

Then, with little warning, a few women stand up, dust off their sarong dresses, and head into the bush. I take Rosy's hand and follow behind the ladies. I look over my right shoulder, and guess who I spot, running to catch up with us? Sweet Belie. The baby is no longer on her back. And I don't see her mom with us. *Hmm, interesting*, I think, *she's out here on her own.*

We walk about fifteen minutes, until one of the women, Kwachacha, stops and points to a small hole in the dirt, no bigger than a quarter. "See how the dirt is here?" Kwachacha says as she pulls up her long red skirt and kneels next to the hole. A young mom in her early twenties, Kwachacha has the most elegant posture I've ever seen. From head to toe, her body is straight as an arrow. Turns out, she's also an incredible hunter.

Using a three-foot-long stick, Kwachacha starts digging around the hole. Brown soil flies into the air. Belie watches her with fierce focus. Soon, Kwachacha has dug a trench about two feet long. She stops, gestures with her hands to another woman, then begins digging again, but now in the perpendicular direction, creating an L-shaped trench in the ground. I'm utterly confused. What is Kwachacha doing?

Suddenly a white thread appears at the back of the trench, sticking out of the brown soil. Kwachacha stops digging, pulls on the thread, and a white mouse pops out!

"What!" I scream in utter shock. I expected a tuber, maybe, but not a mouse. "How on earth did you know it was there in the ground?" I ask naively. Catching a mouse underground was one of the most fantastic feats I have ever seen. Kwachacha hands the mouse to a toddler and walks away nonchalantly.

Meanwhile, the rest of the women have moved under a nearby tree, digging for tubers with sharp wooden sticks. Red, potato-like objects pile up next to them. One woman hands me a stick and makes a gesture toward a deep trench in the ground. I take the invitation, kneel down in the soil, and try to mimic their motion. The moms expect everyone to help with every task, even the out-of-shape journalist.

I look around in search of Belie and see that she's taken charge of three toddlers who followed the group from the huts. She fixes one little boy's shoes that have come un-Velcroed. She nuzzles with another toddler to stop him from crying. Then she feeds them lunch. She takes a tuber, peels it, and hands it to the kids. She goes and collects a few baobab pods, picks up a rock about the size of a cantaloupe, holds it over her head, and smashes it onto one of the green velvety pods. Bam! The pod cracks open and reveals chunks of white fruit. Belie hands pieces of the fruit to the toddlers. Then she comes over and hands the rest to me and Rosy. The white nuggets have the consistency of space ice cream and the tartness of 7Up.

Damn, girl, I think. *You are so strong. And so responsible.*

A few days later, Rosy and I meet up with the women again. This time we go to fetch drinking water down by a river. The trip isn't easy. We have to hike about two miles on rocky, steep terrain. Almost all the babies

and toddlers stay home with the older women because they will be a burden. On the way back, the women will carry twenty-five-pound buckets
of water on their heads—no easy task, even without a baby on your back.

Rosy comes along with us, but she's so exhausted from all the exercise
we've had that she spends the majority of the time on my back, whining
and complaining. "Mama, when are we going to be there?" Or "Mama,
how much longer is it?"

Not Belie. She ties an empty water bottle to her back, hands one to Rosy
to carry, too, and then heads off with the women down to the river. Again,
her mom and dad don't come with us. Left on her own, Belie exudes independence and tenacity.

After about an hour of hiking, we see the river gorge below. We drop
down a steep descent, traverse a dry riverbed, and finally, we arrive at the
watering hole. The young women begin to fill up their buckets with fresh
water. Belie and Rosy help out. But five minutes into the task, I notice
Belie breaks away from the group and starts climbing a cliff at the edge of
the river gorge. It's super steep—about a
hundred feet up.

Aha, I think, *finally, she's playing
and goofing off. She's doing something
just for fun.*

But oh no!

At the top of the cliff is a baobab tree.
Belie walks over to the tree and begins
to gather up the nutritious pods, toss-
ing her finds into a giant silver bowl.

She's not playing. She's foraging!

When we get back home, several
women crack open the baobab pods,
pull out the seeds, and grind them
into a powder, using only a few
rocks as tools. They
mix the white powder
with water, stir it into

a thick, creamy porridge, and then pass the porridge around in small cups, made from a gourd. This is lunch. I try a sip, and it tastes wonderful—tart and refreshing. It also feels incredibly nutritious.

I look over at little Belie. She's sitting nearby on a boulder, with her slender legs straight out in front of her and crossed at the ankles. Her facial expression is calm; her body poised. We have this delicious and nourishing porridge to eat because of her gumption and action; she climbed the cliff to collect the pods, all on her own. At that moment I realize just how remarkable Belie is. She doesn't just take care of herself *and* help with the toddlers. She also helps to feed the entire camp. She's already a huge contributor to her community, and she hasn't even started kindergarten yet. She's already returning the gifts her parents are giving her. And she doesn't seem burdened by the responsibility. Instead it makes her feel good. It makes her confident and relaxed.

How did the Hadzabe moms and dads train her to contribute in this way? Then I think back to my Hadzane name: Wait-a-bit. I start to wonder if maybe the dads, by naming me Wait-a-bit, might actually be trying to teach me something about my parenting. As a mom, do I need to wait-a-bit?

Ancient Antidote for Anxiety and Stress

During our time in Tanzania, I'm constantly surprised by how much freedom children seem to have. Kids of all ages seem to go wherever they want, do whatever they wish, and say whatever they feel.

When I compare, Rosy's life seems confined, even imprisoned, by contrast. She spends her days in our condo or at school; she lives constantly under the watchful eyes of me, Matt, or her teachers; and through it all, she receives a constant stream of instructions.

The Hadzabe kids even have emotional freedom. If a child needs to have a tantrum, so be it. No one rushes over to shush them; no one tells them "to calm down"; no one tells them how to feel. Eventually, a parent or other child will console the child, but no one shows any sense of urgency.

Parents grant even the tiniest toddlers this freedom. Take, for example, Tetite (pronounced tee-tee-teh). She's about eighteen months old, and she's one of the cutest toddlers I've ever met. She has big round eyes, fat cherubic cheeks, and a mischievous little grin. Rocking a baby-doll dress in yellow gingham, Tetite marches around the camp like a teenager. If a big kid takes something from her hands, she screams and grabs it right back. Without a

doubt, Tetite is a full-fledged member of the community, deciding her daily agenda.*

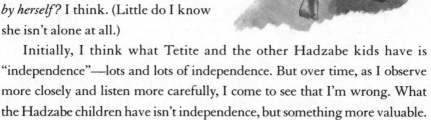

One afternoon, Belie takes Rosy and me to an
overlook, high up the mountainside and about
a quarter mile from the camp. We scramble up
boulders, and Rosy almost falls several times.
When we finally arrive at the top, we are so
high up that I feel a little queasy. Then I look
down, and guess who I see standing at the
bottom of the rocks, alone? Tetite! She's
walked all the way up from the camp, by
herself. *Why is she allowed to go so far
by herself?* I think. (Little do I know
she isn't alone at all.)

Initially, I think what Tetite and the other Hadzabe kids have is
"independence"—lots and lots of independence. But over time, as I observe
more closely and listen more carefully, I come to see that I'm wrong. What
the Hadzabe children have isn't independence, but something more valuable.

In general, hunter-gatherer communities greatly value a person's right to
make their own decisions—that is, their right to self-governance. They believe it's harmful to control another person. This idea forms a cornerstone
of their belief system, including their parenting.

This view extends to children, who are allowed to decide their own action, moment to moment, and set their own agendas. No stream of offers
of help, no issuing of commands, no lecturing. Parents don't feel this ubiquitous urgency to "occupy" a child's time or "keep them busy." Instead,
they feel confident that the child can—and will—figure all that out for
themselves. Why interfere?

---

* I had the same thought, over and over again, in the Maya village of Chan Kajaal. There, children
as young as age five or six could ride their bikes all around town, go to the playground whenever they
wanted, and seem to set their own agendas—when they weren't in school. Even the little two-year-olds
could play outside in their backyard alone, despite the fact that danger seemed to lurk everywhere: fires
still burning from the night before, machetes lying on the ground, and a number of pits and holes for a
little toddler to fall into.

"Deciding what another person should do, no matter what his age, is outside the Yequana vocabulary of behaviors," Jean Liedloff writes about the Yequana tribe in Venezuela. "A child's will is his motive force."

In fact, many parents in hunter-gatherer communities go to great lengths *not* to tell children (or adults) what to do. This doesn't mean that parents don't pay attention, or don't care what children do. Oh no! It's the opposite. A parent—or another caretaker—is definitely watching. (Actually, the Hadzabe parents often watch their children even more intently than I ever do, even as I emit my endless stream of instructions at Rosy, because if you think about it, can you really watch a child when you're talking?) But they parent from a different vantage: they believe that children know best how to learn and grow. Anything a parent says—the vast majority of the time—will only get in the child's way.

"So a one-year-old can be perfectly happy by himself for an hour doing whatever it is he wants to do," says Maya psychological anthropologist Suzanne Gaskins. "A parent or another caretaker watches to make sure he's safe. But he isn't stimulated. His agenda isn't changed by someone intervening. Parents give respect to that one-year-old that he has a legitimate agenda, and the goal is to help facilitate it."

With the !Kung hunter-gatherers in southern Africa, the word for "learning" and "teaching" is the same (n!garo), and parents will often use the phrase "She's teaching/learning herself" while a child is trying to figure out how to do something. Why interrupt their learning?

Let your kid do what they want to do;
it's not your place.
Let them be.

For the Hadzabe supermoms and superdads, exerting control over a child comes as a last resort. They would almost rather do anything else before they would tell a child what to do.

This same belief is so strong among the BaYaka hunter-gatherers in Central Africa that parents will actually stop and shame another parent who they see trying to control a child. "It was one of the few times we saw other parents interfere with others' parenting," says psychologist Sheina Lew-Levy. "When a parent is really trying to change a kid's behavior and make him do something he doesn't want to, another parent will say, 'Let your kid do what they want to do; it's not your place. Let them be.'" (You'll remember that's exactly what David told me on the first hunt with the Hadzabe dads.)

In one study, Sheina counted how many commands parents give children each hour. The results paint a vivid picture of what hunter-gatherer parenting looks like. Sheina followed adults and children around their homes and neighborhoods for nine hours. She tracked how many times an adult assigned a child a task (e.g., "Go get the fire" or "Hold the water cup" or "Go wash your hands"), explained how something worked, praised a child, or gave them negative feedback. (Because, if you think about it, praise is a way of controlling a child.)

Guess how many commands, on average, the BaYaka parents issued *each hour?* Three. That means the parents basically stay silent for more than fifty-seven minutes of every hour. On top of that, more than half of those commands were requests for the children to help the adult or the community. So the parents only choose to instruct when the instruction also helps transmit the value of cooperation.

When parents do need to remind a child of a rule or influence their actions, then the parent does it in a way that's subtle and indirect—and in a way that minimizes conflict. The parent allows the child to maintain a sense of agency so the child doesn't feel controlled or dominated. The parent uses questions, consequences, and puzzles. The parent could also change their own behavior (e.g., walk away from a hitting child instead of telling the child to stop hitting), change the environment around the child (e.g., remove an iPad from the room if the child can't use it wisely, instead of telling them not to use it), or silently help the child handle an unsafe situation (e.g., stand next to a child while they climb a wall and gently hold their hand or spot them, instead of telling them to get down off the wall).

This "no-bossing-around" policy has massive implications for the child's relationship with their parents. For starters, it means fewer conflicts—much fewer conflicts.

One afternoon, around the fire, Thaa and Belie illustrate this point beautifully. As I watch, the father and daughter sit companionably together for about two hours while Thaa sharpens an arrow for the next day's hunt and Belie watches him. They chat a little, but mostly they're silent. They coexist peacefully. Over the two hours, neither of them attempts to boss the other. Neither one tells the other what to do. Or what *not* to do. They seem to share this understood rule: you control yourself and I'll control myself.

As a result, they have no arguments. They have none of the tension and angst that exists between me and Rosy. They simply seem to enjoy each other's company.

Seeing Thaa and Belie together holds a mirror up to my own conflict-inducing behavior with Rosy. Back in my tent while Rosy takes a nap, I try to think if I have ever once gone two hours without telling Rosy what to do. Have I ever gone ten minutes? And could this be a source of our mutual stress?

Every time I tell Rosy what to do, am I, in a way, picking a fight with her?

———————

As an American mom, I think I'm pretty laid-back. Matt and I both try to give Rosy a huge amount of freedom. I definitely value independence and self-sufficiency and want both for Rosy. But in fact, compared to the Hadzabe and Maya moms, I'm a nagging ninny. No, that's an understatement—I'm a bossy pants. My intentions are admirable; I'm trying to teach her to be a good person and do things the right way. But now I'm coming to wonder if this parenting style might actually be doing the opposite—and creating a child who's needier, more demanding, and more dependent.

Watching the Hadzabe parents in action, I realize that I constantly issue commands. In fact, I am even on the lookout for commands. "Rosy, watch the fire." "Don't climb too high on the rocks." "Stop swinging that stick around." "Don't eat too many muffins." "Wipe your face." "Stop at the crosswalk!" I even tell Rosy what to say ("Say, 'Thank you!'"), where to put her body parts ("Rosy, don't suck your thumb"), and what emotions to have ("Rosy, stop crying. Stop being angry"). I tell her not just when she breaks a rule or misbehaves, but also when she's simply trying to help or participate in an activity. And to keep her safe, I physically box her in to a tiny few square feet around me: "Rosy, get down off the wall." "Rosy, don't run on the sidewalk." Rosy, Rosy, Rosy, Rosy. It's a constant stream of commands.*

Come to think about it, even when I *give* Rosy "choices"—or ask her questions that begin with "Do you want"—I'm still, in a way, limiting her experience by directing her attention or managing her behavior. I'm still trying to control her.

The entire time we were in Tanzania and Mexico, I never heard a Hadzabe or Maya parent ask a child, "Do you want . . . ?" And they surely never offered "choices." But I do these things all the time.

Why? Why do I feel the need to control Rosy's behavior so much? To guide and narrow her path through the world? I ask myself this question every night in Tanzania while rubbing Rosy's back as she falls asleep in the tent. I reach a simple conclusion: I think this is what a good parent does. I believe that the more I say to Rosy—and the more I instruct her—the better parent I am. I believe that all these commands will keep Rosy safe and teach her to be a respectful, kind person.

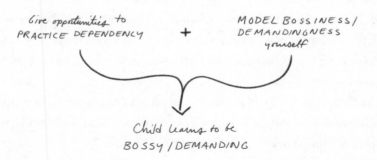

But do my commands really help? Or do they cause the opposite effect? Think back to our formula for training a child: practice, model, and

---

* Back in San Francisco, I counted how many commands I give Rosy each hour. I stopped the experiment early because after ten minutes I was clocking in about one to two commands per minute, or more than a hundred commands per hour.

acknowledge. With these commands, what does Rosy practice and what do I model?

Giving children enormous amounts of freedom and independence must come at a cost, right? Besides the safety concerns, there must be behavioral consequences for letting a child decide moment to moment what they do? I'm not issuing the commands just to hear myself talk. If I stopped supplying clear directives and consistent consequences to Rosy's actions, wouldn't I raise a self-indulgent brat?

As one psychologist wrote, children's freedom seems like a "recipe for disaster . . . for producing spoiled, demanding children who would grow up to be spoiled, demanding adults." Think Veruca Salt in *Charlie and the Chocolate Factory*: "I want a golden goose and I want it now!"

But in fact, during my time in Tanzania, I never saw one instance of Veruca Salt–like behavior. Same goes for the Maya children. In fact, in both places, I saw the opposite. I saw children who do way less whining, demanding, and screaming than kids in the West. Children who are considerate of others; who want to help their friends and family; and who are confident, curious go-getters.

I'm far from the first to notice such a paradox. Many anthropologists, psychologists, and journalists have written about this. After living with the Ju/'hoan hunter-gatherers in the Kalahari Desert, writer Elizabeth Marshall Thomas eloquently summed up the idea: "Free from frustration or anxiety . . . the Ju/'hoan children were every parent's dream. No culture can ever have raised better, more intelligent, more likable, more confident children."

And so what gives? How come a life free of punishment and rules results in confident and cooperative kids with the Hadzabe? While, in our culture, it's linked to self-indulgence and selfishness?

The answer is clearly complex. A child is like a bottle of wine—the final product depends not only on what the winemaker (i.e., the parent) does during the fermentation (i.e., parenting) process, but also the environment under which the grapes are grown (i.e., the community's values). That said, one factor seems to be especially critical to raising confident, kind kids: Hadzabe children don't simply have freedom or independence; they have autonomy. And that makes all the difference in the world.

_____

I grew up in a small, rural town, tucked between the Blue Ridge Mountains on one side and the outer edge of the D.C. suburbs on the other. All and all, I had a quintessential American childhood (including all the conflict and anger that goes along with that). Surrounded by horse ranches and cornfields, we lived on a tree-lined street that ended in a cul-de-sac. Kids zoomed up and down the black pavement in little "biker gangs," and teenagers played tackle football in our front yard. When I wasn't in school, life was all about one thing: adventure. In the summer, I would wake up, eat a bowl of cereal, throw on a pair of cutoff jean shorts, and head out the door. And I loved it! I loved exploring the creek behind our house, often barefoot and in a bikini top. When we kids got hungry, we'd hike across a cow pasture to a nearby 7-Eleven and buy Big Bite hot dogs.

My mom didn't know where I roamed from morning until it was time for dinner. And she never really seemed to care much. She never encouraged me to come home and help her put away groceries or fold the laundry. And I surely didn't look for ways to help her. Sitting on the curb outside the 7-Eleven, munching on a hot dog, I never once thought about picking up some milk or cereal for breakfast in the morning. I was independent, yes. But I wasn't autonomous—at least not in the way Belie is.

It's easy to confuse autonomy and independence. Before writing this book, I certainly thought they were the same. But in fact, the two concepts

AUTONOMY

Go for three commands, requests, questions per hour.

Wait-a-bit before giving a child an instruction; think, is it necessary?

Reserve requests and commands for connecting the child to the family (i.e. for teaching helpfulness and generosity).

have different meanings, and this difference is essential to understanding how hunter-gatherer parents raise such self-reliant *and* kind children. It's also key to understanding a way of parenting that does not involve control—a way of collaborating with your child that smoothes your relationship and helps your child feel less anxious.

The difference has to do with connectivity. Independence means not needing or not being influenced by others. An independent child operates like a solitary planet. They're disconnected. They have no obligations to their family or their community around them. And in return, the family and community have no expectations of the child. Independence is an alley cat in the city who answers to no one but himself, or ten-year-old Michaeleen, barefoot on a hot summer day.

It's not Belie in Tanzania or Angela in the Yucatán.

Hadzabe and Maya children have a huge amount of connections and obligations to many people—old, young, and all in between. And these connections exist at almost every moment in their lives. Even when kids ride their bikes around the village or scramble over boulders far out in the bush, having adventures like I did, they are still powerfully connected to their families and communities. These children are not solitary planets. They belong to a solar system, circling around each other, feeling and stabilized by each other's gravity.

Those connections come in two ways: responsibilities to others and an invisible safety net.

Let's start with the former.

Responsibilities to others

When Hadzabe kids go out to play or hang out around the camp, they have freedom. There's no question about that. But their parents layer that freedom with something else: expectations that the child will help their family.

I notice these expectations the entire time we are with Belie. For starters, the moms and grandmas often call on her to help. They issue small requests, just like we learned about in the previous section. "Belie, go grab a bowl," one of the grandmas says after grinding baobab seeds with a rock. "Belie, bring me him," a mom says when her baby starts crying and needs feeding. Whenever it's time to go into the bush, a mom or older cousin asks Belie to carry something (e.g., firewood, a water bottle), gather something (e.g., baobab pods), or take care of someone (e.g., Tetite). And whenever they sit down to eat, they expect Belie to not only share her food with the younger children, but to give them that share first. (In fact, the moms and dads in the community have trained Belie to do this since she was a baby, through the formula of practice, model, and acknowledge.)

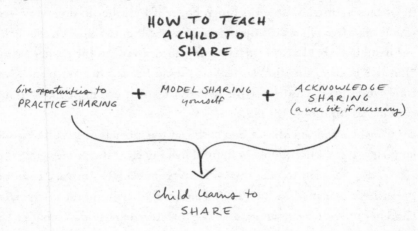

HOW TO TEACH
A CHILD TO
SHARE

Give opportunities to
PRACTICE SHARING
+
MODEL SHARING
yourself
+
ACKNOWLEDGE
SHARING
(a wee bit, if necessary)

Child learns to
SHARE

Basically any time the women do a task, they ask Belie to help and contribute in some small way. They don't issue many commands, maybe only one or two per hour (versus my hundred commands per hour!). Sometimes the moms don't even say anything, but instead simply use their actions to connect Belie to the group and ensure that she contributes to its collective goals. For example, when we head out to look for tubers, one of the moms hands Belie a digging stick to carry. Another time, she gives Belie a baby to hold. Or she points in the direction of the bucket to tell Belie to fill it with water. Belie always seems happy to help and proud to contribute.

Even when Belie plays away from the camp and is not near the adults, she's still committed to the group and helping out. How? She's helping to watch Tetite and the other toddlers. The parents have trained Belie to help with the younger kids, and Belie takes this job seriously. Remember when

Tetite followed us to the boulders? I didn't see Tetite until she needed help. But Belie had kept an eye on the younger girl the whole time. By the time I spotted Tetite, Belie was already scrambling down the rocks and making sure the toddler was safe.

After watching the Hadzabe women with Belie for a few days, I see how easy it is to get kids to help with tasks—and how difficult I was making it. I was way overthinking it.

First, I was giving Rosy tasks that were way too complicated for her (e.g., "Clean up the living room," "Fold the laundry," or "Come help with the dishes"). Instead, it works much better if I ask her to do a very, very small subtask of what I'm already doing (e.g., "Put this book on the shelf," as I hand her a book; "Put this shirt in your drawer," as I hand her a shirt; "Put this bowl in the dishwasher," as I hand her a dish). With such easy commands, Rosy is much less likely to resist, and much more likely to succeed in accomplishing the task.

I was also padding the request with way too much flowery, unnecessary language (e.g., "Rosy, would you mind helping clear the dinner table?" or "Rosy, do you want to take this coffee to your dad?"). Instead, I can put the dirty dinner plate in Rosy's hand and say, "Put this in the kitchen," or hand her the coffee cup and say, "Take this coffee to Dadda." That's it! So simple. So clear. And so much more likely to work.

By sprinkling these requests into daily activities, parents train the children to orient their activities and attention toward others, says psychologist Sheina Lew-Levy. Children learn to be on the lookout for what other people need, and then to hop in and help whenever they can.

Along the way, children learn to make their own decisions. At the same time, there's also an overarching expectation that everyone pitches in and contributes, Sheina says. "So kids and adults are all acting on their own. Nobody is telling them what to do. But at the end of the day, everyone brings your food back to the group. You share the food. You think of the group."[*]

---

[*] You see a similar structure in the Maya village. When kids run and play around the village, older children are expected to care for the younger ones, to watch out and make sure they don't hurt themselves, to protect them. And kids of all ages are expected to pay attention and be around when their parents need their help (they are expected to be *acomedido*). If a child hears the call, as Maria de los Angeles Tun Burgos says, they know to come home and help their family.

This approach really is a beautiful way to parent because it gives a child two things they crave and need: freedom and teamwork.

I always thought of freedom and teamwork as contradictory concepts, but with this parenting approach, the two ideas balance each other out and bring out each other's advantages. It's like a perfectly ripe peach. When you bite into it, your mouth fills with sweetness. But as chef Samin Nosrat points out in her writing, the peach has another element, tartness, which balances the sweetness. It's the combination that makes the peach taste so good.

The same goes for raising kind children. Freedom (sweetness), on its own, can generate selfish kids. But add a pinch of teamwork (tartness) and the child bursts with generosity and confidence. They become the perfect peach.

One night back home in San Francisco, Rosy eloquently sums up this style of parenting at dinner: "Everyone does what they want, but they must be kind, share, and be helpful."

Invisible safety net

Maya and Hadzabe parents don't simply let their children run off from home, cross their fingers, and hope the children will be okay. Instead, the parents have established a structure to keep their kids safe. I think of it as an invisible safety net because the child doesn't know the safety net exists until they need help.

First of all, parents in these cultures rarely leave young children completely alone. To my Western eye, the kids seemed alone, but when I looked a little harder, I saw that wasn't true at all. As the psychological anthropologist Suzanne Gaskins told me once about Chan Kajaal, "Someone is always watching." You think you are alone, but people watch everything.

"My image of a Maya parent—or an older child—is one waiting in the wings and anticipating the help and then providing it in almost a seamless way, an almost invisible way," Suzanne says. "So the younger child may not even see that help has been given."

The same goes for Hadzabe parents, especially the dads. In Tanzania, many times I think that I'm alone in the bush—either doing "my business" or just taking a break from Rosy—until suddenly one of the dads appears in a tree five feet away or runs past me on a trail nearby. *Whoa*, I think. *How does he know I am all the way over here?*

When I return to camp, the dad says something that makes it clear he had been keeping me safe the whole time. Even when we went out hunting with Thaa and his friends early on, I thought Rosy and I had fallen so far behind the group that no one saw what we were doing. Not in the slightest. During the entire hunt, Thaa would quietly circle back behind us to make sure we didn't get lost. He was just so quiet about it that I never noticed him. Indeed, his "invisible safety net" is how I got my Hadzane name: Wait-a-bit (Hon!o!oko).

Come to think of it, Thaa can track down wild cats and impalas in the bush. Keeping an eye on an "Tok'oko"—and her middle-aged mother—is probably no problem.

When the parents can't "keep an eye" on a kid themselves, they ensure that an older child goes along to help. Parents train children to take care of younger siblings as soon as kids start walking. And so, by the time kids reach Belie's age, five or six, they're highly capable caretakers. They know how to keep the toddlers safe, feed them, and settle them when they cry. At the same time, older children (siblings and friends) return the favor by looking after the younger children. So there's a beautiful hierarchy of love and support. Teenagers help the younger kids; younger kids help the toddlers; and everyone helps the babies.

Sometimes parents will even send an older child (or another adult) to follow behind a younger one, stealthily, when a child first tries to run an errand on their own. The older sibling will stay out of sight, so the younger child *feels* like they ran the errand on their own. In the Yucatán, Maria told me she uses this strategy when her kids are first learning to go buy groceries alone. "Alexa [age four at the time] always wants to go to the corner store alone," Maria said. "I let her go, but then I send one of her sisters to follow her because I'm afraid she'll get lost."

And thus, giving children autonomy doesn't mean sacrificing safety. It simply means staying quiet and out of the way. It means watching, from a distance, so kids can explore and learn for themselves. Then if the child gets into danger—real danger—you swoop in to help.

———————

Autonomy has tremendous benefits for kids of all ages. Oodles of studies have linked autonomy to a slew of desired traits for kids, including inner drive, long-term motivation, independence, confidence, and better executive function. Basically, every trait I see in Belie. As a child gets older, autonomy is connected to better performance in school, increased chance of career success, and decreased risk of drug and alcohol abuse. "Like exercise and sleep, it appears to be good for virtually everything," neuropsychologist William Stixrud and educator Ned Johnson write in their book, *The Self-Driven Child.*

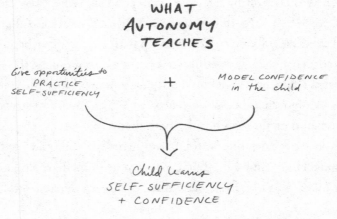

WHAT
AUTONOMY
TEACHES

Give opportunities to
PRACTICE
SELF-SUFFICIENCY

+

MODEL CONFIDENCE
in the child

Child learns
SELF-SUFFICIENCY
+ CONFIDENCE

In essence, when I step back, wait-a-bit, and let Rosy handle the world on her own, I convey several important messages to her. I tell her that she's capable and self-sufficient; that she can solve problems on her own; and that she can handle what life throws at her. Think back to the formula. By letting Rosy act on her own, I give her opportunities to practice being self-sufficient and independent. And I model respect for others.

On the flip side, when I constantly instruct and guide her actions, I undermine her confidence, even as I try to help her. I give her opportunities to practice dependency and neediness. And I model bossy, demanding behavior.

But my bossiness has another disadvantage: it slows down Rosy's growth, both physically and mentally. The Hadzabe families have noticed this effect on children. "Because we give children so much freedom and because they participate in all activities from an early age, our children are independent much earlier than in most societies," a group of elders explained in the book *Hadzabe: By the Light of a Million Fires*.

What's more, when children don't have enough autonomy, they often feel powerless over their lives. "Many [American] kids feel that way all the time," Bill and Ned write in *The Self-Driven Child*. That feeling causes stress, and over time, that chronic stress can turn into anxiety and depression. Lack of autonomy is likely a key reason for the high prevalence of anxiety and depression among American children and teenagers, the pair write.

Here in Western culture, we aren't very good at giving kids autonomy. We think we are. We try. But at the end of the day, many kids have little control of their daily lives. We set them up with strict daily schedules and routines, and ensure that an adult supervises every moment throughout the day. In the end, we somehow both macromanage *and* micromanage their lives. And in the process, we generate a huge amount of stress inside our children and in our relationships with them.

Autonomy provides the "antidote to this stress," Bill and Ned write. When you feel like you have influence over your immediate situation and the direction of your life, stress goes down, the brain relaxes, and life gets easier.

"The biggest gift parents can give their children is the opportunity to make their own decisions," psychologist Holly Schiffrin says. "Parents who 'help' their children too much stress themselves out and leave their kids ill-prepared to be adults."

In other words, Mama Michaeleen, you need to "wait-a-bit" before you instruct, direct, or issue a command. Just wait-a-bit. Because Rosy is highly capable of learning and figuring out the right behavior on her own. And she will often surprise me with what she can do.

Try It 8: Boost Confidence and Self-Reliance

To review, there are two main ways that we can help increase our child's autonomy while also reducing conflict and resistance:

1. Decrease your commands and other verbal input (e.g., questions, requests, choices).
2. Empower the child by training them to handle obstacles and dangers, which in turn allows you to reduce your commands.

Dip Your Toe

- **Try three commands per hour.** Grab your phone and set the timer for twenty minutes. During this time, restrict yourself to one verbal command to your child. Resist the urge to tell the child anything: what to do, eat, say, or how to act. This includes asking questions about what the child wants or what they need. If you absolutely have to change their behavior, do it nonverbally; use actions or facial expressions. Try with all your heart to let the child be, even if they break "rules" or do something you can't stand. (Remember, it's only twenty minutes.)

If the child ends up in what looks like an unsafe situation, wait just a beat and see if the child can help themselves before you intervene. If not, go over and remove the physical danger or move the child.

After the twenty minutes, assess how you and your child feel. Do you feel more relaxed and calm? Does your child feel less stressed? Do you have less conflict?

Try this exercise with any activity that brings stress and conflict in the home (e.g., getting ready for school, getting ready for bed). In the end, the child might not look or behave exactly how you wish. They may end up going to school with tangled hair or mismatching shoes, but the psychological benefits for the family will far outweigh these cosmetic issues.

Once you get comfortable with twenty minutes, try bumping up the time to forty minutes, then an hour. After a month or so, see if you notice a difference in your child's behavior and their relationship with you. Do they have more confidence? Do you experience less conflict?

- **Stop being a ventriloquist.** I didn't realize how much I act as Rosy's ventriloquist until I see how the Hadzabe parents never answer for children or tell them what to say. Never, ever.

Meanwhile, I constantly answer for Rosy ("Yes, Rosy loves school!") or tell her what to say ("Say, thank you, Rosy"). I take away her voice.

So when we return home from Tanzania, I simply stop answering for her or telling her what to say (or at least, I try very hard not to do these things). As a result, sometimes Rosy seems rude to other people. But I'm confident that she'll learn and figure out the appropriate behavior (with the formula). And if I really feel like she should have shown gratitude, I will ask her afterward: "What would a big girl have done?" and leave it at that.

For older children, make it your goal to let your child speak whenever possible and increasingly so as their confidence and abilities grow. Let them order at restaurants, set up after-school activities, settle disputes with friends and, when possible, talk with teachers, coaches, and instructors about successes and mistakes. If the child isn't accustomed to handling these situations on their own, go along with them to help. Let the child know ahead of time that they are capable of speaking for themselves and that you have confidence in them, and then simply go with them as a support if they need it. Resist the urge to interrupt. "At a store, or with an instructor or coach, you might even physically hang back and avoid eye contact so that it's clear to the adult that your child will be doing the talking," former Stanford dean Julie Lythcott-Haims writes in her book *How to Raise an Adult*.

If your child is shy, introverted, or has special needs, you may need to do more of the talking, Julie writes. "You know your kid best. . . . But even if you're speaking for your kid, be mindful that you are not them and are not literally able to speak for them. You can say, 'Jasmine told me she's feeling . . .' or 'Jordan told me he's interested in . . .'"

In all circumstances, let the child take the lead and show you what conversations they can handle on their own. Resist the urge to interrupt your child, no matter what, even if they make mistakes or leave out key points.

Wait-a-bit before talking. One day, your children will have to handle these conversations on their own, Julie points out. Now is the time to practice these skills.

• **Let children handle their own arguments.** Inuit parents in the Arctic told me this advice over and over again. Essentially, when children argue among themselves, just step back and don't interfere. Your meddling will only make the argument worse and prevent children from learning how to settle their own disputes. Jump in only if the children start hurting each other (as in, *really* hurting each other). If one kid comes over and complains about another kid, nod and say, "Hmm." Kids know what to do. They don't need more validations of their feelings. They need autonomy.

Wade In

• **Drop a rule.** Is there something your child really wants to do alone, without your help, but you always tag along or stop them? Maybe it's biking to school or going to the corner market. Maybe it's using the kitchen knife, cooking on the grill, or making pasta. Take a tip from Maria in the Yucatán: Let the child do it! And while they do it, form an invisible safety net around them. If they leave the house, wait-a-bit, then follow stealthily behind (or have an older sibling do it). If they want to use a knife or similar tool, modify the situation so that the child won't hurt themselves. Give the child an easy food to cut (e.g., celery, strawberries), offer a dull knife, or let them use a real knife for thirty seconds or so. Then switch out the sharp knife for a dull one. In all these situations, the goal is the same: give the child a little more freedom and real practice at learning a new skill.

• **Train a child to avoid or handle dangers in your home and neighborhood.** In Western culture, we shield babies, toddlers, and kids from dangers. We cover electric plugs with plastic; keep knives high up on shelves; and when a toddler waddles near a grill, we rush over and scream at them ("Stop! Wait! It's hot!"). This vigilance keeps kids safe. But man-o-man does it cause stress, for everyone.

Meanwhile, in the vast majority of cultures, young children learn—safely—how to use knives, tend to fires, cook over a stove, even shoot bows and arrows or throw harpoons. The specific details of the training depend on the child's age, personal abilities, and the activity's danger level. But the idea remains the same across the board: Use the formula! Practice, model, and acknowledge.

Turns out, children are hungry to learn these skills! They love it. Toddlers and young kids see parents using knives, heat, and electricity for such amazing tasks as chopping, cooking, and generating light. Why wouldn't a kid want to get involved?*

- **For babies and toddlers (crawling and walking).** Let's use fire and electricity as an example.

Start teaching a baby and toddler which items in the home (and around the neighborhood) are "hot." When the stove is on, point and say something like "Hot!" Then act out what would happen if you touch it. "Ouch! That would hurt." Point to the electric socket and say the same thing: "Hot! Ouch!"

Then if you or a family member accidentally burn yourself, show the child the burn so they can see what happens if you're not careful with "hot." Say something like "See what happened when I wasn't careful and touched the stove? Ouch! It hurts."

If a toddler shows interest in a tool that seems too dangerous for them, encourage the child to watch while you use the danger. Then use their interest as an opportunity to teach them safety skills. For example, Rosy was really interested in fire around age 2.5, so my husband taught her how to blow out a candle, how the flame could burn her, and all about how fire extinguishers work. She loved the fire extinguisher so much, she carried it around the house for a week, and we had to set a place at the dinner table for "sting washer."

- **For small children (approximately three and up):** Be sure the child fully understands how to avoid the danger (see steps above). Now a child

---

* If you think about it, the idea makes good sense. We teach young babies to sign words like "milk" and "more" when they can't talk. Why couldn't we teach them words like "hot" and "sharp" so they learn how not to hurt themselves? Then by the time she starts walking, she is already on her way to understanding what to avoid and what to handle carefully. And then by the time she is three or four, like Rosy, not only is she careful around a knife or fire, but she may also be interested in learning how to use the danger properly.

can begin to practice handling the danger. For fire, show the child how to light a burner, turn on the oven, stir a pot of boiling water, flip a pancake, or melt butter in a pan. For knives, give a child a serrated steak knife to start with and let them slowly work their way up to a dull paring knife. The idea is to give the child something sharp enough that it's actually useful but dull enough that they won't hurt themselves with it. Then watch and see how their skills develop. If the child shows aptitude on a given knife and asks to try a sharper one, then let them try it with something easy to cut, like bananas or small cucumbers. But there's no need to rush the process. If the child cuts happily with a butter knife, let them be.

Jump In

- **Find autonomy zones.** Many American families live around busy roads, dangerous intersections, and stranger-filled neighborhoods. That said, we can still find places where children can have (almost) full autonomy and parents can relax (while practicing the new rule of "three commands per hour").

In each autonomy zone, you can use the same strategy: train the child to handle or avoid any dangers that exist in the environment so you don't have to constantly give the child instructions. You can do this in three steps:
  - **Identify dangers.** At the beginning, walk around near the child as they explore the environment. Be the invisible safety net. Keep an eye out for any dangers—steep drop-offs, pools of water, sharp objects. Catalog these dangers in your mind. Don't say anything to the child if they don't notice them or show any interest in them. You're just asking for trouble if you direct a child to a danger.
  - **Step back.** Sit down somewhere, pull out a book (or work), and relax. Let the child explore autonomously. Count your commands and go for three per hour.
  - **Form an invisible safety net.** If the child goes near one of the dangers, start watching more closely. The more time they spend near the danger, the closer you watch. Resist the urge to run over to the child or scream a warning. Wait and watch. If the child seems inter-

ested in the danger, calmly walk over and begin to train them about that danger (e.g., for a sharp object, say, "Sharp. Ow. That would hurt," gently and calmly). If the child already knows about the danger, remind them of the consequences (e.g., for a sharp object, say calmly, "That would cut you. Ow, that would hurt if you step on it"). If the child still doesn't understand, gently take the child's hand and lead them away from the danger. Try the lesson another day.

Aim for kids to spend at least three hours each week in an autonomy zone and work your way up to a few hours each day, using time after school and on the weekends.

What makes a good autonomy zone? For toddlers and smaller children, look for places with wide-open spaces, so you can see the little ones easily from a far distance and you don't have to follow them around. Some great places:

➤ Parks with wide-open spaces
➤ Playgrounds (I like the ones with sand or soft dirt to cushion falls)
➤ Beaches (you can quickly train a child to avoid the ocean)
➤ Community gardens
➤ Grassy fields
➤ Schoolyards
➤ Dog parks
➤ Your house and yard (or porch in the city)

For older children, community pools and community centers make great autonomy zones. Work up toward dropping kids off at these places (and the ones above) and picking them up later. Teach children to help look after themselves and after younger siblings. Tell them to watch out for the little ones and make sure they stay safe.

• **Make your neighborhood an autonomy zone.** The exact age for this autonomy zone really depends on the neighborhood, the child, and the availability of the safety net (i.e., older siblings available to watch after the little ones). That said, it's never too early for children to become acquainted with the area around the home. Start teaching toddlers how to cross busy streets, watch out for traffic, and learn other dangers around a neighborhood. Have them play outside as much as possible, with you on the front porch or by the window. Slowly increase the range they go alone or with you watching from a distance. Boost the invisible safety net by getting to know your neighbors.

a. Introduce your child to your neighbors. This includes neighbors of all ages. Have neighbors over for dinner or for coffee (or a beer). Have your kids bake cookies or meals for neighbors and then deliver them together. (This also makes a great activity for practicing sharing and generosity.)

b. Host a block party. After meeting everyone at a block party, neighbors become acquainted with the kids on the block and will be more likely to keep an eye out for them during their autonomous adventures.

c. Encourage your kids to play with the kids in the neighborhood. Invite the neighbor kids over to play or watch a movie. Become friends with their parents and host dinner parties with them all. Even a young kid, age three or so, can run over to a neighbor's house to play on their own (or with the invisible safety net). As we'll learn in the next section, neighbor kids and parents can become important alloparents, creating a circle of physical and emotional safety around kids.

Summary for Chapter 14:
How to Raise a Confident Child

Ideas to Remember

➤ Like adults, kids and toddlers don't like to be bossed around. Children, at every age, have a natural inclination to learn autonomously without interference.

➤ When we boss kids around, we undermine their confidence and self-reliance.

➤ When we give children autonomy and minimize instruction to them, we send the message that they are self-sufficient and can handle problems on their own.

➤ The best way to protect a child from anxiety and stress is to give them autonomy.

➤ Independence and autonomy are different concepts.
- An independent child is disconnected from others and not responsible for anyone except themselves.
- An autonomous child governs their own actions and makes their own decisions, but they have a constant connection to their family and friends. They are expected to help, share, and be kind. They are expected to give back to the group whenever possible.

Tips and Tools

➤ **Pay attention to how frequently you instruct your child.** Take out your phone and set it for twenty minutes. Count how many questions, comments, and demands you make to your child during that time.

➤ **Go for three commands an hour.** Try to limit your verbal instructions to three per hour, especially during activities that trigger conflict and arguments (e.g., getting ready for school, getting ready for bed). Use commands only to teach children helpfulness, generosity, and other responsibilities to the family.

➤ **Find an autonomy zone.** Identify places around your town where toddlers and kids can practice autonomy, where you can watch them from a distance and interfere minimally. Try parks and playgrounds with open spaces, grassy fields, and beaches. Bring a magazine or work and let the kids play for a few hours.

➤ **Make your yard and neighborhood an autonomy zone.** Train your child to handle dangers around your home and neighborhood. Build an "invisible safety net" by getting to know your neighbors and their children.

➤ **Stop being a ventriloquist.** Make it a goal to stop speaking for your child or telling them what to say. Let them answer questions directed at them, order at restaurants, decide when to say "Please" and "Thank you." Work toward having them handle all conversations themselves, including discussions with teachers, coaches, and instructors.

CHAPTER 15

Ancient Antidote
for Depression

*The mother is rarely alone when her baby cries; others often substitute
or join her in interventions.*

—Ann Cale Kruger and Melvin Konner,
speaking about their time with !Kung women

When Rosy was born, our life looked ideal. Matt and I finally had saved up
enough money to buy a condo, and it seemed perfect. It had beautiful views
of the San Francisco Bay, and when the fog wasn't too thick, you could
watch the sunrises over the East Bay Hills. Plus, the condo was, as Goldi-
locks would say, not too small and not too big. It had just enough space for
a nursery. Before Rosy arrived, I decorated its walls with big yellow owls
and pink letters, spelling out "Rosemary."

On top of that, Matt and I were able to take paid leave from work to be
with our new baby girl. We felt lucky. And happy.

The first six weeks of Rosy's life rolled along without a hitch. Matt
grilled peanut butter and jelly sandwiches for me while I learned how to
breastfeed. Rosy cried a lot. But Matt and I worked together to hold and
soothe her, and my sister visited for ten days, which was wonderful.

Then Matt went back to work. And our world changed in a dangerous way.

From eight in the morning to about six at night—that is, for about ten hours each day—it was just me, Mango the dog, and grumpy, colicky Rosy in the apartment. Day after day. Hour after hour. Minute after minute. Time started to crawl at the most excruciating pace. What on earth would we do all day? And, oh yeah, how was I going to get this baby to nap so I could take a break?

Sometimes I'd turn on NPR just to hear another voice. Other times, if I had the energy, I'd hop in an Uber and attend a lactation support group across the city. One afternoon a friend from college popped by to say hi and brought me lunch. But that was about it. Otherwise I was alone, and as the days went by our perfect condo turned into what felt like an island of isolation. Every time Rosy cried, fussed, and screeched, I was the only one who picked her up, cuddled her, and calmed her down. I provided all her food, comfort, and love. I was her entire world. And she was turning, slowly, day by day, into mine.

On paper, such a close relationship sounds beautiful, bonded, and like a dream come true. That's how I had envisioned it. And that's how it surely looked in friends' photos on Facebook. Peaceful maternity-leave bliss.

But in practice, such isolation and solitariness had a dark side for me. By month three, I felt exhausted to the bone. I averaged three or four hours of sleep per night, at most, because I couldn't get Rosy to sleep in the crib for longer than that. The exhaustion meant I no longer had the energy to do anything except keep this tiny human alive. I no longer wrote or read about science. I no longer went on hikes or cooked dinner. Day by day, I could feel my sense of self slipping out of my skin.

Eventually, I became depressed. And I knew I needed help. But help was so *very* hard to find. I called doctors and therapists for months, until finally I got lucky. I found a psychiatrist who would take our insurance and had openings. By Rosy's six-month birthday, I was taking an antidepressant and seeing a therapist each week. "You have to get some help with Rosy," she said one afternoon. "Can you hire a nanny? Can you go back to work early? You need help."

Then I was lucky—again. We *could* hire help. And we could also pay to fly my mom out for regular visits. But in the end, Rosy had bonded almost exclusively to me (and eventually, Matt and the nanny, after much stress and screaming). I struggled with depression for several years.

I have always blamed this depression on myself—that for some reason, I couldn't handle the life of a new mom. I had residual "baggage" from my childhood. I didn't seek out enough companionship right after Rosy was born. I didn't make the right choices about childcare. Or I had a genetic "flaw" or some other type of disposition.

But while visiting the Hadzabe families, I began to see how the problem was never me. Not at all.

———————

About a million years ago, something extraordinary was happening in Africa. There was a curious-looking ape species who was evolving to have remarkable abilities.

It wasn't just that the ape could walk on two feet. So could some other ape species. Nor was it that she could design and build an impressive set of tools, such as knives and axes. So could those other ape species. Sure, her brain was large—but again, that wasn't super special, either.

On the surface, this ape looked quite similar to a handful of other bipedal, big-brained, humanlike species who lived and wandered around the African continent at about the same time.

But if you spent a few days with this ape and her family, you would start to see something peculiar going on. For starters, the adults were unusually cooperative and empathetic. They worked together on tasks that other apes tended to do alone, such as building homes or tracking down prey. And they almost seemed able to read each other's minds. They could understand another person's goals and then help that person achieve those goals.

Perhaps most curiously, the babies were incredibly needy. The poor lady ape gave birth to babies who were, by all practical purposes, helpless. They couldn't even cling to their mother's body. They needed months of intense care before they could crawl, another year before they could run from danger. And even then, this lady ape wasn't out of the woods. She had to take care of each child for about a decade before the sweet darling could finally become self-sufficient and acquire enough calories to take care of herself.

Anthropologist Sarah Blaffer Hrdy estimates that over those first ten years of life, this ape's child would need about 10 to 13 million calories of energy to mature completely. That's the equivalent of about four thousand jars of Trader Joe's peanut butter. And remember, these ape species were hunter-gatherers. They couldn't pick up sandwiches from a deli or groceries from a market. They would have to forage and track down all the food their offspring required—not just for weeks and months, but for many, many years.

As Sarah asserts, there's no way this mama ape could even come close to supplying her child with this much food, especially given that she likely had another child to feed or she was already pregnant with a second helpless, incredibly demanding soon-to-be baby.

This lady ape had a problem on her hands: her children required way more care, food, and energy than she could handle alone, or even with a competent and loving partner. She needed help—and not just a quick visit from a long-lost aunt over the weekend, but full-time help. Somebody who could stay close to her, night after night. She needed help preparing meals, help foraging for extra berries, and help keeping the place clean. She needed somebody to play with the older children and to hold the babies when she couldn't.

As time went on, the problem only worsened. Over the course of thousands and thousands of generations, the species' babies became more and more helpless, and children took longer and longer to become self-sufficient.

Skip ahead eight hundred thousand years and now this ape species looks essentially like us humans today. It is us.

Eventually, *Homo sapiens* started giving birth to what some scientists call "premature" babies. And I don't mean preterm births. I mean *all* human babies are born premature compared to other primate species. Not only are human infants pretty much squishy blobs, completely vulnerable and without any motor coordination, but their brains hardly work.

Compared to other living primates, humans are born with the least developed brains, ones that are 30 percent smaller than the adult size.

Take, for instance, our closest living relative, chimpanzees. A human baby would have to grow in the womb for another nine to twelve months to be as neurologically and cognitively developed as a newborn chimp.

I remember when Rosy was only a few days old, she could do nothing but cry and poop. She even had problems latching on to breastfeed. I remember holding her over the sink, trying to give her a bath. And she felt like a turkey at Thanksgiving, before you put it in the oven: raw and slippery. Her muscles were so flaccid. Her arms, legs, neck just dangling in space. At every moment, I thought she would slip out of my hands.

No one knows exactly why *Homo sapiens* give birth to such premature infants. Some blame our superlarge brains, which, if allowed to fully develop in the womb, would give mothers some serious problems during childbirth. Scientists also don't know why kids take so darn long to mature into self-sufficient beings. Maybe our extended childhood gives us ample time to learn the powerful skills that make us human, such as mastering languages and navigating complicated social structures. But we know one thing for certain: as humans evolved over hundreds of thousands of years, and our offspring began to require so much more time, attention, and calories, another trait evolved with us—alloparenting, or "other" parenting.

As Sarah Hrdy herself puts it: "An ape that produced such costly, costly slow-maturing offspring as we have could not have evolved unless mothers had had a lot of help."

And when Sarah says a lot of help, she means a hell of a lot of help.

An alloparent can be any person—besides the mother and father— who helps to take care of a child. A relative, a neighbor, a friend, or even another child can be a fantastic alloparent.

Sarah believes that these extra parents were essential for human evolution. Over the course of her career, she has acquired an impressive trove of evidence to back up this hypothesis. She believes that humans evolved to share the duties of childcare as a group. At the same time, human offspring evolved to attach to, bond with, and be raised by a handful of people—not just two.

I once heard this alloparent family referred to as a "circle of love," and it struck me as an appropriate term. Because we're not talking about casual caretakers who come in and out of a child's life. We are talking about five or six key people who work alongside the mother and father, connecting to form a steady stream of unconditional love as a child grows.

Alloparenting is likely one of the key reasons why our species and our ancestors have survived the past million years or so while other human-like species, such as Neanderthal and *Homo heidelbergensis*, didn't make the cut. In other words, *Homo sapien*'s "success" on earth probably has less to do with "man the hunter" than "aunty the helper" and "grandpa the giver."

Ultimately, you are responsible for your own children, but you have to love all the children like your own.

— SUBION

Allo comes from the Greek term for "other." But the phrase "other parent" doesn't do alloparents justice in the slightest. They are not simply the "others" who take a side role or minor role in a child's life. Oh, no. They're central, omnipresent sources of love and care for children, responsible for much more than changing diapers or rocking a baby to sleep.

Take, for instance the Efe, a group of hunter-gatherers who have lived in the rainforest of central Africa for thousands of years. Right after a mom gives birth, other women come over to her house and form a baby SWAT team, ready to respond to every whimper and cry the baby has. They hold, snuggle, rock, and even feed the newborn. As the anthropologist Mel Konner writes: "Dealing with a fussing baby is a group effort." After a few days, the mom can return to work and leave the baby with an allomother.

In the first few weeks of a new baby's life, an infant will move from one caregiver to the next, on average, every fifteen minutes. By the time the baby is three weeks old, allomoms account for 40 percent of the newborn's physical care. By sixteen weeks, allomoms account for a whopping 60 percent. Skip ahead two years, and the child spends more time with others than with their own mother.

All these snuggles, cuddles, and moments of comfort from allomoms have lasting benefits for babies and children. These women know the little dumpling just as well as the mother. And the dumpling feels just as safe and comfortable with these alloparents as they do with mom. As a result, babies attach and bond to many adults, perhaps as many as five or six.

You find similar situations in many hunter-gatherer communities worldwide. Among the BaYaka, who also live in central Africa, children have about twenty different caretakers over the course of a day. Some of these caretakers will casually look after the baby, but others—about half—will aid in such essential tasks as feeding and cleaning the baby.

"So that situation is very different from the Western one, where the mother is to be the sole figure in a baby's life and uses all her energy to take care of the baby," says anthropologist Abigail Page, who studies the Agta, a group of hunter-gatherers in the Philippines.

In southern India, the Nayaka hunter-gatherers value alloparents so much that they have a special name for them: *sonta*, which roughly means a group of people who are as close as siblings. Adults call all the children around their home "son" or "daughter," or *maga(n)*, and all the older people in their community "little father," *cikappa(n)* and "little mother," *cikawa(l)*.

At first blush, you might think that relatives serve as the critical alloparents in hunter-gatherer communities. But in many cultures, families move around frequently and often find themselves living far away from kin.

More recently, researchers began to look *outside* the family for alloparents. And lo and behold, they found a whole menagerie of caretakers who are related to the child only through proximity and love. One study in particular found a surprising source of parental help—one source that Western families can easily tap into and bring back into the fold.

The study took place along the northern coast of the Philippines, a region where Agta families have lived for tens of thousands of years. They spearfish in coral reefs, forage in tidal pools, and when they need to escape violence (or a coronavirus pandemic), they move high up into the mountains.

Abigail Page and her colleague followed a bunch of Agta kids, ages two to six, to see who looked after them throughout the day. The mom did a big portion of the care, about 20 percent of it. But guess who did even more? Other kids! I'm talking about the under-ten crew, who crave responsibility and really want to act like a "big kid." I'm talking about the Belies around the world (and Rosy in a year or two).

These mini-alloparents, ages six to eleven, provided about a quarter of the young children's care, Abigail reported. They freed up the moms so much that the women could go back to work, or just take a break and relax. And these mini-alloparents did more than simply babysit—they took the job more seriously than that. They also did a bunch of teaching.

Abigail thinks that young children, about five years older than another child, can be the best teachers out there—way better than parents themselves. The youngsters have several big advantages over us old folks, she points out. They have more energy than parents. They naturally integrate play and pretend into their "teaching exercises," so learning is more fun. And their skill level at a task more closely matches that of a younger child.

Western culture currently underestimates the value of child-to-child teaching, says psychologist Sheina Lew-Levy, who studies the BaYaka hunter-gatherers in central Africa.

"We think teaching occurs when a more knowledgeable adult instructs a younger individual, but in my research, I found that not to be the case. I found child-to-child teaching to be much more common after infancy," she says.

In the end, these multiage playgroups not only give parents extra time to themselves, they also give children a physical and mental boost, Sheina says. "These playgroups are really important for social learning and development. In these groups, kids learn to expand their horizons; they learn social and emotional skills; and they learn how to function in society."

———————

Back with the Hadzabe families, I see alloparenting everywhere. From sunup to sundown, every single day, a group of about a dozen women and men work together to take care of each other's babies and toddlers. Every woman and every man holds, carries, and dotes on each other's kids so much that, at first, I had a hard time telling which kid belonged to which parents. The kids move between adults with so much ease and comfort that they seem equally comfortable with a handful of adults.

One mom of four kids, Subion, summed up alloparenting perfectly: "Ultimately, you are responsible for your own children, but you have to love all the children like your own."

With a sweet face and a gentle voice, Subion radiates tenderness and compassion. When she smiles and laughs, which she does often, two dimples appear on either side of her plump cheeks. But Subion is tough as nails. She's a single mom. One of her sons is disabled and can't walk. The day before our conversation, I saw her carry a bucket full of water on top of her head for about 1.5 miles up a steep river gorge, with a baby on her back and a toddler tugging at her skirt.

"Subion, do you think being a mom is hard?" I ask her.

"Yes," she says quickly, with a serious tone. "Because you have to work hard to take care of them, but I am proud of being a parent."

Watching Subion laugh and joke with the other women at the camp while they pass around each other's babies, I realize these Hadzabe moms have not only an enormous amount of help with childcare, but they also have an enormous amount of camaraderie. I'm lucky to spend two or three hours a week with my girlfriends. These Hadzabe women see each other for eight to ten hours each day! You can tell that the women have deeply rewarding and fulfilling relationships.

Scientists hypothesize that alloparenting evolved to help parents provide for their children. But what if, along with ensuring kids have full tummies, alloparenting also provided something else essential to parents: friendship?

Subion and the other Hadzabe men and women have in abundance what I was missing as a new mom: social support. They have a rich network of people to whom they can turn when they feel down or need help. When life gets rough, they have each other's back.

For *Homo sapiens*, social support works a bit like a miracle drug. It provides health benefits that ripple through our entire bodies, from our minds into our blood, through our hearts, and into our bones. Over the past decades, study after study has linked meaningful friendships and camaraderie to all kinds of health benefits. They decrease our risk for cardiovascular disease; boost our immune systems; and protect us from stress, anxiety, and depression. And when we do find ourselves trapped with a mental health problem, the more that we believe we have friends and families supporting us, the better chance we have of recovering from anxiety and depression.

"Just spending time with others, even if you aren't interacting, can lower your blood pressure and have a calming effect," says psychologist Bert Uchino, at the University of Utah, who studies how loneliness affects our physical health.

On the flip side, a lack of social support worsens mental health problems, forming a sort of snowball effect, Bert says. Loneliness can cause anxiety, depression, and sleep problems, which in turn cause more loneliness. "When people don't have social support, their bodies have signs of physical stress. They look like they're being threatened. Like people are out to get them," Bert says.

Social support is so important for physical health that, in one study, having strong relationships correlated just as strongly with a longer life expectancy as being physically active or cutting out smoking. In other words, the time and energy you spend planting and cultivating deep, fulfilling friendships is likely just as crucial to your overall well-being as your afternoon run (or even not smoking).

Most of these studies examine adults, but social support, especially from family members, may be even more important for children, Bert says. "The quality of our early family relationships is tied to whether we suffer from loneliness and social isolation as an adult. If a child feels nurtured by their parents and feels like they can count on them, then the child carries that with them for the rest of their lives."

If that's the case, then what happens when a child feels loved and nurtured not by just two parents, but by three, four, even five alloparents?

Some anthropologists believe that alloparenting gives children something that sounds almost magical: trust in the world. Trust that your family will take care of you. Trust that the people in your neighborhood will take care of you. Trust that the forest will take care of you. Trust that people you meet will be kind, warm, and helpful. Trust that the world will provide for you.

"So the close relationships between alloparents and an infant early in life builds a high level of trust, and then that trust gets projected onto the whole world," says Sheina Lew-Levy.

And so the circle of love that a young child experiences prepares them to better carry love, confidence, and a sense of security into the world.

Back in San Francisco, I can't stop thinking about Subion and the other Hadzabe moms and the days they spend together, helping with each other's babies and toddlers. I begin to imagine how my experience as a new mother would have been different if I'd had so much help. What if our family had five alloparents available, let alone ten?

How nice it would have been to have a close aunt teach me how to swaddle Rosy, or a grandpa show me how to rock her to sleep. Or if a neighbor could have come over on the nights when Rosy was colicky and we couldn't stop her crying. Or if my sister could have stayed three months instead of a week.

With all these extra hands, hugs, and hearts, Rosy would have cried much less, I'm certain. But what about the mama and papa? I probably would have felt more like a human being instead of a milk-producing, diaper-changing machine. Both Matt and I would have felt less exhausted and alone. Having alloparents would have lifted us up physically and mentally. Would I still have developed postpartum depression? I doubt it.

Maybe the problem wasn't me, after all. Instead, maybe the problem lies in Western culture—how we think parenting should work and how we bring new babies into this world. By isolating new parents and focusing so heavily on the nuclear family as the primary caretakers, we set up moms and dads for postpartum anxiety and depression. (And that's with a family like ours, who are extremely fortunate and privileged to have a home, stable income, and medical insurance. What about families without such financial security? I can only imagine how much harder our culture's practices make it for them.)

And as we're learning, this isolated style of parenting isn't great for children, either, despite our good intentions. As parents, we want to do everything we can to provide our kids with all that they'll need in the future—but by focusing so much on school, grades, and "accomplishments," are we, perhaps, also shutting children away inside the condo—and thus making them vulnerable to the same anxiety and depression that I felt as a new mom?

Perhaps, I am coming to see that what Rosy needs isn't another extra-curricular activity after school or an extra study session on the weekends. Rather, she needs time with a few key adults and children who know and love her just as much as her father and I do. What she needs is a circle of love that will lift her up and give her trust in the world.

Try It 9: Build Emotional Support for the Family (and Give Yourself a Break)

A little alloparenting goes a long way. Even just a couple of extra caring adults can make a profound difference in any child's life, no matter their age.

Dip Your Toe

- **Value the "little mothers" and "little fathers" in your child's life.** In Western culture, we already have many alloparents around us—ones who work extremely hard to help our children. I'm talking about nannies, day care providers, teachers, and babysitters. Some of these alloparents spend more time with our children than we do. They are linchpins for our children's emotional development and health.

And yet, over the past hundred years or so, our culture has pushed many of these alloparents to the periphery of the parenting landscape. But we can easily shift the focus back on their contributions and importance.

First of all, we can show these people how much we value and appreciate the work they do for our families. For teachers and day care providers, we can regularly acknowledge their efforts by encouraging our children to make them thank-you cards and bake them thank-you treats. We can honor their birthdays or prepare homemade gifts for the holidays. And if a teacher or coach shows special interest in a child, we can even offer to have them over for dinner or bring them a special meal.

For nannies and babysitters, who regularly work in our homes, we can treat them less as paid help and more as valued family members. We can take an interest in their lives and families. We can be as generous as possible with compensation and offer help to their own families whenever they may need it. If the caretaker seems interested, we can invite them—and their families—over for meals or parties. (Just make clear that the offer is not meant as "additional work," but rather as a gesture of appreciation and a genuine desire to build a relationship.)

Even after the child grows out of the person's care, we can continue to cultivate the relationship. We can check in regularly with them and their families, through emails or calls. We can meet up for visits, if they would like, or bring them homemade gifts and goodies. Above all, we can treat caretakers with as much respect and gratitude as we give close family members. Their contributions to our families are just as important.

Wade In

- **Train up a mini-alloparent.** Recruit an older sibling to look after the younger ones. Start training them when they are young, say three or four. At that age, a child is eager to learn and help—and acting as the caretaker will become second nature for them as they grow up.

For children of any age, simply use the formula: provide opportunities to practice, model the behavior you want, and connect the care to maturity. Tell the child that they are responsible for the baby and "need to be the mama/daddy" or the "big kid." Then slowly, over time, give the child more responsibilities. Provide the invisible safety net, as needed.

Jump In

• **Build an auntie and uncle network.** Suzanne Gaskins gave me this idea, and it's brilliant. Basically, for each child, you pick three or four close friends. And then all the families work together to provide after-school care. Each day, a different family picks up the kids (if needed) and provides snacks and parental supervision (if needed). "Then my boys had a bunch of aunts and uncles," Suzanne says. Children flex their autonomy muscles while also building social support with their friends and their family. Over time, everyone becomes one giant extended family. And parents get a break!

• **Build a MAP.** That's my own acronym for "multi-age playgroup" or "mixed-age playgroup."

MAPs help children grow emotionally by leaps and bounds. Younger children learn more sophisticated behavior from the older children. Older kids learn through teaching the younger kids, while also flexing their leadership and nurturing skills.

You can try several ways to create MAPs. You can keep it simple and encourage kids in your neighborhood to play together after school and weekends. I often tell Rosy, "Go get Marat [the boy who lives next door]," which I alternate with "Go play at Marat's house."

Or you can organize a weekly neighborhood playgroup in your backyard or a nearby park. Invite all the kids in the neighborhood to come for a few hours on a Saturday or Sunday. One or two other parents are all you need. And the ones who come should try to form the "invisible safety net." Ideally, parents would disappear into the background and interfere only if a child is going to get hurt.

Try hosting the MAP each week. Or ask other parents to host and supervise. After a few months, the kids will likely be playing together on their own, with very little organization. And your neighborhood safety net will be strong and wide.

• **Tolerate your relatives (or learn to value their contributions).** Depending on your family, this can be a tough one. In my own family, there can be conflict and tension. But I see how much everyone loves Rosy—and how much she loves them. And so I decided to stop picking fights, and learn to coexist peacefully (most of the time).

In general, Matt and I have made it a priority to include our families in Rosy's life as much as possible. We try to visit extended family for holidays and always welcome them into our home. Each summer we help organize a vacation with Matt's siblings and all their kids. And these reunions have been a blast!

If this isn't possible with your own family, focus on cultivating your "uncle and auntie" network with friends and neighbors. The goal here is to build deep, high-quality connections, not necessarily *more* connections.

Summary for Chapter 15:
How to Protect Children from Depression

Ideas to Remember

➤ Babies and children are designed to be raised by many types of people. From grandparents and aunties to nannies and neighbors, they are all important.

➤ This network of love and support helps the child see the world as supportive and kind, which protects them from depression and mental health problems.

➤ One or two extra alloparents can make a big difference in a child's life.

➤ Other children make fantastic alloparents and tend to be better teachers and playmates than adults. Children naturally integrate play into learning and have skill levels closer to other children than adults have.

➤ Deep, close friendships are likely just as important for you and your child's health as exercising and eating healthy.

Tips and Tools

➤ **Build a network of aunts and uncles.** Work together with three or four other families to share after-school care. Have each family be responsible for a day each week. This network provides emotional support for kids and breaks for parents.

➤ **Create MAPs (Multi-age playgroups).** Encourage your child to play with kids, of all ages, around the neighborhood. Invite other families over for dinner or cocktails. Organize big neighborhood playgroups on the weekend, where kids of all ages are invited to play in your yard or at a nearby park.

➤ **Train up mini-alloparents.** Teach older children to take care of younger siblings, starting at a young age. Connect their care to their growing maturity (e.g., "You're helping your brother because you're a big girl now"). Reward the child for their care by increasing their responsibility over time.

➤ **Value the alloparents you already have.** Work together with your child to show appreciation for nannies, day care providers, teachers, and coaches. Make them thank-you notes, treats, and special meals. Treat them as valued family members. Model generosity and respect.

Western Parenting 2.0

T
E
A
Minimal interference

A New Paradigm for Western Parents

Imagine, for a second, a little toddler learning to walk. Perhaps you picture the mother holding the baby's hands. In the U.S., that's often how it happens, Suzanne Gaskins observes. "Or she's out in front, saying, 'Come to me, come to me,' with a verbal instruction."

But in the Yucatán, the same situation looks quite different.

"The Maya mom goes right behind the child with arms stretched out, ready to catch her if they fall," Suzanne continues. "From the child's perspective, they're walking on their own with no help whatsoever."

———————

When I set out to write this book, I had a couple of big questions to answer: How did Maria in the Yucatán raise such helpful and respectful children? And how does her relationship with her kids feature so little conflict and resistance?

Over the course of this book, we've gradually gathered all the pieces to answer those questions. Maria values togetherness, encouragement (instead of force), autonomy, and minimal interference. She practices TEAM parenting.

HELICOPTER
PARENTING

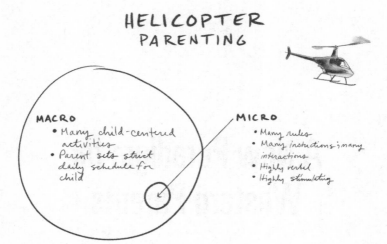

MACRO
- Many child-centered activities
- Parent sets strict daily schedule for child

MICRO
- Many rules
- Many instructions; many interactions
- Highly verbal
- Highly stimulating

If we think about our roles as parents, we can divide our job into two categories: Macro- and micro-parenting (a bit like economists do with their field). Macro-parenting is all about the big picture—how we structure the child's days, schedule activities, and organize their time. Micro-parenting, on the other hand, is what we do moment to moment during those activities. It's what we say, how much we say, and how much we attempt to influence a child's behavior in real time.

FREE-RANGE
PARENTING

MACRO
- Many child-centered activities
- Low structure
- Child sets schedule

MICRO
- Few rules
- Few exceptions; few responsibilities
- Minimal instruction
- Child is in charge

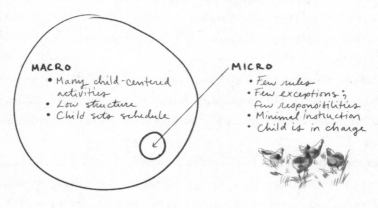

So, for example, helicopter parents strictly control a child's overall schedule (macro-parenting), and they strictly control the child's actions during those activities (micro-parenting). By contrast, free-range parents allow a child to set their own schedule, and they let the child decide how to act during those activities. They take a laissez-faire approach on both the macro- and micro-parenting fronts.

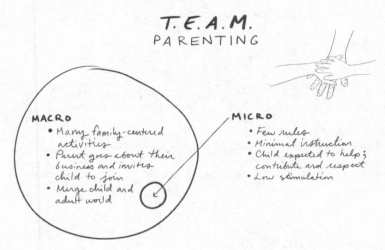

T.E.A.M. PARENTING

MACRO
- Many family-centered activities
- Parent goes about their business and invites child to join
- Merge child and adult world

MICRO
- Few rules
- Minimal instruction
- Child expected to help; contribute and respect
- Low stimulation

In this book, we've learned an alternative approach to these two dichotomies. With TEAM parenting, the mom and dad set the daily agenda and overall schedule for the whole family. They go about their business around the home and community, and expect the kids to follow along, more or less.* They welcome the children into their world.

So in terms of macro-parenting, mom and dad take charge. The family does activities *together*, and the children have little influence on the overall schedule.

But during those family-centered activities, the child is largely in charge of their own behavior. The child has an enormous amount of *autonomy*, and the parent *minimally interferes*. The parent watches the child and carefully chooses when to influence the child's behavior (e.g., when the

---

* If a child doesn't want to participate in a family activity, parents typically don't force the child to join in; instead, they leave the child with another caretaker or alloparent.

child is unsafe, or when the parent is transmitting a key cultural value, such as helpfulness or generosity). Even then, the parent uses a light touch. They *encourage* the child, with a whole suite of tools, instead of coercing through punishments or threats. They know that actions and modeling will prove much more effective—and much less stressful—than issuing instructions and commands. And whenever possible, the parent harnesses a child's own interest or enthusiasm to motivate them.

MINIMAL INTERFERENCE

Avoid feeling like you have to push or pull a child along.

Make the knee-jerk reaction to step back and watch (instead of telling a child what to do).

Have confidence a child can entertain and occupy themselves.

Demand little of a child's attention and they will demand little of yours.

Minimal interference not only reduces conflict, it also gives children oodles of practice at entertaining and taking care of themselves. They become incredibly skilled at the art of solitary absorption and self-generated fun. They learn to figure out problems on their own, settle their own disputes, make up their own games, prepare their own snacks, even get their own gosh-darn milk. And they become much less demanding along the way. In essence, if a parent doesn't demand and control a child's attention, the child won't demand and control the parent's attention.

I don't often get it right—this whole book I've wanted to show you that we all struggle. But when I do manage to pull off the TEAM parenting approach with Rosy, the results have consistently been magic. And I can see our relationship improving "little by little," as Maria says.

One evening, while making dinner, I nail it—just absolutely nail it. While I cook salmon in the kitchen, Rosy dances to *The Lion King* soundtrack in the living room. I'm doing a great job at maintaining three-commands-per-hour. In return, Rosy demands little of me. We are peace-fully coexisting (almost like Thaa and Belie by the fire).

Then Rosy tries to disturb the peace. She comes over and says, "Mama, can we have a picnic in the living room for dinner? Please, please, Mama?"

The old Michaeleen would have instantly said, "No way, sister! That sounds like it's going to make a huge mess." Rosy and I would have ended up in a full-blown screamfest about why a picnic is too much trouble. But the new Michaeleen waits a bit and thinks, *Hmm, this is a good opportunity for Rosy to practice setting the table.*

"Okay, Rosy. Let's do it. Here, set the table," I say as I hand her the plates. She grabs them, rushes back into the living room, and a few min-utes later, a beautiful "picnic" setting appears on the living room rug. Rosy even goes up to our porch, picks a few purple petunias, and creates a floral centerpiece for the picnic.

We repeat the process for about a week. Each night, Rosy sets the "pic-nic" table. And then when we finally move dinner back into the room, guess who sets the table without me asking? Little Roro.

In the U.S., we feel this enormous responsibility to "optimize" our chil-dren. That often means filling their days with nonstop activities or enter-tainment. I sure felt this way with Rosy (sometimes I still do). This feeling places a heavy burden on our shoulders and fills our minds with an omni-present anxiety (e.g., "Oh my gosh, what am I going to do with Rosy for the entire Saturday?"). But the feeling also supercharges our parenting—both the macro and micro. Our knee-jerk reaction is maximal interference.

"Parents have taken on all these extra obligations because someone has convinced us that they are essential for optimizing a child," anthropologist David Lancy says.

But there's no scientific evidence showing that this approach works best for kids. It's certainly not optimal for all children (certainly not for Rosy). One could argue that this approach goes against children's natural inclination for autonomy, self-exploration, and cooperation. Not to men-tion, this parenting style is exhausting for everyone. Every time the parent manages a child's behavior, the parent runs the risk of resistance.

Before I began writing this book, Suzanne Gaskins warned me that "maximal interference" was only making my life harder. And also holding back Rosy, physically and emotionally. "I think American parents are picking fights they don't need to," she said. "It's actually really stressful for a child when a parent is always pulling the child forward into places the child's not yet ready to go or hasn't decided they want to go."

As you've been reading this book, I hope you've seen how parenting doesn't have to be that way. Not in the least. In fact, if we want to raise confident, self-sufficient kids, we don't want it to be that way. We don't want to pull and push our kids so much; to constantly entertain and keep them busy. And most of all, we don't *need* to always try so hard.

We can release our grip. We can release our grip on our children's behavior and on what we think parents need to do. We can be confident that our children know better than we do about what they need to grow and learn.

We can join the millions of parents around the world—and across history—who step behind the child, wait-a-bit, and let the child make their own decisions; let them make their own mistakes; and let them make their own types of kebabs. We, or an alloparent, will be standing behind them with our arms outstretched, ready to catch them if they fall.

CHAPTER 16

Sleep

When Rosy and I finally finish traveling for this book, I return to San Francisco still puzzling over one thing: Why does Rosy have such a hard time going to sleep at night? She gets plenty of exercise, light, and "stimulation." She should be tired. And yet bedtime is a chronic struggle in the Doucleff household.

Every single night, there's drama and conflict. Rosy and I often end up screaming at each other, while Matt ends up chasing Rosy around the room as she chants a protest mantra. Something like "No, no, no. I will never go to sleep. No, no, no."

And yet, everywhere Rosy and I traveled for this book, we never encountered such nighttime theatrics. Children didn't seem to have any problems at all going to bed. I never once heard a child cry, scream, or throw a fit at bedtime. For some kids, going to sleep seemed like something they *wanted* to do, even looked forward to doing.

One night in the Arctic, I saw a three-year-old girl put herself to sleep, with no help from an adult, whatsoever. We were sitting in Maria's living room in Kugaaruk, while a bunch of kids played video games. Around

7:30 p.m., when the sun still had a good five hours left before it set, little Tessa stood up from the sofa, walked down the hall, and didn't return.

I asked Sally what Tessa was doing in the bedroom.

"She went to sleep," Sally said.

"She just put herself to sleep, all by herself?"

"Yes, she does that a lot," Sally responded. "She's a good sleeper."

You don't say, I thought.

Everywhere Rosy and I traveled, I asked parents, what do you do for bedtime routines? What do you do if children don't want to sleep? All the parents shrugged off the questions and basically indicated that sleep was no big deal. "Sometimes Ernesto needs a little push to finish his homework before going to bed," Teresa told me in the Yucatán.

That's it? Nothing else?

"Nothing else," she said calmly.

And so back in San Francisco, I become determined to fix our sleep problem. I know that Rosy would never magically turn into Tessa, but she has room for improvement. Lots of room.

After several weeks of research and experiments, I hit a wall. Rosy has made no progress whatsoever, and some nights, all my meddling only worsens the problem. So I pretty much give up and accept that bedtime mayhem is a burden that our family has to bear. *She'll grow out of it, eventually*, I say to myself. *And really, is it that bad?*

Then one night, right before Rosy's bedtime, I'm sitting at our kitchen table, drawing an illustration for this book. I sketch out the "formula"— the three ingredients for training a child to do anything you want: 1 cup of practice + 1 cup of modeling + 1 teaspoon of acknowledging = skill learned.

Around 8:30 p.m., I hear the small wildcat upstairs screeching in the bedroom. I put the sketch into a notebook, take a deep breath, and head up the stairs. When I arrive on scene, I see Rosy jumping on the bed while Matt holds her pajamas in his hand, trying to convince her to calm down.

Right before I can open my mouth and launch into my usual script of commands ("Rosy, we are serious . . ."), the sketch of the formula flashes through my thoughts—practice, modeling, acknowledge—and a realization hits me like a brick in the face. *Oh, no*, I think. *I have trained Rosy at bedtime. And the training has worked well. Super well. The only problem is, I have been training her to do exactly the opposite of what I want.*

Twenty years ago, Benjamin Reiss was writing a book about the history of insane asylums when he stumbled upon an intriguing observation about sleep. "In the nineteenth century, the doctors at these asylums were really obsessed with controlling their patients' sleep," Ben says. The doctors strictly dictated when patients slept, how long they slept, and what the sleeping environment was like. Sound familiar? They also meticulously tracked the patients' sleep with charts and logs.

Ben chairs the English department at Emory University, and he's a fantastic historian. He likes to take ideas that we think of as "biological truths" and track down how we came to see them that way. Then he figures out what our biology might actually be telling us.

And so Ben wondered: Why were the doctors and nurses in these asylums so concerned about the patients' sleep? Why were they so obsessed?

He dug into the history of sleep around the world and quickly realized that this obsession with sleep—this need to track and control the process—isn't exclusive to insane asylums. "It's pervasive across all of Western society," Ben says. And it causes big problems with our kids.

In Western culture, we have an extremely narrow view of what constitutes "normal" sleep, and if you vary from that "normal," you set yourself up for problems, he says. "We have these rigid rules that people take as if they are God given or that our biology dictates," he says.

We think that in order to be healthy, we *have* to sleep about eight hours each night, in one uninterrupted chunk. And yet, not that long ago, the vast majority of people in Western culture didn't sleep like this at all. Up until the late nineteenth century, "normal" sleep was segmented. Most people slept in two chunks, each for about four hours. One segment occurred before midnight, the other after midnight. And in between people did all sorts of tasks. As historian A. Roger Ekirch writes: "They rose to perform chores, tend to sick children, raid a neighbor's apple orchard. Others, remaining abed, recited prayers and pondered dreams."

There's even evidence that segmented sleep dates back thousands of years in Western culture. In the first century BC, the Roman poet Virgil wrote about the "hour which terminates the first sleep, when the car of Night had as yet performed but half its course," in his epic poem the *Aeneid*.

So if you tend to wake up in the middle of the night and have a hard time falling back to sleep, maybe you don't have insomnia. You just sleep like your ancestors did for thousands of years. They would think you're normal.

Basically all the "sleep rules," as we know them now, came into fashion in the nineteenth century. During the Industrial Revolution, workers needed to arrive at factories at a certain time in the morning, no matter when the sun rose or set. As a result, "sleep had to be subjected to increasing levels of control," Ben writes in his book *Wild Nights: How Taming Sleep Created Our Restless World*.

Before then, people tended to follow their biological signals: Sleep when you're tired and wake up when you're rested. "This is worth reiterating: virtually nothing about our standard model of sleep existed as we know it two centuries ago," Ben writes.

Human sleep is actually quite flexible, adaptable, and personalized. Sleep patterns vary enormously from culture to culture, location to location, and even season to season. There's no "right way" to sleep. Scientists can measure an "average" sleep regime, but it's by no means the "normal" one.

"Some societies nap while some don't; some sleep in large groups, others more or less alone; some naked, some clothed; some in public, some hidden," Ben writes. Many different regimes can be healthy for different people—or even for the same person during different seasons.

And if you think everyone needs eight hours a day, think again. Back in 2015, researchers tracked the sleep habits of more than eighty people in three indigenous communities that live without electricity: the Hadzabe in Tanzania, the San in Namibia, and the Tsimane in Bolivia. The results were remarkably similar across all three groups: people, on average, slept about six to seven hours a night (which is remarkably close to the amount of zzz's many Americans clock each night).

What makes Americans such WEIRD sleepers, Ben says, isn't how much we sleep, but rather how much we try to control each other's sleep and how rigid we are in our thinking. We set strict schedules for ourselves and our children, which often don't comport with our basic biology. Then we expend an enormous amount of energy to follow these schedules. And when the schedules don't work—or our children don't follow them—our minds fill with anxiety. We worry that we aren't normal, or we aren't good parents.

And so at bedtime, Ben says, we end up doing the opposite of what we want to do. Instead of creating a calm, relaxing environment and mind-set, we generate struggle and conflict. We manufacture mayhem. And we teach our children, over years and years, to become stressed and anxious at bedtime.

That's exactly what was happening at the Doucleff household.

———————

And so watching Rosy jump on the bed, chanting, "No, no, no sleep!" I see exactly what I have trained her to do at 8:30 p.m. every night. I have trained her to strip, scream, and jump on the bed. Basically, I have trained her that bedtime means party time!

Think back to the formula: practice, model, and acknowledge. At bed-time, I have given Rosy the opportunity to *practice* arguing, screaming, and issuing demands (e.g., "I need food," "I need milk," "I need another book"). I have *modeled* impatience and bossiness—some might even say demanding behavior ("You have to brush your teeth right now, Rosemary Jane"). Finally, I have given so much attention to the wrong behaviors. I have *acknowledged* (negatively, but intensely) all of Rosy's antics. I have met Rosy's high energy with high energy. And thus, day after day, month after month, and year after year, bedtime has become harder and harder.

Oh my gosh, I feel like such a fool, I think as Rosy jumps off the bed to race naked across the room. I feel like I have been duped by all the parent-ing books that have admonished me to "keep a strict bedtime," to "stick to the routine," and to add more and more structure to our lives. For Rosy, all that structure and control has backfired. It has triggered anxiety, conflict, and party time! And it has disconnected her from her biological clock.

If you recognize your own household in this story, take heart, tired parent. One great thing about kids is how quickly they can change. No matter how deep you've dug yourself into a hole, you can always get out of it. You can always retrain a child—and retrain them quite easily. How? By using the formula for good.

Think back to little Tessa up in Kugaaruk. At only three years old, she had already mastered a skill I didn't have until I reached my thirties: she knew what her body felt like when she was tired and she knew what she needed to do about it. She went to bed.

I can train Rosy to have the same skill, to detect her tired signals and then take herself to bed when she feels them. But to do that, I have to "let her go," as the interpreter David Mark Makia told me in Tanzania. I have to give up (almost all) control over Rosy's sleep schedule. I have to throw out the bedtime routine in favor of giving Rosy the space to develop the skill of listening to her biological cues. I can help her learn that skill, but I have to *minimally interfere*. At the end of the day (no pun intended), it will be up to her when she goes to sleep.

I'm not going to lie to you. That whole plan scares the bejesus out of me. *But what if she never goes to sleep? Or what if she doesn't get up in the morning? We are headed into Dante's* Inferno, *for sure.*

And so I decide to try the scheme for a week, and if it doesn't work, I will go back to our routine.

With great trepidation, I close my eyes, grab Rosy's hand, and jump off the sleep schedule cliff.

To my utmost surprise, Rosy flies!

———

The formula works way better—and faster—than I predict. The first few nights, Rosy stays up late, until about 10:30 or 11:00 p.m. But she still wakes up easily in the morning. By night four, she goes to bed on time, and by day seven, she gets ready for bed almost entirely on her own. No more arguments. No more screaming. No more running around like a wild cat.

Then on day ten, a miracle occurs at the Doucleff household. At around seven p.m., Rosy walks upstairs, all by herself, gets in bed, and goes to sleep.

"Did you see that?" Matt asks.

"Yes," I say cautiously.

"Nights have been so easy."

"I know. I know. Don't jinx it."

Since that night, we have had essentially zero problems with Rosy at bedtime. Zero. The formula transformed her into a super sleeper.

So how did I do it?

Around eight o'clock each night, I began to watch Rosy like a hawk. When I detected her tired signals (e.g., rubbing her eyes, sucking her thumb, whining more), I turned down the lights in the house. I'd noticed how the darkness in Tanzania really calmed her down. Then I executed the following procedure:

1. **Model**. I said, very calmly, "I'm tired. My body is telling me I'm tired. I'm going to bed." I went upstairs and got myself ready for bed (although I wasn't going to sleep). I brushed my teeth. Flossed. Put on my pajamas. Then I got into her bed, and started reading a book. And I waited.

2. **Acknowledge**. When she came upstairs and laid next to me, I gave her a bit of positive attention. I hugged her and smiled at her. Then I connected the desired behavior to maturity with one question: "Rosy, what would a big girl do now?" I stayed in the bed and continued to model what I wanted her to do. I never forced her to get ready for bed but rather encouraged her with the tools we've learned.

3. **Practice**. Once she got her pj's on and brushed her teeth, I helped her fall asleep by rubbing her back. I stayed calm the whole time and never pushed. If she talked or whined, I simply said, "Let's be quiet and still so our bodies and minds can calm down and go to sleep. I'm tired."

Night after night, we both practiced being calm and feeling tiredness in our bodies. A few nights, I actually fell asleep myself.

In a matter of three weeks, we turned one of the most difficult parent-

ing issues in our lives into a nothing burger. And along the way, I sharp-
ened my TEAM parenting skills:

Togetherness: We did bedtime together.

Encourage: I encouraged Rosy to go to sleep instead of forcing her at a
particular time.

Autonomy: Rosy decided, on her own, when to go upstairs to go to sleep.

Minimize interference: Instead of controlling Rosy's behavior, I did
what was minimally required to help her learn a valuable life skill.

EPILOGUE

Over the course of my writing this book, Rosy has changed so much. She grew by leaps and bounds, emotionally and physically—way more than I had expected. She went from being my "enemy" to becoming one of my most favorite people in the world.

First of all, she has turned into a fantastic travel companion. Seriously. Who else would fly forty hours and drive another ten hours, only to arrive at a place without showers or electricity, and then turn to you and say: "I love this place, Mama. It's so beautiful!"

Second, she has embraced *acomedido* with gusto. She volunteers to help cook meals (who knew a three-year-old could scramble eggs in a hot pan?), to make the beds, and even, sometimes, to do the laundry. One day she said, "Mama, what should I do now?" And without missing a beat, I blurted out, "A load of wash." Lo and behold, the little half-pint went and put in a load of laundry. *Wow, I've been totally overthinking this parenting thing*, I thought.

But most of all, Rosy tries. Oh goodness, she tries so hard. She tries to be kind, to be calm, and most pointedly, she tries to please me. One day a few months ago, she got mad and hit me on my leg. She didn't hit hard. And I wasn't angry. But she ran away and went into another room. I peeked around the door, and there she was, with her little hands over her face, shaking her head. I could see that she was upset with herself for not controlling her emotions. And she was thinking hard about what to do next. I could see how much she wanted to grow up and be a "big girl." Her heartache broke my heart. So I walked into the room to console her. But to my surprise, she consoled me. She looked at me and said, "I'm sorry, Mama. Can we start over? I want to start over."

Because I had control of my own emotions, I could meet Rosy's calmness with my own calmness. I could let go of the hitting, and indeed, I could start over. In that moment, I realized how much I, too, had changed, as well, while writing this book.

Maria, Sally, Thaa, and the other superparents taught me an unbelievable amount about raising Rosy. They taught me that simple actions and gentle touches are way more powerful with children than commands. They taught me that if I meet Rosy's emotional outburst with my own emotional outburst I will only make the situation worse. But if I meet her high energy with calm energy, she will settle down, and tantrums will stop.

Perhaps most important, Maria, Sally, and Thaa taught me to see what I couldn't see before: that all children, including Rosy, are inherently kind and helpful. Our species might not be here on earth if they weren't.

One can view a child's behavior like a glass of water: Is it half helpful, or half hurtful? Half generous, or half selfish? Once I shifted my view and could see Rosy's kind intentions and her eagerness to help, I could nurture and amplify those qualities. I could help her see those traits in herself. And as I did, those parts of her began to grow in size and strength. The glass began to fill up the rest of the way, and the clear liquid began to glow and sparkle with love and light.

I truly believe that Rosy never wants to "push my buttons," "test boundaries," or "manipulate" me. I believe that she is simply trying her best to figure out the rules of this crazy, WEIRD culture into which she was born. And in many instances, that's exactly what I am trying to do as well.

In her wonderful book, *How to Do Nothing*, Jenny Odell writes about what happens when people first begin to watch birds. The practice of trying to hear and see birds changes their senses. They become more aware of all the sounds around them. And eventually, they realize, holy cow! Birdsong is an omnipresent symphony outside. "Of course, it had been there all along," Jenny writes, "but now that I was paying attention to it, I realized that it was almost everywhere, all day, all the time."

I think the same is true of children and kindness. Once you slow down and stop trying to change a child's behavior so much, your sensitivity for their love grows by volumes. You see the child rushing over to help her friend who fell off her bike; you see the child collecting limes from a tree for dinner; and you see all the helpfulness in her eyes when she grabs the spatula from your hands and says, "Mama, that's not how you flip pancakes. Here, let me show you how."

Rosy's kindness "had been there all along . . . but now that I was paying attention to it, I realized that it was almost everywhere, all day, all the time."

ACKNOWLEDGMENTS

Throughout this book, I've tried to acknowledge all the people who've made it possible, including the wonderful families and parents who welcomed us into their homes, the interpreters who helped us get to know those families better, and the scientists who helped to explain how their parenting tools work. I'm incredibly grateful for their time, expertise, and thoughtful discussions.

In addition, a few people worked extremely hard behind the scenes to bring this project to fruition. Editor Carrie Frye infused every page of this book with her remarkable skill, spirit, and intellect. Illustrator Ella Trujillo brought the people and ideas to life with her beautiful, warm art. The incomparable Corina Kramer explained, very patiently and gently, all the holes in my thinking—and what I'm still getting wrong as a Western mom. Editor and publisher Jofie Ferrari-Adler worked tirelessly to make this book the best it could be, and then, along with Alexandra Primiani, to spread all these ideas as far and wide as possible, like the fluff of a dandelion in the wind.

None of this would have happened without the outstanding literary agent Alex Glass, who got the whole project rolling with one quick email, asking me, "Have you thought about writing a parenting book?" (And then persevered for months, even though I kept turning him down.)

Finally, I thank my partner, Matthew Doucleff, who has always supported my ideas as a writer and mom, although begrudgingly at first (and often with an eye roll), no matter how cockamamy they may sound.

NOTES

Prologue

7 *Today about a third of all teenagers*: Ronald C. Kessler et al., "Prevalence, severity, and comorbidity of 12-month DSM-IV disorders in the National Comorbidity Survey Replication," *Archives of General Psychiatry* 62, no. 7 (July 2005).

7 *More than 60 percent of college undergraduates*: American College Health Association-National College Health Assessment II, Undergraduate Student Reference Group Data Report, Fall 2018, https://www.acha.org/documents/ncha/NCHA-II_Fall_2018_Undergraduate_Reference_Group_Data_Report.pdf.

7 *Generation Z, which includes adults*: Cigna, "Cigna's U.S. Loneliness Index, Survey of 20,000 Americans Examining Behaviors Driving Loneliness in the United States," 2018, https://www.multivu.com/players/English/8294451-cigna-us-loneliness-survey/.

7 *"Parents have gone into a control mode"*: "College Students (And Their Parents) Face A Campus Mental Health 'Epidemic,'" NPR, *Fresh Air*, Terry Gross interview with Dr. Anthony Rostain and Dr. B. Janet Hibbs, May 28, 2019, https://www.npr.org/transcripts/727509438.

8 *They have developed a sophisticated*: Lucia Alcalá, Barbara Rogoff, and Angélica López Fraire, "Sophisticated collaboration is common among Mexican-heritage US children," *Proceedings of the National Academies of Sciences* 115, no. 45 (November 2018).

8 *Hadzabe parents are world experts*: Daudi Peterson, *Hadzabe: By the Light of a Million Fires* (Dar es Salaam, Tanzania: Mkuki na Nyota Publishers Ltd, 2013), 152.

8 *And Inuit have developed a remarkably effective approach*: Jean L. Briggs, *Never in Anger: Portrait of an Eskimo Family* (Cambridge, MA: Harvard University Press, 1970).

9 *one aspect of the parent-child relationship*: This idea comes originally from an interview with psychologist Barbara Rogoff, University of California, Santa Cruz.

Chapter 1: The WEIRDest Parents in the World

19 *Back in the 1880s, a young*: Ross H. Day and Hannelore Knuth, "The Contributions of F C Müller-Lyer," *Perception* 10, no. 2 (1981).

20 *The vast majority of studies—about 96 percent*: Joseph Henrich, Steven J. Heine, and Ana Norenzayan, "The weirdest people in the world?" *Behavioral and Brain Sciences* 33, no. 2–3 (June 2010).

21 *The conclusion from these analyses was startling*: Ibid.

21 *In the 1950s and '60s, scientists tested out the Müller-Lyer illusion*: Marshall H. Segall, Donald T. Campbell, and Melville J. Herskovits, *The Influence of Culture on Visual Perception* (Indianapolis: Bobbs-Merrill, 1966), 158; Robert N. McCauley and Joseph Henrich, "Susceptibility to the Müller-Lyer Illusion, Theory-Neutral Observation, and the Diachronic Penetrability of the Visual Input System," *Philosophical Psychology* 19, no. 1 (August 2006).

21 *What the researchers found was so surprising*: Ibid.

21 *In some indigenous cultures, such as hunter-gatherers in southern Africa*: Ibid.

22 *The researchers hypothesized that the illusion tricks Americans*: Ibid.

22 *Scientists hypothesize that all this exposure to boxes trains our brains*: Ibid.

24 *anthropologist David Lancy was wondering if the same was true about our parenting*: Author interview with David Lancy, January 9, 2018.

25 *For 99.9 percent of the time humans have been on earth, the nuclear family simply didn't exist*: Author interview with John Gillis, April 12, 2018; John R. Gillis, *A World of Their Own Making: Myth, Ritual, and the Quest for Family Values* (Cambridge, MA: Harvard University Press, 1997), 20.

25 *you might think that the idea of a mom at home sounds antiquated*: Pew Research Center, "Fewer Mothers Prefer Full-time Work: From 1997 to 2007," July 12, 2007, https://www.pewsocialtrends.org/2007/07/12/fewer-mothers-prefer-full -time-work/#:~:text=Married%20mothers%20are%20somewhat%20more ,a%20decade%20ago%20(49%25).

26 *"There is every reason to believe that modern living conditions"*: David F. Lancy, *The Anthropology of Childhood: Cherubs, Chattel, Changelings* (Cambridge, UK: Cambridge University Press, 2008), 248.

26 *"an instinct that comes as naturally to women"*: Gillis, *A World of Their Own Making*, 177.

28 *A few thousand years ago, families in Europe looked a lot like they do*: Rhitu Chatterjee, "Western Individualism May Have Roots In The Medieval Church's Obsession With Incest," NPR, November 7, 2019, https://www.npr.org/sec tions/goatsandsoda/2019/11/07/777276474/western-individualism-may-have -roots-in-the-medieval-churchs-obsession-with-ince.

28 *As a result, children in the Middle Ages*: Author interview with Michael Zuckerman, April 11, 2018.

28 *parents strongly encouraged (or coaxed) their children to marry*: Chatterjee, "Western Individualism May Have Roots In The Medieval Church's Obsession With Incest"; Judith Shulevitz, "A New Theory of Western Civilization," *The Atlantic*, October 2020.

29 *Then, sometime around 600 AD, the Catholic Church began tugging on this tapestry*: Joseph Henrich, *The WEIRDest People in the World: How the West Became Psychologically Peculiar and Particularly Prosperous* (New York: Farrar, Straus and Giroux, 2020) 169; Shulevitz, "A New Theory of Western Civilization."

29 *Innumerable repercussions followed from these laws*: Jonathan Schulz et al., "The church, intensive kinship and global psychological variation," *Science* 366, no. 707 (November 2009).

Chapter 2: Why Do We Parent the Way We Do?

33 *In the early 1980s, the British writer Christina Hardyment found herself*: Christina Hardyment, *Dream Babies: Childcare Advice from John Locke to Gina Ford* (London: Jonathan Cape Ltd., 1983), xiv.

33 *the field of pediatrics began to emerge as a distinct discipline*: P. M. Dunn, "Michael Underwood, MD (1737–1820): physician-accoucheur of London," *Archives of Disease in Childhood* 91, no. 2 (April 2006), F150–F152.

33 *"swollen descendants of terse little booklets"*: Hardyment, *Dream Babies*, 9.

34 *That advice dates back at least to 1748, when Dr. William Cadogan penned an essay*: William Cadogan, "An Essay upon Nursing and the Management of Children, from their Birth to Three Years of Age," 1749, J. Roberts, http://www .neonatology.org/classics/cadogan.html.

34 *"It is with great Pleasure I see at last"*: Hardyment, *Dream Babies*; Cadogan, "An Essay upon Nursing and the Management of Children, from their Birth to Three Years of Age."

35 *A rocker, he wrote, was an apparatus "contrived and at one time"*: Hardyment, *Dream Babies*, 53.

35 *"Although the baby's instinctive craving for its mother's presence"*: Ibid.

35 *If babies "are left to go to sleep in their cots"*: Ibid.

35 *"Bedtime was now an opportunity to show who was boss"*: Ibid.

37 *"A lack of store-bought toys was no disadvantage"*: Howard P. Chudacoff, *Children at Play: An American History* (New York: New York University Press, 2007), 59.

37 *"use of blocks, in school and at home, to teach values"*: Ibid., 44.

37 *At the same time, psychologists began*: Ibid., 74.

37 *Toys, once thought to be completely unnecessary*: Ibid., 74–75.

38 *"like a spitball in the eyes of American child-raising experts"*: Barbara Ehrenreich and Deirdre English, *For Her Own Good: Two Centuries of the Experts' Advice to Women* (New York: Anchor Books, 2005), 283.

38 *"at least some of them [Russian children] were* more *creatively daring"*: Ibid.

38 *Sputnik 1 generated an almost instantaneous national mood of panic*: Ibid.

39 *"It was her job to keep the child's sensory apparatus employed"*: Ibid., 284–85.

40 *But when you actually look at the data*: Peggy J. Miller and Grace E. Cho, *Self-Esteem in Time and Place: How American Families Imagine, Enact, and Personalize a Cultural Ideal* (New York: Oxford University Press, 2018), 21–51.

40 *In America, parents are made to feel like they must nurture*: Andrew W. Mecca, Neil J. Smelser, and John Vasconcello, eds., *The Social Importance of Self-Esteem* (Berkeley, CA: University of California Press, 1989).

40 *"Parents were told to praise their young children"*: Miller and Cho, *Self-Esteem in Time and Place*, 24.

41 *parents may be making their own lives harder in the long run*: Ibid., 232.

41 *requires that parents "spend a great deal of time and energy"*: Ibid., 232.

42 *"We thought we were saving time [with new technologies]"*: Yuval Noah Harari, *Sapiens: A Brief History of Humankind* (New York: HarperCollins, 2015), 88.

44 *"Parenting questions are some of the hardest problems out there for science"*: Author interview with Brian Nosek, February 10, 2020.

45 *"It's a bit like having an underpowered telescope to study the galaxy"*: Ibid.

45 *American Academy of Pediatrics advised parents not to give babies peanut butter*: Scott H. Sicherer, "New guidelines detail use of 'infant-safe' peanut to prevent allergy," AAP News, January 5, 2017, https://www.aappublications.org /news/2017/01/05/PeanutAllergy010517; Alessandro Fiocchi et al., "Food allergy and the introduction of solid foods to infants: a consensus document. Adverse Reactions to Foods Committee, American College of Allergy, Asthma

and Immunology," *Annals of Allergy, Asthma & Immunology* 97, no. 1 (July 2006).

45 *But eventually larger, more powerful studies followed*: G. Du Toit et al., "Randomized Trial of Peanut Consumption in Infants at Risk for Peanut Allergy," *New England Journal of Medicine* 372, no. 9 (February 2015).

45 *Twenty years after the initial advice, the medical community*: "NIAID Addendum Guidelines for the Prevention of Peanut Allergy in the United States," National Institute of Allergy and Infectious Diseases, January 2017, https://www.niaid.nih.gov/sites/default/files/peanut-allergy-prevention-guide lines-parent-summary.pdf.

45 *From 1999 to 2010, peanut allergies in children rose*: Ruchi S. Gupta et al., "Assessment of Pediatrician Awareness and Implementation of the Addendum Guidelines for the Prevention of Peanut Allergy in the United States," *JAMA Network Open* 3, no. 7 (July 2020); National Academies of Sciences, Engineering, and Medicine, Maria P. Oria and Virginia A. Stallings, eds., "Finding a Path to Safety in Food Allergy: Assessment of the Global Burden, Causes, Prevention, Management, and Public Policy," The National Academies Press, Washington, D.C., November 30, 2016, https://www.nap.edu/catalog/23658 /finding-a-path-to-safety-in-food-allergy-assessment-of.

46 *recommends that moms and dads be wary of new ideas that arise from studies*: Author interview with Brian Nosek, February 10, 2020.

Chapter 3: The Most Helpful Kids in the World

52 *In one study, Lucia and her colleagues interviewed nineteen mothers*: Lucia Alcalá et al., "Children's Initiative in Contributions to Family Work in Indigenous-Heritage and Cosmopolitan Communities in Mexico," *Human Development* 57, no. 2–3 (2014).

52 *"Mom, I'm going to help you do everything"*: Ibid.

52 *"The mom comes home from work, and she's really tired"*: Author interview with Barbara Rogoff, February 1, 2018.

53 *Lucia tells me that parents are teaching their children*: Author interview with Lucia Alcalá, May 22, 2019.

53 *three-quarters of the mothers said that their children routinely*: Alcalá et al., "Children's Initiative in Contributions to Family Work in Indigenous-Heritage and Cosmopolitan Communities in Mexico."

53 *This skill—of paying attention and then acting*: Angélica López et al., "Attentive Helping as a Cultural Practice of Mexican-heritage Families," in *Mexican*

American Children and Families: Multidisciplinary Perspectives, eds. Yvonne M. Caldera and Eric W. Lindsey (New York: Routledge, 2015), 60–75.

53 *The idea is complex: It's not just doing a chore or task*: Author interview with Andrew Coppens, February 23, 2018.

53 *In the same study, Lucia and her team also interviewed fourteen moms*: Alcalá et al., "Children's Initiative in Contributions to Family Work in Indigenous-Heritage and Cosmopolitan Communities in Mexico."

54 *they have also taught the children to value their work*: Author interviews with Suzanne Gaskins, April 4 to April 6, 2018.

Chapter 4: How to Teach Kids to Do Chores, Voluntarily

58 *The first is tantrums*: Author interview with David Lancy, June 1, 2018.

58 *Toddlers everywhere are eager to be helpful*: David F. Lancy, *Anthropological Perspectives on Children as Helpers, Workers, Artisans, and Laborers* (New York: Palgrave Macmillan, 2018), 217.

58 *Toddlers are born assistants*: Felix Warneken and Michael Tomasello, "The roots of human altruism," *British Journal of Psychology* 100:3 (August 2009).

58 *"Doing things with other people makes them happy"*: Author interview with Rebeca Mejía-Arauz, February 28, 2018.

59 *"We have mothers tell us things"*: Ibid.

59 *If the child literally grabs the tools*: Andrew D. Coppens et al., "Beyond Behavior: Linguistic Evidence of Cultural Variation in Parental Ethnotheories of Children's Prosocial Helping," *Frontiers in Psychology*, 11 (2020).

59 *Take, for example, a two-year-old toddler who is eager*: Mariëtte de Haan, *Learning as Cultural Practice: How Children Learn in a Mexican Mazahua Community* (West Lafayette, IN: Purdue University Press, 2000), 77–78.

60 *many indigenous parents are happy*: Coppens et al.

60 *"One mom told us: 'When my toddler was doing the dishes'"*: Author interview with Rebeca Mejía-Arauz, February 28, 2018.

60 *In one Maya community in Chiapas, Mexico, parents* intentionally: Margarita Martínez-Pérez, "Adults' Orientation of Children—And Children's Initiative to Pitch In—To Everyday Adult Activities in a Tsotsil Maya Community," *Advances in Child Development and Behavior* 49 (2015).

61 *Psychologists believe that the more a young child practices helping the family*: Author interview with Andrew Coppens, February 23, 2018.

61 *In one experiment, she and her team gave pairs of siblings a task*: Author interview with Lucia Alcalá, May 22, 2019.

63 *"Children can really be involved in household chores way earlier"*: Author interview with Rebeca Mejía-Arauz, February 28, 2018.

63 *The tiniest little staggerer has tasks to perform*: Margaret Mead, "Samoan children at work and play," *Natural History* 28 (1928).

64 *she followed children and their parents around for hours*: Adam H. Boyette and Sheina Lew-Levy, "Learning Is Imperative: The Socialization of Cooperative Autonomy among BaYaka Foragers," forthcoming.

65 *"As early as the child can sit, sit him next to you"*: Lucia Alcalá et al., "Children's Initiative in Contributions to Family Work in Indigenous-Heritage and Cosmopolitan Communities in Mexico," *Human Development* 57, no. 2–3 (2014).

66 *"Once the child starts walking, you can begin to ask"*: Author interview with Rebeca Mejía-Arauz, February 23, 2018.

66 *"Many moms will say something like, 'Come, my child' "*: Ibid.

66 *in a Maya community in Chiapas*: Margarita Martínez-Pérez, "Adults' Orientation of Children—And Children's Initiative to Pitch In—To Everyday Adult Activities in a Tsotsil Maya Community."

67 *"Depending on the activity, sometimes children observe"*: Author interview with Lucia Alcalá, May 22, 2019.

67 *"A barely mobile toddler may be asked to carry a cup"*: David F. Lancy, *The Anthropology of Childhood: Cherubs, Chattel, Changelings* (Cambridge, UK: Cambridge University Press, 2008), 264.

67 *David calls this the "chore curriculum"*: Ibid., 265.

68 *" 'Run and fetch me' is one of the commonest phrases heard"*: Raymond Firth, *We the Tikopia: A Sociological Study of Kinship in Primitive Polynesia* (London: George Allen & Unwin Ltd., 1936), 80.

71 *"The invitation is for doing things together"*: Author interview with Rebeca Mejía-Arauz, February 28, 2018.

72 *50 percent of the Nahua-heritage moms said that they'll sometimes use this approach*: Alcalá et al., "Children's Initiative in Contributions to Family Work in Indigenous-Heritage and Cosmopolitan Communities in Mexico."

Chapter 5: How to Raise Flexible, Cooperative Kids

76 *"In Maya culture, there's a belief that everybody has a purpose"*: Author interview with Barbara Rogoff, March 30, 2018.

84 *Children are welcome to run over to watch and pitch in*: Suzanne Gaskins, "Childhood Practices Across Cultures: Play and Household Work," in *The Oxford*

Handbook of Human Development and Culture: An Interdisciplinary Perspective, ed. Lene Arnett Jensen (London: Oxford University Press, 2015), 185–97.

85 *Children don't see a difference between adult work and play*: Author interview with Rebeca Mejía-Arauz, February 28, 2018.

85 *"It's a pretty sophisticated way to look at child development"*: Author interview with Lucia Alcalá, May 22, 2019.

86 *Children as young as eight or nine years old are fully conscious of this motivation*: Ibid.

86 *Kids are acutely aware of their relationship to others*: Michael Tomasello et al., *Why We Cooperate* (Cambridge, MA: The MIT Press, 2009), 45.

89 *"The trouble, I think, is that children have been brought up"*: Author interview with Barbara Rogoff, March 30, 2018.

90 *"If you start out early, or wean an older child into a situation"*: Ibid.

94 *And if they don't participate or fail to pick them up on a regular basis*: Lucia Alcalá et al., "Children's Initiative in Contributions to Family Work in Indigenous-Heritage and Cosmopolitan Communities in Mexico," *Human Development* 57, no. 2–3 (2014).

95 *If they resist, remind them that they're part of the family*: Ibid.

99 *"Apart from language . . . the last outstanding distinction between us"*: Sarah Blaffer Hrdy, *Mothers and Others: The Evolutionary Origins of Mutual Understanding* (Cambridge, MA: The Belknap Press of Harvard University Press, 2009), 9.

99 *To be helpful in such diverse ways, toddlers must already possess*: Tomasello, *Why We Cooperate*.

100 *among the Ese'Eja hunter-gatherer tribe in the Bolivian Amazon*: Daniela Peluso, "Children's Instrumentality and Agency in Amazonia," *Tipití: Journal of the Society for the Anthropology of Lowland South America* 13, no. 1 (2015).

Chapter 6: Master Motivators: What's Better Than Praise?

110 *With intrinsic motivation, the activity is enjoyable on its own*: Richard M. Ryan and Edward L. Deci, "Brick by Brick: The Origins, Development, and Future of Self-Determination Theory," chapter in *Advances in Motivation Science*, vol. 6, ed. Andrew J. Elliot (Cambridge, MA: Academic Press, 2019), 118.

110 *And it likely lasts longer than its counterpart, extrinsic motivation*: Richard M. Ryan and Edward L. Deci, "Self-Determination Theory and the Facilitation of Intrinsic Motivation, Social Development, and Well-Being," *American Psychologist* 55, no. 1 (January 2000).

110 *External influences, such as rewards and punishments, can actually weaken*: William Stixrud, PhD, and Ned Johnson, *The Self-Driven Child: The Science and*

Sense of Giving Your Kids More Control Over Their Lives (New York: Viking, 2018), 107.

111 *Studies show that when a child feels connected to a teacher*: Ibid., 175.

111 *This sweet spot is where intrinsic motivation likely occurs*: Kennon Sheldon and Mike Prentice, "Self-Determination Theory as a Foundation for Personality Researchers," *Journal of Personality* 87, no. 1 (November 2017).

112 *"Sometimes they may use facial expressions"*: Author interview with Rebeca Mejía-Arauz, February 28, 2018.

112 *Psychologists have found that when young children grow up hearing*: Peggy J. Miller and Grace E. Cho, *Self-Esteem in Time and Place: How American Families Imagine, Enact, and Personalize a Cultural Ideal* (New York: Oxford University Press, 2018), 218.

113 *Instead of praising children, Maya parents acknowledge or accept*: Author interview with Lucia Alcalá, May 22, 2019.

114 *Lucia calls this "fluid collaboration"*: Barbara Rogoff, "Collaboration as an Ensemble," National Science Foundation video, 2019, https://stemforall2019.videohall.com/presentations/1346.

117 *A Maya parent could say*: Email to author from Suzanne Gaskins, December 9, 2020.

117 *Nahua-heritage parents sometimes acknowledge children's work*: Lucia Alcalá et al., "Children's Initiative in Contributions to Family Work in Indigenous-Heritage and Cosmopolitan Communities in Mexico," *Human Development* 57, no. 2–3 (2014).

118 *Anthropologist Jean Briggs has documented a similar type of acknowledgment*: Patricia D'Souza, "the book of Gjoa," *Nunatsiaq News*, November 22, 2002, https://nunatsiaq.com/stories/article/the_book_of_gjoa/.

118 *Up in the Arctic, one Inuit mom connects*: Jean L. Briggs, *Inuit Morality Play: The Emotional Education of a Three-Year-Old* (New Haven, CT: Yale University Press, 1998), 49.

119 *One Nahua-heritage mom told Lucia that she never punishes her daughter*: Alcalá et al., "Children's Initiative in Contributions to Family Work in Indigenous-Heritage and Cosmopolitan Communities in Mexico."

Chapter 7: Never in Anger

129 *"I really wanted to go to the most remote"*: Jean Briggs interview with Paul Kennedy on *Ideas*, Canadian Broadcasting Corporation, 2011.

131 *"Often twenty and occasionally as many as forty"*: Jean L. Briggs, *Never in Anger:*

Portrait of an Eskimo Family (Cambridge, MA: Harvard University Press, 1970), 31.

132 *"They never acted in anger toward me"*: Briggs interview with Paul Kennedy on *Ideas*.

132 *"Indeed, the maintenance of equanimity"*: Briggs, *Never in Anger*, 4.

132 *"I felt no unusual intensity even in the general"*: Ibid., 258.

132 *Allaq laughed a little*: Ibid., 258.

132 *"shot impulsively at a bird"*: Ibid., 258.

133 *"My ways were so much cruder"*: Briggs interview with Paul Kennedy on *Ideas*.

133 *"Allaq had spent the evening frying bannock"*: Briggs, *Never in Anger*, 154.

140 *Studies suggest that better executive function*: Adele Diamond, "Executive Functions," *Annual Review of Psychology* 64 (2013): 135–68.

Chapter 8: How to Teach Children to Control Their Anger

146 *So to help a child learn emotional regulation*: Laura Markham, "7 Tips To Help Kids Learn to Control Their Emotions," Aha! Parenting, June 21, 2018, https://www.ahaparenting.com/blog/How_Kids_Learn_to_Control_Their _Emotions.

Chapter 9: How to Stop Being Angry at Your Child

156 *The Utku [Inuit] expect little children to be easily angered*: Jean L. Briggs, *Never in Anger: Portrait of an Eskimo Family* (Cambridge, MA: Harvard University Press, 1970), 111.

156 *"Kids are considered to be extremely bossy"*: Richard G. Condon, *Inuit Youth: Growth and Change in the Canadian Arctic* (New Brunswick, NJ: Rutgers University Press, 1987), 61.

Chapter 10: Introduction to Parenting Tools

166 *some Maya parents will tap into the child's desire to be a "big sister"*: Author interview with Suzanne Gaskins, June 23, 2019.

169 *"There was consistency also in the calmly rational quality"*: Jean L. Briggs, *Never in Anger: Portrait of an Eskimo Family* (Cambridge, MA: Harvard University Press, 1970), 141.

169 *She launched a "storm of wails and slaps"*: Ibid., 157.

170 *children's emotions—and energy level—mirror those of their parents*: Author interview with Tina Payne Bryson, November 8, 2019.

174 *"touch is good for your health"*: Lisa Feldman Barrett, *How Emotions Are Made: The Secret Life of the Brain* (New York: Houghton Mifflin Harcourt, 2017), 178.

175 *"Our right brain cares about the big picture"*: Daniel J. Siegel, MD, and Tina Payne Bryson, PhD, *The Whole-Brain Child: 12 Revolutionary Strategies to Nurture Your Child's Developing Mind* (New York: Random House, 2011), 31.

175 *"In our society, we're trained to work things out using our words"*: Ibid., 24.

180 *"which means roughly, to seek thought, to seek mind"*: Jean Briggs interview with Paul Kennedy on *Ideas*, Canadian Broadcasting Corporation, 2011.

183 *"The goal of Inuit education is to cause thought"*: Ibid.

Chapter 11: Tools for Sculpting Behavior: Stories

202 *Oral storytelling is a human universal*: Ferris Jabr, "The Story of Storytelling," *Harper's Magazine*, March 2019, https://harpers.org/archive/2019/03/the-story -of-storytelling/.

203 *Today, modern hunter-gatherer groups use stories to teach sharing*: Daniel Smith et al., "Cooperation and the evolution of hunter-gatherer storytelling," *Nature Communications* 8, no. 1 (December 5, 2017).

204 *A big part of childhood, in both traditional Celtic and traditional Inuit cultures*: Author interview with Sharon P. MacLeod, November 5, 2019; author interview with Myna Ishulutak, December 8, 2018.

208 *Several studies have found that learning about their family's history*: Marshall P. Duke, Amber Lazarus, and Robyn Fivush, "Knowledge of family history as a clinically useful index of psychological well-being and prognosis: A brief report," *Psychotherapy: Theory, Research, Practice, Training* 45, no. 2 (June 2008).

208 *The scientists point out that what's important here is that parents share stories*: Robyn Fivush, PhD, "The 'Do You Know?' 20 Questions About Family Stories," *Psychology Today*, November 19, 2016, https://www.psychologytoday .com/us/blog/the-stories-our-lives/201611/the-do-you-know-20-questions -about-family-stories.

Chapter 12: Tools for Sculpting Behavior: Dramas

215 *In the 1960s, the Canadian government forced or coerced*: Qikiqtani Inuit Association, *Qikiqtani Truth Commission: Thematic Reports and Special Studies, 1950–*

1975, "QTC Final Report: Achieving Saimaqatigiingniq" (Iqualit, Nunavut: Inhabit Media, 2013), https://www.qtcommission.ca/sites/default/files/public /thematic_reports/thematic_reports_english_final_report.pdf; Sara Frizzell, "Federal government apologizes to Baffin Inuit for sled dog killings, forced relocations," CBC News, August 14, 2019, https://www.cbc.ca/news/canada /north/apology-qikiqtani-truth-commission-1.5245173.

219 *In these dramas, children get to try out different responses*: Jean L. Briggs, *Inuit Morality Play: The Emotional Education of a Three-Year-Old* (New Haven: Yale University Press, 1998), 6.

220 *For children, the dramas give them the chance to flex and strengthen*: Author interview with Peggy Miller, January 10, 2019.

220 *Play makes a powerful parenting tool for changing behavior*: Author interview with Laura Markham, January 10, 2019.

222 *Then she can think about the experience in a new, rational way*: Ibid.

Chapter 13: How Did Our Ancient Ancestors Parent?

234 *but ancient stone tools and rock paintings suggest*: Frank W. Marlowe, *The Hazda: Hunter-Gatherers of Tanzania* (Berkeley, CA: University of California Press, 2010), 18.

235 *In 2000, anthropologists estimated that the population numbered*: Peter M. Gardner, "Understanding Anomalous Distribution of Hunter-Gatherers: The Indian Case," *Current Anthropology* 54, no. 4 (August 2013); Peter P. Schweitzer, Megan Biesele, and Robert K. Hitchcock, eds., *Hunters and Gatherers in the Modern World: Conflict, Resistance, and Self-Determination* (New York: Berghahn Books, April 2000), 5.

236 *In 1995, archaeologist Robert Kelly compiled a summary of Western knowledge*: Robert L. Kelly, *The Lifeways of Hunter-Gatherers: The Foraging Spectrum* (New York: Cambridge University Press, 1995), 2.

236 *belonged to a group of highly skilled hunter-gatherers called the Ramaytush Ohlone*: Jonathan Cordero, "Impact of Spanish Colonization: Golden Gate National Recreation Area," National Park Service, https://www.nps.gov/articles/impact-of-spanish-colonization.htm.

237 *"The reader should know that many of these 'hunter-gatherers'"*: Kelly, *The Lifeways of Hunter-Gatherers*, 2.

237 *The Hadzabe in northern Tanzania are no different*: Marlowe, *The Hazda*, 97.

237 *the Hadzabe have lived similar to the way their ancestors have lived*: Daudi Peter-

son, *Hadzabe: By the Light of a Million Fires* (Dar es Salaam, Tanzania: Mkuki na Nyota Publishers, 2013), 18.

238 *"In the gift economy, gifts are not free"*: Robin Wall Kimmerer, *Braiding Sweet-grass: Indigenous Wisdom, Scientific Knowledge, and the Teachings of Plants* (Min-neapolis, MN: Milkweed Editions, 2013), 31.

Chapter 14: The Most Confident Kids in the World

251 *In general, hunter-gatherer communities greatly value a person's right*: Daudi Peterson, *Hadzabe: By the Light of a Million Fires* (Dar es Salaam, Tanzania: Mkuki na Nyota Publishers, 2013), 147.

252 *"Deciding what another person should do, no matter what his age"*: Jean Liedloff, *The Continuum Concept: In Search of Happiness Lost* (Cambridge, MA: Perseus Books, 1977), 90.

252 *"So a one-year-old can be perfectly happy by himself for an hour"*: Author inter-view with Suzanne Gaskins, June 23, 2019.

252 *With the !Kung hunter-gatherers in southern Africa*: Melvin Konner, *The Evo-lution of Childhood: Relationships, Emotions, Mind* (Cambridge, MA: The Belknap Press of Harvard University Press, 2010), 637.

252 *"It was one of the few times we saw other parents interfere"*: Author interview with Sheina Lew-Levy, November 15, 2019.

253 *In one study, Sheina counted how many commands parents give children*: Adam H. Boyette and Sheina Lew-Levy, "Learning Is Imperative: The Socialization of Cooperative Autonomy among BaYaka Foragers," forthcoming.

256 *As one psychologist wrote, children's freedom seems like a "recipe for disaster"*: Peter Gray, "Play as a Foundation for Hunter-Gatherer Social Existence," *American Journal of Play* 1, no. 4 (Spring 2009).

256 *"Free from frustration or anxiety . . . the Jul'hoan children"*: Elizabeth Marshall Thomas, *The Old Way: A Story of the First People* (New York: Picador, 2006), 199.

260 *"So kids and adults are all acting on their own"*: Author interview with Sheina Lew-Levy, November 15, 2019.

260 *You see a similar structure in the Maya village*: Author interview with Suzanne Gaskins, June 23, 2019.

261 *But as chef Samin Nosrat points out*: Samin Nosrat, *Salt, Fat, Acid, Heat: Master-ing the Elements of Good Cooking* (New York: Simon & Schuster, 2017), 126.

261 *"My image of a Maya parent—or an older child"*: Author interview with Su-zanne Gaskins, June 23, 2019.

262 *In the Yucátan, Maria told me she uses this strategy*: Author interview with Maria
     de los Angeles Tun Burgos, April 5, 2018.

263 *"Like exercise and sleep, it appears to be good"*: William Stixrud, PhD, and Ned
     Johnson, *The Self-Driven Child: The Science and Sense of Giving Your Kids More
     Control Over Their Lives* (New York: Viking, 2018), 12.

263 *On the flip side, when I constantly instruct and guide her actions*: Holly H. Schif-
     frin et al., "Helping or Hovering? The Effects of Helicopter Parenting on Col-
     lege Students' Well-Being," *Journal of Child and Family Studies* 23 (2014).

264 *"Because we give children so much freedom"*: Peterson, *Hadzabe*, 152.

264 *"Many [American] kids feel that way all the time"*: Stixrud and Johnson, *The Self-
     Driven Child*, 11.

264 *Autonomy provides the "antidote to this stress"*: Ibid., 8.

264 *"The biggest gift parents can give their children is the opportunity"*: Holly Schif-
     frin, "Helping or Hovering? The Effects of Helicopter Parenting on College
     Students' Well-Being," University of Mary Washington, August 15, 2018,
     https://expertfile.com/spotlight/5983/helping-or-hovering-the-effects-of-heli
     copter-parenting-on-college-students-wellbeing.

266 *"At a store, or with an instructor or coach, you might even physically hang back"*:
     Julie Lythcott-Haims, *How to Raise an Adult: Break Free of the Overparenting
     Trap and Prepare Your Kid for Success* (New York: Henry Holt and Company,
     2015), 193.

266 *"You know your kid best"*: Ibid., 196–97.

266 *In all circumstances, let the child take*: Ibid., 196–97.

Chapter 15: Ancient Antidote for Depression

274 *"The mother is rarely alone when her baby cries"*: Ann Cale Kruger and Melvin
     Konner, "Who Responds to Crying? Maternal Care and Allocare Among the
     !Kung," *Human Nature* 21, no. 3 (October 2010).

276 *On the surface, this ape looked quite similar to a handful of other bipedal*: Sarah
     Blaffer Hrdy, *Mothers and Others: The Evolutionary Origins of Mutual Under-
     standing* (Cambridge, MA: The Belknap Press of Harvard University Press,
     2009), 7–10.

278 *Compared to other living primates, humans are born with the least developed brains*:
     Holly M. Dunsworth et al., "Metabolic hypothesis for human altriciality," *Pro-
     ceedings of the National Academy of Sciences of the United States of America* 109,
     no. 38 (September 18, 2012).

278 *A human baby would have to grow in the womb for another nine to twelve months*:

Adolf Portmann, *A Zoologist Looks at Humankind*, trans. Judith Schaefer (New York: Columbia University Press, 1990).

278 *"An ape that produced such costly, costly slow-maturing offspring"*: John Poole, "Why Grandmothers May Hold The Key To Human Evolution," NPR, *All Things Considered*, Goats and Soda blog, June 7, 2018, https://www.npr.org /transcripts/617097908.

279 *"Dealing with a fussing baby is a group effort"*: Melvin Konner, *The Evolution of Childhood: Relationships, Emotions, Mind* (Cambridge, MA: The Belknap Press of Harvard University Press, 2010), 437.

280 *You find similar situations in many hunter-gatherer communities worldwide*: Courtney L. Meehan, Robert Quinlan, and Courtney D. Malcom, "Cooperative Breeding and Maternal Energy Expenditure Among Aka Foragers," *American Journal of Human Biology* 25, no. 1 (January/February 2013).

280 *"So that situation is very different from the Western one"*: Author interview with Abigail Page, November 22, 2019.

280 *In southern India, the Nayaka hunter-gatherers value alloparents*: Nurit Bird-David, "The Giving Environment: Another Perspective on the Economic System of Gatherer-Hunters," *Current Anthropology* 31, no. 2 (April 1990).

281 *Abigail Page and her colleague followed a bunch of Agta kids*: Abigail Page et al., "Children are important too: juvenile playgroups and maternal childcare in a foraging population, the Agta," *Philosophical Transactions of the Royal Society B: Biological Sciences* (2020).

281 *Abigail thinks that young children, about five years older than another child*: Author interview with Abigail Page, November 22, 2019.

281 *"We think teaching occurs when a more knowledgeable adult instructs"*: Author interview with Sheina Lew-Levy, November 15, 2019.

283 *"Just spending time with others, even if you aren't interacting"*: Author interview with Bert Uchino, January 24, 2020.

284 *"So the close relationships between alloparents and an infant"*: Author interview with Sheina Lew-Levy, November 15, 2019.

285 *Even just a couple of extra caring adults*: Christina Bethell, Jennifer Jones, and Narangerel Gombojav, "Positive Childhood Experiences and Adult Mental and Relational Health in a Statewide Sample," *JAMA Pediatrics* 173, no. 11 (2019); Selena Simmons-Duffin, "Positive Childhood Experiences May Buffer Against Health Effects Of Adverse Ones," NPR, *All Things Considered*, Shots blog, September 9, 2019, https://www.npr.org/sections/ health-shots/2019/09/09/759031061/positive-childhood-experiences-may -buffer-against-health-effects-of-adverse-ones.

285 *And yet, over the past hundred years or so, our culture*: John R. Gillis, *A World of Their Own Making: Myth, Ritual, and the Quest for Family Values* (Cambridge, MA: Harvard University Press, 1997), 20.

287 *"Then my boys had a bunch of aunts"*: Author interview with Suzanne Gaskins, June 23, 2019.

287 *Younger children learn more sophisticated behavior from the older children*: Peter Gray, "The Special Value of Children's Age-Mixed Play," *American Journal of Play* 3, no. 4 (Spring 2011).

293 *"Or she's out in front, saying, 'Come to me, come to me,' "*: Author interview with Suzanne Gaskins, April 6, 2018.

295 *So in terms of macro-parenting, mom and dad take charge*: Suzanne Gaskins, "Childhood Practices Across Cultures: Play and Household Work," in *The Oxford Handbook of Human Development and Culture: An Interdisciplinary Perspective*, ed. Lene Arnett Jensen (New York: Oxford University Press, 2015), 185–97.

297 *"Parents have taken on all these extra obligations"*: Author interview with David Lancy, January 9, 2018.

298 *"maximal interference" was only making my life harder*: Author interview with Suzanne Gaskins, April 6, 2018.

Chapter 16: Sleep

301 *"In the nineteenth century, the doctors at these asylums were really obsessed"*: Author interview with Benjamin Reiss, June 5, 2018.

301 *Up until the late nineteenth century, "normal" sleep was segmented*: A. Roger Ekirch, "Segmented Sleep," *Harper's Magazine*, August 2013, https://harpers .org/archive/2013/08/segmented-sleep/.

302 *"sleep had to be subjected to increasing levels of control"*: Benjamin Reiss, *Wild Nights: How Taming Sleep Created Our Restless World* (New York: Basic Books, 2017), 12.

302 *"This is worth reiterating: virtually nothing about our standard model"*: Ibid., 24.

302 *"Some societies nap while some don't; some sleep in large groups"*: Ibid., 11.

302 *researchers tracked the sleep habits of more than eighty people*: Gandhi Yetish et al., "Natural Sleep and Its Seasonal Variations in Three Pre-Industrial Societies," *Current Biology* 25, no. 21 (October 2015).

Epilogue

309 *"Of course, it had been there all along"*: Jenny Odell, *How to Do Nothing: Resisting the Attention Economy* (Brooklyn, NY: Melville House, 2019), 28.

INDEX

ABOUT THE AUTHOR

Michaeleen Doucleff is a correspondent for NPR's Science Desk. In 2015, she was part of the team that earned a George Foster Peabody Award for its coverage of the Ebola outbreak in West Africa. Prior to joining NPR, Doucleff was an editor at the journal *Cell*, where she wrote about the science behind pop culture. She has a doctorate in chemistry from the University of California, Berkeley, and a master's degree in viticulture and enology from the University of California, Davis. She lives with her husband and daughter in San Francisco.